Omnec Onec
Anja Schäfer

Simply Wisdom and Love

Venusian Spirituality

DISCUS
PUBLISHING

Omnec Onec and Anja Schäfer:
Simply Wisdom and Love – Venusian Spirituality

Omnec Onec Official Website: **www.omnec-onec.com**

Copyright © 2015 Discus Publishing
Publisher: Anja Schäfer

Visit us on the internet: **www.discuspublishing.com**

Thank you to the proofreaders Helga Klötzer, Elizabeth Whitney,
and Brad Markus

Front cover design by Anja Schäfer with the use of images by © Laurent
Renault/Fotolia.com and © Diane Labombarbe/istockphoto.com

ISBN: 978-3-9817441-0-1

The Light Bearers

Those who chose to carry the light of truth for mankind, all too
often may find the winds of change blow and cause the light to
dim and lose its original glow.

Sometimes fate will close in like a fog causing even the carrier
not to see the light.

There are the dark ones, making life seem like eternal night.

Then, deep inside the carrier is Soul, the Eternal Light - whose
knowledge of truth, once again, gives power to the light.

Because the Lightbearer keeps lighting the way for other Souls
who seek truth in a world of darkness, will find a whole host of
truth bearers, who join in with their lights, creating a blending
light that shields the truth seekers from darkness, and makes the
way much easier for all mankind.

Omnec Onec

Contents

PART TWO
Unpublished Texts

PART THREE
Transcripts

PART FOUR
Projects

Preface from the Publisher

$\mathcal{M}$ y first encounter with Omnec Onec was in 1994 – through the TV. Coincidentally, I tuned into a talkshow and right away was fascinated by Omnec's charisma and her calm, pleasant way of putting spiritual messages in a nutshell. "Imagination is the key to creation" was my personal key phrase that was seeded into my consciousness. It needed some time to grow, because it was not before 1997 when I consciously thought of Omnec again, namely when I opened my esoteric bookstore "Lichtblick" in Landshut, Bavaria and ordered books for the initial equipment. I remembered Omnec Onec and her book "From Venus I Came" that I had heard of a couple of years before in the talkshow. I ordered the book for myself and devoured it. Omnec's descriptions of the astral Venus and the continuous love and wisdom in this extraordinary autobiography touched me deeply. I felt like I had arrived at home. Some months later I read her second book that was available at that time titled "Handbook of Venusian Spirituality". This time, I decided that I had to meet this woman in person and contacted her publisher to ask for tour dates. I was directly forwarded to Wulf Wemmje, who was Omnec's manager at that time, and he offered me to come to Landshut with Omnec, if I was willing to organize a lecture and workshop for her. Of course, I was thrilled and accepted right away.

When Omnec stood in front of me only three weeks later, I was very nervous. She was dressed all in white and looked fantastic. Her calm, loving charisma and the information that she shared with us in her lecture and workshop moved me deeply. During this first meeting, I was too excited to have a closer contact with her. Our amicable, almost familiar relationship started to develop about half a year later, when she and Wulf came to Landshut again. When Omnec and I exchanged glances in the workshop, I realized what real love is for the first time in my life. My heart was wide open, I was very relaxed and well-balanced. This memorable experience was the starting point for our long-term future collaboration.

From this time on, Omnec and I met more and more frequently. The experiences that I had personally with her and triggered by her presence in my life could fill an entire book. One day I found myself in the situation of translating her lecture into German. This was followed by the first trips together to workshop locations, and later we discovered that we share the Oasis-Vision. Obviously it is a part of my self-chosen life task to support and spread Omnec's information, because this is what I have been doing since then. Again and again I traveled with Omnec in the German speaking countries and organized lectures and workshops. In 2008, I created her website www.omnec-onec.com, followed by social media activities and video uploads on YouTube. As Omnec's books were sold out and I myself unable to re-publish them at that time, I found a new publisher for her who not only published her books as a compilation edition, but also her CDs and a lecture-DVD. As an employee at the publisher's house, I edited Omnec's books, typeset them, spoke the German versions of her CDs and DVD and went on a reading tour with her in fall 2011.

During this reading tour, I recorded all book presentations and transcribed them afterwards. This resulted in the idea to compile the present book and to complement it with unpublished material.

Since 2012 I am self-employed with my publishing service. The present book is the first book that I have published through my newly founded publishing house DISCUS PUBLISHING. I hope that it reaches many interested readers for whom the messages from "The Woman from Venus" are as valuable as they are for me.

Anja Schäfer

PS: To be able to distinguish throughout the book whether a text was written by Omnec or by me, the name of the author stands on top of every text.

About Omnec Onec
– The Woman from Venus –

Author: Anja Schäfer

Omnec Onec is the only recorded living Venusian in our societies who came to Earth from the astral dimension of Venus with her own physical body. She became publicly known by her autobiography *From Venus I Came*. In this book, Omnec portrays in detail the history of Venus and describes why and how she was born on the astral level and why as a child of seven she was given the opportunity to lower her vibrations, to manifest a physical body. She came to Earth in order to later in her life work as a spiritual teacher and to fulfill her earthly life cycles.

> *"As I was born on the planet Venus in another dimension and came to your planet as a young child, I was able to retain the knowledge and information that I had gathered as a Soul through many incarnations and lifetimes. I can keep this information intact, and what I teach people is actually what I KNOW and not what I've read about or what I've heard, but what I have experienced through many different life cycles on Earth and in other dimensions."* Omnec Onec

The astral plane is a dimension of higher vibration that cannot be seen or proven with physical means. According to Omnec, a long time ago Venus[1] supported physical life very similar to the Earth today. Natural evolutionary cycles and changing living conditions

---

1 Omnec speaks about Venus, Mars, Saturn and Jupiter as the planets whose inhabitants colonized the Earth millions of years ago. They all still carry life in a higher frequency. (Publisher's comment)

made physical life on Venus impossible, but due to the spiritual development of the people, their societies continued to exist in finer levels of vibration.

The Venusians live in tune with natural laws and the "Laws of the Supreme Deity". They are fully aware of their connection with creation and handle their spiritual powers with responsibility.

Omnec wrote the manuscript of her autobiography in the Sixties already. The book was first published by the U.S. Colonel and UFO investigator Wendelle C. Stevens in 1991 in the USA. As Omnec was guided to focus her teachings to the German speaking countries since 1993, this first book and the next ones – the continuation of Omnec's autobiography on Earth with the title *Angels Don't Cry* and the condensed essence of Omnec's spiritual teachings with the new title *My Message*[2] have not been published in English before 2012. In 2012, these three books came out as a compilation edition with the title *The Venusian Trilogy*.

The spiritual name "Omnec Onec" means "spiritual rebound". It's Omnec's task and talent to help people reconnect with their true selves as Soul. Her Earth name is Sheila Gipson. For karmic reasons and to fulfill her mission, Omnec physically replaced the girl Sheila at the age of seven. In her autobiography and in her public appearances (see PART ONE of this book), Omnec describes the circumstances of her arrival in Sheila's Earth family.

In 2009, Omnec Onec had a stroke. Since then, she has reduced her public activities to a minimum.

Omnec was married twice. She has four adult children and three grandchildren.

---

2   Original title *Handbook of Venusian Spirituality* (Publisher's comment)

PART ONE

The Unknown History of our Solar System and the Spiritual Transformation of the Earth

Author: Anja Schäfer

*I*n the mid-nineties, Omnec Onec shared the information about *The Unknown History of our Solar System and The Spiritual Transformation of the Earth* with people for the first time.

> *"I first heard about the Transformation and the history of the solar system at a meeting on the astral plane to which I was invited in 1994 and which I attended with the help of a long meditation. There, the connections were made clear.*
> *Thousands of human and non-human beings from different galaxies, all intelligent and highly evolved beings, attended this meeting. It was just one of countless occasions when they got together in order to coordinate their efforts to save the Earth. Since about 1930, they tried to increase the vibration step by step in order to prevent a further destruction of the planet."*
> Omnec Onec

After Omnec told in lectures the story of mankind on Earth and the interrelationship with today's times of changes, many people wanted to know more – so the "Transformation-Workshop" was started. In the course of weekend seminars, Omnec shared universal truths for many years. Her information not only made a lot of sense to many people, but also touched their Souls and caused consciousness-expanding experiences.

When it became clear in 2004 that Omnec would return to the USA for an extended period of time, it was uncertain when and if she would come back to hold lectures and workshops in the German-speaking countries, so this video[3] was created.

Besides the unusual biography of "The Woman from Venus", one can say that this information encompasses the essence of what Omnec Onec has to share with people. *The Unknown History of the Solar System and the Spiritual Transformation of the Earth* covers the gigantic spectrum beginning with the origin of mankind over the descent of consciousness up to far into the future of the Earth

---

3   The video recording of this transcript is available as a double-DVD. (Publisher's comment)

– the future of this planet that after the completion of the currently ongoing Transformation Process will be a total positively changed place and home of free people, people who live in harmony with nature and with the universe just as they are determined to live by nature: as free, unlimited, and creative Souls who are fully conscious of themselves and their connection with creation.

The first part of *The Unknown History of our Solar System and The Spiritual Transformation of the Earth* contains the complete information about the inhabitation of our solar system and the currently ongoing Transformation Process of the Earth. This text corresponds to the lectures that Omnec Onec held about fifteen years until she had a stroke in 2009.

In the second part of this transcript, Omnec Onec gives a short introduction into her life story and speaks about her origin, before she goes more into detail about the Transformation Process and the future of the Earth.

The Unknown History of our Solar System and the Spiritual Transformation of the Earth – Transcript Part 1 –

Author: Omnec Onec

The Inhabitation of our Solar System

*H*ello, my name is Omnec Onec. I'm known as Omnec Onec, that is my Venusian name. I am going to tell the story of how the human beings came into this system and eventually inhabited the planet Earth. I would like to explain in kind of a story way like I know it myself, and then I can tell you of course eventually how I came into the picture and how I came to be on your planet. It was a spiritual decision that was made by my spiritual masters and I had the decision to make whether to come here or not.

But the story began a long time ago, before the Earth was even a planet. In faraway galaxies, four different galaxies, that's what I've heard of, the first human beings came in great space ships. They were sent by the spiritual hierarchy. They were told they had to come to this system and inhabit this system, because there were no human beings at that time in this system.

There was the white race, the yellow race, the black, and the red. They have all been given the same information that they would inhabit this system here. So they travelled with their ships, and they encountered one another. They were very well understanding of all physical life. They were in communication with minerals, plants, animals. They were very consciously spiritually aware people. They

18

communicated without speech, by telepathic means. They considered themselves as a part of the human race and not by the skin color, or the cultures or whatever.

They created kind of a – what you would call – cooperative friendship with one another, and they worked in harmony with each other.

They arrived in this system, and they had to create new homes and new beginnings for themselves, because they knew that the thousands that they had brought with them from their home system would never return – that this was to be their new system and their new home. But they carried, of course, the wisdom and the information and cultural ways to this system. They had to choose new homes, and the four oldest planets that were inhabitable at this time were Mars, Venus, Saturn, and Jupiter. The black race chose Jupiter, because of the similarities of the system to where they were from. The red race chose Saturn for the same reasons, and the yellow race chose Mars, and the white race Venus. This was all depending ecologically on their genetics and on what they were used to as far as their environment goes. So they settled on these planets and created new lives, new homes, new communities, and they located the power places on each planet, and on each planet they decided to build a temple, and this temple on their home systems always served as a doorway to the other dimensions, because they communicated with beings higher than they were and more spiritually evolved who no longer lived in the physical. This way they could manifest through these temples technology, crystals, and different things that they needed to survive in their societies. These temples were always located at a power place, at a very special location, and they were able to determine this because of their technology and because of their knowledge.

The Earth Emerges and is Filled with Life Forms

They communicated very well with each other and decided that there was a new planet that was in the process of forming into a planet. It was at this time a comet. The Earth didn't yet exist. They were all waiting for this comet to take its place in rotation around the sun and to become a new planet in this system. They all knew of this, and for generations, they watched, and they waited until this comet actually formed into a planet and took its place in the system. This planet now, of course, is known as Earth.

When they came into this system, there wasn't any human life, and this was why that they came. Their mission was to bring human life into this system that only had plants, minerals, and animals. They went to other systems, when the Earth became a planet and cooled down and took its rotation place. They decided that they would bring all manner of life to this Earth. They would bring plants, minerals, and animals of the most exotic nature and the most beautiful from different locations in our system. So they travelled with their ships and they communicated with these different and various life forms and got permission to bring them to Earth to live in cooperation and harmony for the planet Earth's benefit and beauty.

And crystals and things – they were aware of their properties as far as healing, as far as spiritual evolvement goes, so they balanced the Earth very well with these kind of life forms.

That turned out to be a very beautiful kind of a paradise, this Earth. It had all kinds of exotic fish, and bird life – at this time the Earth didn't have desert areas or frozen areas.

It had two moons, and so that they had a very harmonized environment, and they didn't have these diverse weather conditions that the Earth now has.

Word got out about this new planet Earth, and people and visitors came from different systems and different planets. There were non-human and human forms of life, but they were intelligent, and they came to see this wonder, the new Earth. The four beings were very happy with what they had created and what they had done. And they had vowed that they would protect this planet, because it would serve a special purpose of where various different life forms could live in complete harmony and cooperation. So they were happy with this planet.

The Battle for the Earth

Then there came some visitors, who weren't so spiritually evolved and weren't even in the form of human beings. They were reptilian and dinoid beings. They walked on two legs and they traveled with space crafts, they had great technology, and they were intelligent. But they weren't at all evolved as far as the spiritual understanding goes. They looked at every life form that wasn't the same as them as beneath them. And they had no respect. They started to take things from the Earth, some of the beautiful plants, some of the animals, some of the minerals, and then they got into a war with one another over who would own this planet, who would rule this planet. They created this terrible war that lasted for, I think maybe 30 or 40 years. They had nuclear weapons, and they had weapons that you only see now in science-fiction movies.

One of them made a base on the moon, and one of them on the Earth. During this war, they almost totally destroyed the planet Earth. A lot of the life forms lay in ruin and waste. And the moon that they created their base on, was totally destroyed. So the Earth only had one moon left. And after the ruin, of course, they actually left the planet, they had no use for it anymore. It wasn't beautiful, it wasn't rich anymore. And they even left the wounded behind, because they had no use for their own wounded. So they went back to their home systems.

And then the four original races had to decide what they could do to help planet Earth, and even the wounded that were left here. So they made the decision that they would take small ships and they would investigate. They only took several small crafts from each planet, and several beings, like scientists, ecologists, medical people, and tried to see what they can do for the Earth and for the wounded.

After they got to the Earth, they realized the damage was much worse than they thought. There was nuclear radiation over the whole Earth, and they couldn't even return to their home planets. The people, who came to investigate, were stranded along with the wounded.

So they sent word back to their home planets that they couldn't return, because they would spread the radiation. They had to reside on the Earth, they tried to help the wounded, and cared for the plants and the animals that were left intact. It was a sorry state. The poor Earth was in such ruins, and the effect of the one moon was creating volcanoes, earthquakes, and various weather conditions that were very difficult to deal with. But these people, they had to seek shelter, and they had to live on this Earth.

Over a period of hundreds of years, it took for the Earth to heal itself and to become much better, the life forms, that were left on this Earth in these radiation surroundings mutated into the forms of Neanderthals that you know of as the cave men and into the dinosaurs, the giant beings that you know of from history. These all were mutated species that mutated because of the radiation here on the Earth. And they lived for periods of time, and of course, the Earth was not able to feed all these life forms. The human beings were left without the intelligence that they once had, and with no memory of where their origin was. It was not a very ideal kind of life style. It was mostly – they lived by their instincts. And they had to hunt the animals, and eat from the vegetables as well as the animals. And the animals were killing one another and also preying on the human beings.

So the other planets, they thought about it and they said "Well, we have to do something. This Earth cannot survive much longer, because it cannot support these kind of giant life beings". So they decided that they would consult the beings in the higher dimensions as to what they could do for the Earth, and when it would be possible to heal the Earth and once again bring different life forms there, and what they could do about the mutated species.

There was like a radiation cloud around the Earth from this nuclear war that had taken place. And they decided that there was a comet that was coming near to the Earth. With their technology they could direct it. With special laser techniques and magnetic systems that they had, they could divert it to crash into one of the Earth's oceans. This way, it would create a big cloud of steam around the Earth. With this cloud of steam, they could freeze these particles, the vapor particles of the steam. They could then neutralize the radiation and cleanse the Earth.

Also, the radiation cloud and the steam cloud would create such a darkness on the Earth, that the sun couldn't interact with the gravitational field, and there would be a darkness on the Earth and then it would create ice that encased the whole Earth. This way, there would also cease to live these mutated life forms.

This was the way that they ended the time of destruction and were able to cleanse the atmosphere and the mutated life forms had died. And they could continue to clean the Earth and to replenish the Earth with plants and animals and make it beautiful as it once was.

Of course, there was nothing they could do about the effects of the one moon. That would mean that the Earth would still have diverse weather conditions and volcanoes and earthquakes. They just did the best they could to cleanse the planet and make the planet beautiful once again.

The First Populations on Earth

Then later on, they discovered that the planets that they lived on were going into a natural phase of a dormant state where that physical life could no longer be supported. They had to make a decision. Since they had replenished the Earth once again and brought animals and minerals and plants there, they decided they would take small colonies from each planet, because they could not take all of the human beings. This was too much for this small planet. So they would bring special scientists, teachers, spiritual beings, and doctors, and all of the younger generations.

They brought them, and they located them on different parts of the Earth and created the first colonies of human beings on the Earth. Some of the first colonies you know about – I can't name all of them, because you are not familiar with them anyway – there were the Aztecs, Lemuria, Mu, Atlantis, the Egyptians, and some cultures in Africa as well, I think they were also part of the Egyptian culture. So they created all these different colonies, located all over the Earth, so the Earth had its first human beings.

They lived in harmony with one another, and they created beautiful cities with great temples. And they located the different power places, of course they built the temples for interdimensional travel, so that they could manifest their technology to survive on the Earth, everything that they needed. They created a giant community, I guess you would call it, because they were in contact with one another and they cooperated with one another to keep the Earth, the planet, in harmony.

When they first came to the Earth, they had to maintain a calendar, and they had to drink different amounts of liquids at different phases of the moon to maintain the harmony and the balance within the physical body, but they couldn't do anything about the weather and the oceans.

But eventually they came to the conclusion and an idea that they got from the higher dimensions of how to create a kind of harmony where the environment would be balanced on Earth once again. They wouldn't have to deal with these diverse weather conditions.

They were instructed to manifest certain kinds of crystals through the temples, and they were to build structures out of these temples around the equator of the Earth, and then they were to build around the Earth frozen ice particle structures, too. This would help to reflect the moon's effects and also create more of a harmonic and protected environment for the Earth. So they worked on this.

Of course, none of this happened over night, it took years and years to create and to finish the whole structures of the Earth whether to be in harmony. It was a wonder to behold. Through their technology, they could change the frequency of any visitor's ships so that they could pass through the ice particle shields without damage. And they could still visit the colonies here on Earth. So this was a wonder, of course, for the visitors, who were not as technically advanced or as spiritually advanced as the people on Earth.

A Group of Visitors Wants to Gain
Technological Knowledge

Eventually, there developed a problem, because a group of human beings from a nearby star system refused to accept that they wouldn't share this technical information with them. This went over a long period of time, there were problems created within the people that lived in the colonies instigated by these people who wanted the technical information. Eventually these people declared war on the colonies because they were going to take the technology by force if they had to.

The people on Earth, not being aggressive or warlike, even in self-defense, decided that the only thing they could do was to send the younger people and some of the teachers and the caretakers and the spiritual beings into a hiding in nature. Their last thing, the only thing they could do was destroy the cities and all the technology so that it wouldn't fall into the hands of the invaders.

So the war began. The people were in hiding and they were thinking: "OK, after the war is over, we can return to the hidden temples and rebuild our colonies, if we have to." During the war, the crystal structures were damaged that held up the two frozen ice particle structures that surrounded the Earth. They got reports from the spiritual hierarchy that there was going to be a great flood on the Earth, because the ice particles would melt and fall to the Earth. The people didn't have time, the ones that were in hiding, to build ships or space ships or get to their technology in the hidden temples, so the only choice they had was to build giant wooden ships from nature, and of course they were given the instructions of how to build these properly. They had to put as many human beings and animals and plants and whatever else kind of life forms that they could save until the flood was over. They build huge arks. You read of Noah's ark, but there were many of these, there were hundreds of these ships built all over the planet to protect some life forms.

So they had to survive during the flood on these ships and wait for the waters to recede before they could rebuild and continue with their cultures and their spiritual ideas. The invaders were also waiting for the flood to recede, because they knew that the human beings on Earth were a little different than themselves. They had abilities and powers, such as mental telepathy and communication with beings in higher dimensions and in the physical realm they could communicate with the Souls of the plants, the animals and minerals. So they were determined to capture these people, so they began to land when the flood receded to gather up these people.

Of course, they were telling the people they were only going to be questioned, they didn't tell them that they would go into the hidden temples and take some of the technology.

The Genetic Manipulation and its Consequences until Today

This technology that they took, they also used for surgery and for genetic manipulation on the people to divide the brain into two halves, so that one part of the brain would be nullified and they could no longer communicate in a telepathic way, or have the memory of their greatness, where they came from, their ability for space travel, anything – this was all nullified, and they only left intact the half of the brain that functioned within the physical realm. When they genetically manipulated the people, then the people lost their memories and were given new identities. These invaders then created a – I don't know how you would call it – a ruling society. They set themselves up as kings, and they divided the people by the skin, and into different cultures, and created new religions for the people, based on their beliefs. So these people had to start all over again. Then eventually, because of the stealing of some of the things from the hidden temples, manifesting technology and so on, the spiritual hierarchy and the people in the other dimensions determined that they had to close down all the temples and deactivate them, so that they could no longer function. Then began the control and manipulation of the human beings. The human beings were forced into a certain belief system, religious and culture wise. They created conflicts among the people and even war among the people themselves, depending on their skin and what land they were existing on. The rulers were in charge of everything including creating the new religions and the societies and the laws. So the people lost a lot of their free will and their abilities to remember where they came from, or communicate with their beings in the other dimensions.

The ones that remained on the other planets eventually learned that their destiny as beings so unselfish and caring so much for life forms in the physical was that their cultures instead of just ending on the physical planets when they could no longer support life that they would be taken into another frequency, so that their cultures and everything could still exist and they could communicate with the people on the Earth. They left intact one city on each planet that was a doorway to the other dimensions, so that the beings also could manifest spaceships and come into the physical and keep up the communication and try as best as they could to support the people in this physical realm on Earth who had lost everything, all their abilities, and their connection with them even, with their forefathers. So the people on Earth were in a very sad state, and this condition still exists today.

It's so much deep in the genetic system ¬ involved in there ¬ that the manipulation and the controlling is more on the subconscious level, because the people were forced by losing their lives and torture to adhere to these new cultures and these new ideas. Eventually it became a part that they obeyed without questioning. It was all based on fear, and it's still the same way today. Everything is based on fear. Even the religions teach you that you even have to fear if this life is over what takes place in the other realms, because the people don't know any better, they accept this as concepts and belief systems. They obey automatically. They baptize their children in certain religions, they adhere to their cultural societies, and work for the overseers, the ones, who are in charge. They are convinced that they need these people in order to exist, because they have lost their ability to be self-reliant and independent and rely on their own powers. A lot of them don't have these powers anymore. And if these powers crop up in the genetic system, it's considered a gift to have psychic abilities, or healing abilities. This all was common to those people at one time, but they have lost all this information and knowledge, so they adhere to these different belief systems and concepts that are created by the leaders. The world still exists that way.

There are wars, all kinds of conditions, illnesses that are created by the ruling forces. They convince the people that this is true, and these people accept it and create their own conditions and situations here on Earth according to what they believe.

The belief is true. And they don't realize that they can create exactly what they want and they could live a lot more free and more powerful independently, supported by themselves, sharing, but the world has been divided for so long that it's very hard to get this information to the people. That's the reason that I came, in the 1950s, to Earth. I didn't realize at the time that I was going to play a big role in the Transformation of the Earth.

The current Transformation Process and the Return of Lost Knowledge

The Transformation was created to free the people and to return to them once again the powers that they had naturally. This is a big process that takes a lot of beings on many different levels, physical and non-physical levels cooperating, including the nature system and everything, the overseers of the nature system. The natural beings also have been informed, so that they are all working in harmony to create this Transformation for the Earth.

When I came in 1955, there was a question whether or not that a child could come from another dimension, manifest a physical body and live in the physical societies without any real damage to the body, to the thinking and to the emotions and so on. Of course, they keep track of me and every five years I undergo an examination and a balancing[4].

4   These examinations do not take place any further. The reason is that it is against spiritual laws if she is treated differently than other human beings on

I had to become used to the societies and the mistreatment and the controlling that subtly is woven into the structures. Most people don't see it and are not aware of it, because they have been doing it over and over for so many thousands of years, that it's now deep in the genetic system.

When we tried to send teachers and prophets in the past, they always ended up being massacred by the controlling forces here, so that the truth could not be given to the people - about the genetic manipulation and so on. The people couldn't get the true knowledge of what happened to the societies and why it is so difficult. Of course, it's very difficult to explain, because on the other hand, each individual Soul, before it's born into the physical realm makes a decision as to what its destiny will be and what lessons it will learn.

So it's all pre-chosen by each individual, but on the other hand, living in the societies, where there is so much control over the individual, and the religion, and your status in life – you know, people identify with their professions, they identify with their country, they identify with their religion, with their race and they don't retain their individuality that I AM A SOUL and that I AM LIVING IN A PHYSICAL BODY and this is only a temporary existence. Most of them have no idea of what will happen to them when this life is finished. They rely on the religions and the information that they receive from school, from science, from the structures and so on. All this has been controlled, the information, and what has been allowed to learn about the human being has been controlled by the controlling forces. Most people are not aware of it, so that they weren't allowed to ever receive their real truth about themselves, about their heritage, and about the greatness and their connection to the one Supreme God.

We on other planets, we still have the same concepts and beliefs that we had in the beginning, when we had all these powers. We understand God not as a being, but as the source of the energy for all of creation. And we don't have fear of death, because it's just a transition from one existence to another. This is why I formulated

Earth. Omnec herself decided to spend the rest of her life on Earth without special support, so that she has to deal with the same conditions like every other person on Earth and for her own spiritual growth. (Publisher's comment)

workshops to help the people. In the beginning, I was just thinking that my book would be the information, but apparently it wasn't enough, and the people wanted more. Out of this wanting came my spiritual work, which I wasn't expecting to do. But on the other hand, it must have been my destiny, because that's what I do.

Meanwhile, of course, I was married and had children and husbands on Earth, but I never would allow myself to become really a part of the systems that exist here. It's very difficult, of course, to try to exist within so many different systems and cultures and everything, and retain your individuality and your knowledge.

And that's why I was born on the planet Venus in another dimension and came to your planet as a young child, to retain the knowledge and information that I had gathered as a Soul through many incarnations and lifetimes on Earth. I can keep this information intact, and what I teach people is actually from what I KNOW and not what I've read about or what I've heard, but what I have experienced through many different life cycles on Earth and in other dimensions.

And to make the people aware there is a Christian heaven, but this Christian heaven has been created by the summed total consciousness of all the Christians that exist and that put their energy into this belief system. They don't realize that they have created this Christian heaven, and as well the place of torture, that if you don't live according to your religious beliefs and everything, if you commit suicide or you break some other spiritual law, they believe that after they die they have to be tortured and they have to suffer for that. Many of them find themselves in this situation after death[5].

The other dimensions are just as vast as the physical world, with all the galaxies and all the systems. It's no different, except that it's not material.

I try to explain our concept of God and our understanding of the human being in connection to these other dimensions and what it means to the individual, and to realize the power that the individual possesses. Each thought is energy, and every thought has an effect

---

5 Since 1999, Omnec has shared her information about the life of Jesus Christ and the Christian Heaven in lectures and workshops. The text *The True Story of Christ* is included in PART TWO of this book. (Publisher's comment)

on the environment, on the world, on your society, on your life, on other human beings. People are not aware of that, and they don't control their thinking, they have no control. Usually, their thoughts are directed by media, by societies, by school, by mother, by father, by religious groups, and so the human being doesn't direct their thoughts and energy toward building and creating the world that they would like to have. They live in fear, and they give their energy to support this fear and the negative things that exist in our society. With their thoughts and their fear, they make stronger the negative forces that have ruled this world for so long. But it's coming to an end, and that's why we are in the Transformation Process.

The Transformation Process was created so that the world – the Earth – and the societies and the people wouldn't cease to exist but will have another chance to create the world as it was once and as it should be.

It started with mass meetings of all the spiritual overlords and masters, advanced beyond the physical realm. They all together along with other beings who had a lot to do with what the Earth is now, including the manipulation and control, these beings have evolved to a spiritual point where now they want to correct what they have done here on Earth. All this controlling and manipulating. They want to give the people a chance individually to retain their Soul freedom and their own spiritual power.

Love is the basis for all of creation. In reality, it's the strongest power on Earth, except for fear. Fear is the opposite. Fear is destructive, and fear is just as strong as love, but love is something that exists forever. It's not limited to the physical world. It doesn't have any borders, and it doesn't see unequalness. Love works on an equal basis, and it's healing, and it's what gives the people the hope and the ability to create a beautiful life for themselves.

You have a choice in every situation to give up and become a victim of circumstances or you can become a master of your own destiny and choose what you wish to put your energy into and what you wish to have as part of this world here. Individually, we have these energies and these abilities, and they will become stronger during the Transformation Process. But the people have to be taught how to use these thought forms, how to send this energy in a positive way to support the structures that exist here, because at one time there is coming the day when the negative structures and everything that was created by the controlling forces on the Earth have to give up their rule. And everything that they have created, the banking systems, the computers, the factories, everything that's organized and controlled by money will collapse physically in these structures. And we have to then create the kind of world that we want to have.

Our Concept of the Creator

I am going to give you an example, I will try to create a little concept for you of how that we see creation and the Creator and ourselves in the theme of everything that exists.

The Creator is a source of energy that everything was created from. At one time, the Creator decided: I love myself, and I don't want to cease to exist, so with my power and energy, I will create everything, every kind of life form that they can use each other for their existence in the physical world, and they can learn lessons here by being exposed to the opposite of what it is. And itself can realize through its existence and experiences the total sum of what the energy is from the Creator.

The Creator created everything, every mineral, every plant, every animal, every human, because everything is a Soul, and this Soul is from this pure energy in non-ending cycles. So everything creates from itself and continues creating, so there is no end to existence, and there is no end to the Creator. So therefore the Creator loved itself and created from itself all that there is in never-ending cycles of continuum, so that itself continued to exist through what it has created, including each individual Soul. Every mineral, every plant, every animal, every drop of water, is living and is a part of this living energy source, and we are part of it.

We are more highly evolved in our individual evolution, because we have gone through the process of being a mineral and being a plant and being an animal. And as a human being we need all of these life forms for our physical existence, and yet we also have to care for these other life forms, because it is our existence, and we would cease to exist without them for our nourishment, for our physical bodies, for our environment, for the world that we live in. We depend on these other life forms.

It's easier in the other realms. You can just collect this energy and you can create what you wish from this energy. We have this ability. In the physical world, it's the same process, but of course, you have to manually and physically do this. If you want to create something, you have to have a concept, and then you have to have the material to create what you have created in your mind. Imagination is the key to creation. Whatever you can imagine becomes reality or is reality. That's the way it works. Every glass, every table, every home, every material that exists in this world was once a concept and idea that was somewhere in a person's imagination, before it became reality. So that is the key to everything that exists, first it has to be in your mind, in your imagination. And if you have so many concepts and so many ideas that are not your own, then eventually you become blocked and you cannot accept that everything is possible. Whatever you want and whatever you wish to create is possible. It can be. But when you don't believe it, then you have blocked it, because you have accepted another belief system – from scientists, from school, from whatever. But this is not the reality of what is. It hinders the creation, the freedom of creating and building what we wish to have, when you think that these are all the possibilities there are. Allow yourself to say: Yes, everything is possible, and therefore anything I imagine can be. When you have that idea, and when you can look at any Soul in any form, whether it's mineral, plant, animal, or human form, and not see the physical but see the Soul on an equal level and love this Soul, no matter how horrible their life choice might be, then you love unconconditionally. That's how the Creator intended it and how the Creator loves its creation.

As human beings, you go through an evolution, too, in your intelligence. You start out in a more primitive state, and you accept more easily and follow and obey the rules. Then eventually you reach a state as a human being where you start to question the reality and the validity of reality. Why are there wars? Why is there suffering?

Why is this, why is that? Because we create it! We create it, because we put our energy into these belief systems, and that's the way the world is. Of course, we choose a lot of the suffering, because it is learning for us. As a Soul, there is no negative or positive, everything is a valuable lesson. If you are a mass murderer, if you are a homeless person, if you are rich and you are talented and you are famous, if you are beautiful or ugly, it doesn't make any difference. It is an experience that you have chosen, so that you as a Soul can understand creation and your part in it.

Good and bad have been created by the societies. These are concepts. In reality, there is nothing good or bad. Everything is valuable, everything is for a purpose. We have to accept that it is for a purpose. We have to accept sometimes that we chose to have cancer or to be crippled or to have our brain not correct or whatever. This is a way that we learn. Until you've experienced everything, you can sit there and say: "Oh yes, I have done that, I have been there", and you can have compassion and understanding and love, real love, unconditional.

Our love in our societies is based on concepts and standards. What is beautiful, what is ugly, what is acceptable, what is good, what is bad, but these are not concepts that we create, this is what we have picked up from everybody else, or from television, magazines, other people. But in reality, every Soul is beautiful and perfect.

The physical body reflects what you are as a Soul. When you can see the beauty and not see the physical structures, then you are starting to be on the evolutionary step of developing consciously whether maybe you won't have to come back to this world and experience at all. But that's just as individual as you are.

The Design of Creation and the Birth of the Soul

The energy source that I call God ¬ or you can call God, and there are many different Gods in many different religions with many different names, but I think in total, it has the same meaning – this energy source is the center of creation. Imagine there is a centrifuge and everything is spinning at a high rate. Now if you put in stones, and sand, and water, you will find that the heavy materials fall to the outer edge. In relation to existence, this outer edge will be where the physical world is relating to the center of creation, where is just pure energy, and there is no material. The more toward the center of creation you go, the less and less material you find and the more and more energy there is. Everything is energy, it's just vibrating at a different frequency, that we cannot perceive with our physical eyes. We assume that everything is solid and material, because we have created it to be so in our environment and in our world. But in reality it's a collection of atoms, and it's only energy. And if you also are energy, then you can become aware that reality is a perception.

In the beginning, when you were first created as a Soul, you had no form, you had no experience, you were just energy. The only thing you knew is that you came from a greater source of energy. That is the reason why God created the different dimensions and the physical world. It's for the Soul to go down through these different dimensions to the physical world and to start to experience the opposite of what it is. It's like a little Soul that is born, and he is jumping around and he is happy, he is a light. But then, when he looks to the great light, the great source, he wonders: "Am I really a light?", and God says: "Well, then you have to go down and encounter the darkness to experience the opposite of what you are. You don't become that darkness. You are a light in the darkness. But to encounter the opposite of what you are, is a way of learning what you are." The Soul learns through experience of being, not from hearing something, not from reading books, or gathering information, but from actually experiencing everything. And the Soul wants to experience everything, because then it can become as great as as that what you came from, and a part of that what you came from.

Since the basis of our creation is love, that's a greater part of our existence. Love is something, that ... if you understand unconditional love, it's love for no reason. The Creator loves you just because you exist, and that's how we have to learn to love, too. To love the most terrible person that creates such hell in your life, that you can love them and be thankful for the lessons that they have given you, for the hard times that they have created. And when you can reach that point, then you are on your way to really becoming a higher consciousness.

Most people live by their emotions, and they cannot control their emotions, and they cannot let go of things, pain, trauma. When somebody does something to them, then they want to do something back.

This is the nature of our learning process. When we learn to understand ourselves, our emotions, our physical body versus ourselves as a Soul, and when we can learn to have an overview of everything, then we don't have to be here anymore.

The Complexity of Human Experiences and the Meaning of Unconditional Love

When you are first created as Soul, you just know you are energy. And then, you start your journey, down to the physical realms, for your experience, and for your evolution as a Soul. In the physical realm, you go through the physical evolution of mineral, plant, animal, and human. On a Soul level, every experience that you have in every state of your existence is collected by the Soul and becomes a part of what you are. Every Soul is different, every experience is different. No two Souls can have the same experience. They can have similar experiences, or they can choose to be born at the same time, or created at the same time and go through many many evolutions of life encountering one another and experiencing together. This is like a Soul family, I call it. And they encounter them until eventually, they become connected somehow in their physical life, because they are a family. They belong together, they have experienced things together.

After a while, you have experienced with so many thousands and millions of Souls, that the whole entire human race – they are your family in reality. Because you have had encounters with them, you have had experiences. You may have killed them, you may have had children, or been their lovers or whatever. The human state is very complex. It is not simple anymore, because it involves emotions, connections, creating families, responsibilities, so every human being is a complex of all these situations and all these experiences within their own lives, within their own surroundings. And they are so different. But on the other hand, if you can learn to see each human being as a Soul rather than how they look, if you can experience that, you can experience the love of creation.

I love every individual, and I don't judge anyone. We have to learn not to judge one another and accept. This is the problem. Most of the people on Earth, they pay more attention to other people and interfere in their individual lives rather than paying attention to themselves. It's a process of learning to accept others and to allow the others to be what they are. On the other planets, this is just a part of our societies, that we don't interfere and that we accept and love the individual whatever experiences they have chosen.

This is what it's coming to on the Earth. Of course, we haven't reached really the process of this understanding yet. I think that's the reason, too, for the workshops, so that people have an opportunity to have a different perception and to learn to see from another perception. I think, each individual has to go through a Transformation Process, and it's part of developing a higher consciousness.

As a Soul on the Journey through the Levels of Creation

Your journey down to the different dimensions: Every dimension has an important effect upon the individual, because they carry certain energies, and these energies are instilled within the Soul, and also they supply you with a certain kind of life energy and abilities that you need in the physical world to experience and to be. When you are first created as a Soul, as I said, you didn't have any consciousness or no awareness, because you had no experience. That's why you take the journey down into the physical realm. It's for experiencing, and it's for collecting these experiences. And as

I said before, you can't really learn unless you ARE. You have to experience and to BE THAT, in order to know what IT IS.

As Soul[6], when you are first created, the first dimension that you go into, where the energy is divided into the positive and the negative effects, is called the ETHERIC DIMENSION. This is where the division of this energy began. It's only for experiencing, for understanding. When you come into the etheric dimension, you collect energy from this dimension, and this energy is to protect the Soul, because the pure energy of Soul cannot exist in another dimension or in the dual energy without being a part of that. So the first body that it takes on is the etheric body. It's like you collected like a magnet, you gather this energy, when you enter into this realm, and also this energy provides a protecting energy and body for you that you can experience everything that is possible in this existence. Also, the energy from this dimension gives you the ability as a Soul to know that you are divine, that you are connected to the Creator, to creation. It's where many of the saints in the past here on the physical world collected their information, their spiritual information, the divine information is from this dimension. So you collect the energy to provide yourself with a body and protection and you collect also the energy that allows you to have the awareness that you are a part of something divine, to creation.

The next dimension that you cross into as a Soul then will be the CAUSAL DIMENSION. This dimension is also called the place of the Akashic records. In reality, you as a Soul collect all the information from every experience that you have, so the experience is carried within you. But also the energy from this dimension allows the Soul to have access to every existence that it has had, every experience that it has had in different time lapses or whatever in the physical realm. So the causal dimension gives you the causal body, the protection for the Soul, and the body that you can exist in this

6   Dimension / Mantra / Sound / Color
Anami Lok (God Plane) / HU / Music of the Universe / White
Soul / SHANTI / Stark wind / Yellow
Etheric / BAJU / Humming of bees / Gold
Causal / AUM (OM) / Ringing of little bells / Purple
Mental / MANA / Flowing of water / Blue
Astral / KALA / Ocean breeze / Rose/Pink
Physical / ALAYA / Thunderstorm / Green

CAUSAL DIMENSION. A lot of the religious heavens that they have created for their after death experiences are also located in the causal realm. There are many temples of learning, and it's a very vast dimension. Many people have experienced this dimension and the beings that exist there in between lives in a near death experience.

The next dimension that you cross into then is the MENTAL DIMENSION. Also, you collect a body, a protection for the Soul, it's called the mental body, and the energy from this dimension also allows you to have the ability to visualize and create with your thoughts – it's called the mental dimension.

And the dimension that's next for the Soul before it enters in the physical realm is the astral. The ASTRAL DIMENSION also gives you a body, a protection. See, the Soul is in the middle, and everybody that you collect on the way down, is another body that's over another body – it's like many layers of an onion or whatever. The Soul is the center, this is the source of your existence, of your being. The astral dimension gives you an astral body that you collect from this realm, this energy and you create a body. And the energy from this dimension also allows the physical body to have the experience of feelings – emotions, physical feelings and so on. It deals with the senses.

Then, of course, you come to the PHYSICAL REALM. And when you first enter, as a Soul, into the physical realm, you enter into the mineral state. You don't enter into a physical human body, because you have to go through – in the physical realm you have to go through a certain evolution, and you have to be every kind of mineral there is on every physical planet, and serve every purpose that a mineral can serve, before you are free then to go back to the other dimensions, and collect energy in between each life cycle. As a certain mineral, when you serve a certain purpose, then you are free to collect more energy and choose your next existence. Then you come back as another mineral. This goes on until you are finished with the mineral realm of existence, and then you are free to go on your evolution into the plant stage, and it goes on and on. And it's the same procedure that you have to experience being a plant, and you have to serve a certain purpose in the physical realm, maybe for a higher life force or whatever. When you have served a certain purpose, then you are free to go and choose the next stage that you will serve as a plant. Whether it's to be eaten, or for beauty, or for nourishment for the air, or whatever. The different plants that serve under the ocean, and on the surface on the planet and people's gardens. So you experience everything that's possible in that realm of existence, and then you enter into the animal kingdom.

There, of course, you can be a fish, a fowl, you can be something in the ocean, or a land creature. You go through your whole evolution as an animal, and experiencing, serving as food, or to work for men to help them do their gardens, create their houses, or then eventually as a pet.

I believe that, when you have a pet, it is preparing to be a human being, and that is why it lives in such close contact with human beings. So it can learn the way that we behave and interact with one another, and they can learn their place.

Then eventually, of course, you come into the human state, and when you reach the human state, then you realize that you need all of these other life forms that live in the physical to exist yourself, for your substance, for your physical body. At the same time, you are still connected to the other dimensions, the energy flows continuously from the other dimensions, through different chakras that are correlated to these dimensions. This supplies you with your life force and your energy and your abilities to function in this physical world.

No one can actually contemplate how old a Soul actually can be, because it's almost impossible. Our existence is forever, and there is no end, and when it began, you know, that depends on when you were created individually as a Soul, and when you began your journey. Souls are created almost every second of our time in the physical world by the thousands. It's always an endless procedure of new Souls being created and beginning their journey into the physical realm. The new Souls start with being minerals, and the older Souls that no longer can have anything to experience in the physical realm as a human being have to go on their evolution a little bit higher in their consciousness. Then, they serve different purposes and do different kinds of work on the other dimensions, or they can choose to be nature spirits and still live in the physical world. There is an endless variety of experiences that the Soul can have after the physical life experiences are finished.

Being a human is very complex and more difficult, because you have to be every race, you have to be both sexes, you have to experience everything that you can experience as a human being. The variation is endless. Until eventually you reach a consciousness level and you start your search then for the truth rather than accepting the conventional truths and religions and information that is given. I believe that most people who are searching now for various kinds of truth for themselves have reached this level where they are toward the end of their existence as a human being. It depends on you individually, what you can learn, what you can experience and how much you can accept the way things are and the function of all creation and everything. And you can find your place and your – you know, when you realize your connection to all that is, and you realize your relationship to all of creation, and the power that you have as a human being, and when you have lived and you can no longer experience any human realm, then you have to begin your experiences in the other dimensions as a highly evolved Soul.

You can think about your existence, when you are first created as a Soul and where you are now. You can't calculate how long your existence has been. Some people learn more than others, and some advance faster than others, it's all individual, depending on your experiences that you have chosen. Sometimes, people choose to come back into the physical realm to be a teacher for others, to help the people who are still searching or still looking for the truth. Like I said, it's always free will and choice.

The greatest gift that the Creator gave us is our individuality and our ability to have our choice and free will. That is something that we don't want taken away from the Soul. If we left societies to their own development, eventually, human beings would lose more and more of their free will and abilities. But that was their plan. And the reason for the Transformation is that we have to put an end to this controlling and manipulating and give the free will and the power back to the people.

The Creation of a Consciously Desired World

That's another whole subject, the Transformation Process and its effects on your environment, on yourself individually and physically, and the changes that you can be prepared for ... that's another whole subject that takes a lot of concentration. Of course, you have to be willing to participate, consciously aware that there is a Transformation. There are people that reject the idea, that cannot accept it and they're so tied into the structures of the controlling forces, and the computers, and the bank, and the genetic lines, and so on, and they don't want to give up the power. They can't accept that. As I say, they have to die in the physical realm and come back – I call it "recycling", they go through a process where they're in a body that they can accept the Transformation and become a part of the process consciously.

There will be a lot of suicides, people who can't accept the changes that are happening, when the political structures, and the organized religions and the money system and the computer systems, and electricity – everything that people have come to rely on – when it no longer exists, then they have to rely on their own intuition and creative abilities to exist. But they CAN! It's just a matter of letting go of the fear and learning to live and accept the new world as it will be.

This new world will be created by you and your thoughts and your energy that you help to supply for this process. Later on, we will discuss these energy techniques and what you can do, and the Transformation Process. The more people know and participate, the faster the procedure can take place. It all depends on YOU. You have the free will and choice.

If you hear prophecies ... of course, there have always been prophecies about the end of the world and destruction and so on, you only have to make a decision: What do you want? Because, really, it's up to you. And if you put your belief and your power in this phenomena happening, then it will happen. But don't forget that you create whatever you wish to experience!

I am hoping that this information can help you to understand step by step how you can develop and use your power for what you will and what you wish and have.

This is just the explanation of how people came into this solar system, this universe, and how that Soul came into this world and what part that I play in it. The part I play is much more than I thought. Apparently, I have a lot more to do, and a lot more information to give to the people. But this all has to be given at exactly the right time. Otherwise, it's useless information, because it won't do any good.

You have to learn to accept the development of the consciousness. And that the consciousness can't always take all the information and put it into the Soul and into the system where it becomes a part of you. This takes work, concentration, and the will from the individual person to really participate and take place in what is happening, and not just be blind and walk around, and things are happening, and you don't understand.

But if you want the answers, you can have those answers. I can't give you all the answers, because some of the answers you have to find for yourself. Because everyone of you has a master, you have spiritual teachers in other dimensions, you have relatives that are in other dimensions, and connections from other lifetimes, and these all serve to guide and protect you while you are in the physical world and give you the information.

Everything I teach is from my own experience and knowledge. It's not guesswork, and it's not information that I have gathered through years of reading, it's purely experience and knowledge from my own existence, or existences.

To really become advanced, you have to learn to tolerate each other and to accept each other as you are, and not judge, but be open to other people and other ideas and concepts, because the only way that you can create your own concepts is if you can understand the other persons point of view and if you can take the information that's good for you. Everybody has to decide for themselves. I can't tell a person what religion is best, or what teaching ¬ this has to be an individual choice, too. If you reject the information, that's your free will, and that's OK as well. I am not here to prove anything to anybody, but just to give you information. That's what's important, not to be an example for everybody, and I won't tell anybody how to live their life, and I don't fit into concepts that people create of what a spiritual teacher should be or what they have expectations of, because I also have to live my life according to what I think is correct for myself and make choices. And of course, I never have tried to express to people that I am perfect in any way, because I believe, when you reach this state of perfection, then you don't live in the physical anymore. Because this is a physical world, and you have to find the best way for yourself to exist in this reality and to deal with the societies. But if you can learn to do it in peace and without fear, and sharing the information and helping others, that's the best that you can do to help yourself and to help the world that you live in.

The Unknown History of our Solar System and the Spiritual Transformation of the Earth – Transcript Part 2 –

Author: Omnec Onec

My Journey from the Astral Level of Venus to the Physical Earth

When I first came to Earth in 1955, I had to enter through a city called Retz that exists on the physical realm as well as on the other dimensions. This is a doorway where we can manifest a physical body in a certain temple. Then I walked into a small space craft with my uncle Odin and we took our journey to the Earth. When we came into a certain parameter of the Earth, we landed in a special temple in Tibet. It's also a monastery. This has served for thousands of years for extraterrestrials to adjust to the gravity and the atmosphere of the Earth. I was kept there for a year just to learn how the physical body functions and how to speak, to use my vocal chords and of course to adjust to the Earth itself and the atmosphere and to learn to eat, just basic things that people know from the time they were a child. My having a new physical body, I wasn't adjusted or acclimated to this environment. Because it is isolated from the regular human beings in the cultures and the cities, I am not so much affected by the emotions and the aggressions and things that I am not used to. Of course, this was a learning process and it was very strange being a little girl – in the body of a little girl – even though I had existed 130 Earth years in the city on Venus where I lived. But this is a non-physical dimension, it's the astral dimension. We don't have a need to eat, we just absorb the energy and we also can absorb the energy and manifest whatever we need or for our environment perhaps. We have several learning temples there. There is this one special temple which is the entrance into the physical world. But once we make the decision to manifest a physical body and to live in the physical world, we can't return to our home except through astral travel or Soul travel, when one leaves the body. It's a decision you make for the rest of your life and that means that you take the responsibility that you will reside here until your life cycle is finished. It was an adventure for me at first.

I knew of my karmic ties to this little girl and her family. After they got my permission that I would go through this procedure, we had to make sure that I was there as in the Soul to accompany the birth of the little girl even though I was not physical. I had to accompany her during the birth as if I were a twin to receive the genetic patterns and everything for the future here, and so that I would have similarities to her and I could be adjusted to the physical world and have a body that was similar to herself. Also, this gave me the ability to use her birth date as my birth date when I'm here on Earth.

On Venus, we have a different time perception, existence, we live to be 500 physical years. Our development is much slower in the physical process or aging process and on the other hand, our bodily functions are much faster, it's very strange, I had to adjust to this.

The family that I was living with just thought that I was Sheila, because she had perished in a bus accident. The bus had burned and her body with it, and then I was placed with people that were waiting for the ambulances and transport to a hospital for examinations with a duplicate of the note that she had to give to her grandmother. She hadn't seen her grandmother in two or three years, so the similarity was enough that the grandmother thought that I was her little granddaughter.

Later on I myself informed my Earth mother and later my grandmother, but I wasn't publicly known at the time. I was trying to really adjust to the environment, the culture, the thinking process, the emotions. Meanwhile I was also observing some of the problematic difficulties that exist here on Earth with people's consciousness and with their emotions and connection to others.

I knew that one day I would have a book and I really thought that this was all that was required, that I write this book and inform the people. At first it was an experiment to see if a child could survive on the Earth, growing up here, coming from another dimension and everything and adjust. Of course it was very difficult and there were some comical and amusing things that happened to me as I grew up which are explained in my book. There were even funny things that happened at the monastery.

Eventually I married an Earth man and had two children. And later I divorced him and remarried. Altogether I have four children. I lived a normal life, and worked at many different jobs, because I didn't continue my education. I wasn't preparing to be a spiritual teacher, this was not something that was in my thoughts or awareness. But I often was working with children, with their Souls, either before they were physical or while they were sleeping. On the other dimensions it was quite common that I was studying with them or playing with them there to make a connection. I didn't realize that this connection in the future would be a way that they could recognize me and come to get the teachings that were necessary for these special Souls.

The Preparation of my Spiritual Work

So I lived kind of an incognito life, nobody knew about me except my husband, close friends and eventually Paul Twitchell who brought Eckankar, the same teachings as I know, to America. It was decided when I was a child still on Venus that I will be working with him and help to establish this organization, this teaching. In my early twenties I was working very close with Paul, doing dancing and starting youth organizations, establishing the courses and making information available for people, doing meditations at my home. It was a very important step, because we were bringing this information that had been hidden for thousands of years in the monasteries in Tibet.

After the manipulation of the human beings we decided that these teachings will be protected so that they would not be manipulated or that pieces wouldn't be taken out. For centuries, it was only passed down from master to student, it wasn't a written script, because as you know, many people, when they translate things from the ancient languages, they – if they don't agree with certain aspects of the teachings – they may remove this from the information. That is part of the controlling and manipulation of the information that people receive here on Earth. Including the bible. The bible has been translated several times and the first translator into English was King James. King James didn't agree with reincarnation and other dimensions and a lot of the explanations that Christ had explained to people. So this information actually was just removed from the bible. That's why the bible sometimes is really very confusing, because parts are missing and you don't get the whole story.

In the early years, like I said, I was preparing for my spiritual work individually which came later after my book was published and when my children were in college or working. I had no responsibilities to a family at the time, not every day like I usually did. So I was free to travel and to give more information, and when I was invited to Germany, I had my first lecture at a UFO-Congress in Düsseldorf. There I met my basically supporting first Soul family which is still in contact with me here in Germany today and supports me.

As a matter of fact, today I still live with these people, many of them. Actually, when I returned to America after the lecture, I was still working in a regular job, although I had done some TV interviews and different things for my book being published in America. Of course I had done many interviews with different countries, with Russia, Germany, Italy, I don't know how many interviews there were. There was a lot of TV, and I was in the media for a couple of years and on television shows in America. But then I returned to my job. In between working a regular job, I was selling books as well from the restaurant where I worked. This was kind of amusing, because the people in the restaurant had no idea that I had a book until it was published and you can imagine the surprise and the disbelief.

Reasons for Being Here

But on the other hand, this is the whole purpose, that I am here to make you aware that the extraterrestrials within this solar system are actually the ancestors of the people on Earth. This was my intention when I was making my appearances here in Germany and America to make the people overcome the fear. Because what you hear in the media is really the events that are mostly negative about abductions, about negative aliens, scary looking aliens. And of course there is the influence from science-fiction movies which represent kind of horror to the people that every alien is trying to take over the world and that the human beings also will be taken over and losing their abilities. So to deal with the people who have got this information first it's not easy and you have to be very strong to overcome the fun they make and that they don't take you seriously. On the other hand I can understand their perception and what they have learned, and I can deal with that, you know, because I have a sense of humor, and of course, when I do close-ups on television I was always making a joke, that they were still looking for my antennas. Because humor is one of the things that has helped me on Earth to deal with a lot of things to be happy and not to become offended and to understand that people have the right to decide what they believe. I have had scientists, psychiatrists and everybody, you know, examining me and evaluating my mental capacity. Sometimes that was very amusing to see the situations that I ended up in, but I overcame all that, because I was continuously very serious and I retained my dignity. I wouldn't resort to behaving in a way that a lot of people behave when they get very upset and they try to force someone to believe what they are saying, they can become very aggressive, and then all of a sudden you are in a conflict, and I think it's totally unnecessary to spend energy to try to convince somebody of something, if they don't want to believe it. That has to come from inside, and that has to come from a feeling. So I have determined that I will continually be dignified and nice and treat them with respect and I ask for that in return. Usually, the television people and the public media treat me with a lot of respect and dignity, even if they laugh behind my back, it doesn't matter. But on the other hand I have had an opportunity to reach a lot of people. I am still continuously contacted by people who feel a connection to me before they even meet me. So they follow their intuition and they organize workshops, and of course I go. When the people ask and they want more information and want a contact, then I try my best to be there and to do that.

I am planning to return to America, so we started to create this series of information for people who would like to get this information that can't contact me for the next years or so. Because also they need this information elsewhere in the world. I have been in Germany for 10 years working and so I have to start a new chapter in my life. I have the opportunity to present this information to you and make it available for you to have it privately in your own home and take your time to study or listen to what I have to present. That's what we are in the process of doing, and I am in the process of changing, going back to my grandchildren and my daughter. And probably for a while I'll just be Grandma Sheila. And then when I get my book republished, then I'll start working in America.

The Transformation Process of the Earth and Each Individual

I wanted to extend a little bit of information about myself before I begin to speak about the Transformation Process which is now happening, we are in the midst of it, how it came about and then the reasons why, because it's very important that people are prepared when this change starts happening in our societies. I can't give you a definite date, because this all depends on each individual themselves how much energy they put into the Transformation Process and how much fear they can let go of and go forward with a positive attitude and feeling good that the Earth will be once again healed and free of these negative forces that control and manipulate the societies and the people here. I can't give you all the information about the Transformation, but I can give you some and maybe touch upon the most important aspects of the Transformation Process and help prepare you individually for what will happen in your societies, so that you can have a chance to do something about what's happening rather than being afraid and panicking.

Change always is at first chaotic and creates confusion, but usually change means that it's a new beginning, it's a chance to readjust and relocate yourself – think your situation out and figure out the best way to survive mentally, emotionally, and physically of course. So I am going to try to go over this process with you today step by step – why the decision was made, how it began, the effects it will have on you and your societies here, and why it is necessary.

Each of you of course must go through a Transformation Process within individuals – it's not just an overnight thing when the world is going to change drastically. Things will get worse before they get better. That's the way it goes, if you get a wound, it usually has to come to a point where it's very bad, and then the poison is released, and then the wound can heal. And the Earth and the societies here are the same way. Before the healing takes place, there has to be a releasing of the poison, of the negative information, and a lot of things will come to light and be exposed that people kept undercover, things that lead this world and control our societies. So you'll have a lot of shock and a lot of recovering to do. And that's what I am trying to help you to – I want to prepare you with this transformation information.

The Transformation Process began centuries ago – the idea. And then there were lots of beings that had to participate and cooperate to make it really possible. It was an alternative to former methods of informing people with spiritual information and they found that a person that was born on Earth, whether his father was an extraterrestrial or whether he came from a higher dimension, somehow still had the genetic manipulation with the brain, and therefore they didn't retain all the information. Then we had a lot of interference from the government, because when the people from other planets appeared to them and spoke with the leaders of the countries, it was the same results as in the beginning. They were interested in the technology, but not at all into informing the people of the Earth, the masses, of what the manipulation was that took place and the difficulties and how that the societies originally were divided and the races set in conflict with one another. To overcome these old concepts is very difficult, and especially when you don't have any support.

So we decided that the other alternative was that the people on Earth and the planet itself go through a Transformation Process in order to shut down all of the existing structures that were erected and are now part of our societies and that were created by the negative forces. The structures that still control and manipulate the people, like they are working for the ones who are rich and they use all their energy and their time, so that they can survive in the society. So we decided that the people had to be freed and the consciousness had to be changed drastically. There was an influx of information coming from the 1800's up until this point, and the esoteric movement grew in the societies and became more and more popular and common. Peoples' interest in this information and knowledge was very active, so we decided that the only thing that we could do was work on changing the frequency of the Earth in order to protect the existing cultures and provide more spiritual information. People are now turning to natural methods of healing, such as healing with energy, with stones and crystals, and eating. These are old methods that were originally the people's way of life. And now it's being reintroduced to the people. They call it the New Age, but on the other hand it's something that was common in the original colonies on Earth and on other planets.

We are very aware that a lot of the illnesses are created, because the people believe that they going to get ill if they eat something or do something, and they are convinced that they will get cancer or get ill, and sometimes needlessly they create the illnesses within their own selves. When the people realize that they have the power of healing themselves, they don't have to adhere to the fact anymore, that when they are 65, they are old and useless. The aging process is also a part of the concepts of what has been instilled in the people.

In former times, people had much longer lives, and it was quite common and average, but nowadays, it has been shortened quite a bit, because the people believe this and accept that they are getting old at a certain age. Age is a concept also.

Everything is a matter of perception. Even reality. I try to explain to people that reality is a perception. And what you see and what you experience depends on your consciousness or your awareness. To explain that, I usually give you a simple concept: You just take a chair, and you try to figure out – OK – this chair is relatively small in comparison to being a human being, that we can sit on it and be comfortable. But for an insect, this chair is a relatively large structure which takes many hours to scrabble over, to crawl over. And to you the chair is solid material, but to a photon, this chair is a collection of atoms that it can pass right through. You think the chair is still. It seems to be still, but if you are in a spaceship, looking at the Earth, then this chair is rotating with the Earth. So it's a matter of your perception.

And in countries where they don't have chairs, it's not common, then the reality of the chair really doesn't exist. So this is one reality, one concept in different perceptions of one reality. And this is a small reality.

But this world is very big. Even to a Soul, you know, when you are looking at a certain lifetime, it looks like a grain of sand. But if you enter into this, and you conform your body and your size to the environment, then it's overwhelming. You are overwhelmed by the surroundings, by the emotions, by the evolvement with every person, and the cultures, and the information. So people only have one perception of their reality.

I have never questioned anyone's reality, whatever their experience is. Even if they have a phenomenal ability to see other dimensions and other beings, this doesn't mean that it doesn't exist, it's only that we don't have this perception. So we have to allow ourselves to relate to each other and accept each other's reality.

That's the problem in this world, because everybody is busy trying to convince the other one through conflicts, through aggression – to accept their reality and what they see and what they feel. If people would learn to accept each other and each other's reality, each others choices in life, and pay more attention to their own development, there would be less conflicts and less problems. This is something that comes with the raising of the consciousness.

So we decided to ... I say "We", because every person that's involved in the Transformation or a part of it, is included. It's not one person doing something, it's all the spirits that rule over the nature spirits here on Earth and each individual nature spirit themselves. They exist, even though they are not visible to every person. But some people have the perception and awareness to actually visualize or to see them or have a connection to them. They are very important because they are the guardians of the plant kingdom, the mineral kingdom, or the animal kingdom. There are individual entities that protect and take care of these different life forms here on Earth. And they live within our environment with us. The Indians often communicated with them, that was a part of their teachings to have a connection to the nature spirits and to respect them. We are coming more and more back to that in our cultures, where the old teachings and ideas from different cultures are being integrated into our belief system. This is allowing the different consciousnesses to be more vast rather than so closed.

I can see the change in the consciousness of the people, because of the reaction and reception of different information. And people no longer think that things are impossible. With the computers, for instance, with television, with films, and being able to receive information of anything that happens on the Earth in a matter of minutes now. This helps to change the perception of all the possibilities that there are.

When I first started talking about different dimensions in the sixties and seventies, people had no concept or idea of that. But with science-fiction movies, often presenting ideas and concepts of other dimensions, of holograms, of parallel dimensions, people are being more and more exposed to this information, and it's becoming quite a normality and something they can accept readily. At one time this was beyond their imagination or perception, and they absolutely couldn't understand or accept this possibility.

So I can see the changes over the years by existing here and watching society, and I can see that the people are losing their faith in the organized religions, because it doesn't provide them with enough information about their past and about Soul itself and about what will happen after this life is over. This confusion is ... the veil is being lifted so that the people have a clearer view and an understanding that even after death, that you still exist, but in a different way. Your consciousness doesn't cease, your awareness and your ability to perceive. It's just a different awareness, perception, and abilities. There are more and more books about near-death-experiences, out-of-the-body-travel. Our governments have been aware of this for years. They have been doing research secretly, and now it's that you can contact different groups and receive all kinds of information.

Even about the Transformation. The Transformation is a widespread knowledge. It started – I think in the 1930s or so – they started the process, where that people were creating meditation groups for instance. And this also helps to change the frequency. They realized that meditation is a way to calm yourself, and then later on they realized that spirit has an effect on nature, that you can write something on a glass of water and you can change the energy of this glass of water. They are realizing more and more the non-physical worlds and possibilities and how the energy from us as human beings can actually transfer the things that are surrounding us and create a different energy.

Operation Peace Meditation Program

I know that I was asked to create a meditation by the spiritual hierarchy and my people. All I had to do was choose a day, and I got a group together from all over Europe, and all ages, children up to adults, and older people. We decided that we would choose a day during the week, because that didn't interfere with the holidays of the churches and the organized religions, where most people put their attention on church and prayer and attending services. So we chose a day between Monday and Friday. Everybody wrote their request on a piece of paper. Some people thought Monday, the beginning of the week, was the best, some thought Friday, because it was the end of the week. Everybody had their own ideas. I decided on Wednesday, because it's a neutral day, it's in the middle of the week. Apparently, when we counted the votes, there were more requests for Wednesday. So Wednesday became the chosen day for what we call "Operation Peace".

I chose this name, because everybody takes 10 minutes in their own time, and focuses their attention on peace for this Earth, and healing the Earth. You can choose any kind of project, you can take the rainforest, you can take the whales, you can take different projects that involve the Earth, or you can just picture the whole Earth itself. You do a 10-minutes-meditation. And this day, everybody choses their own time, there is not a set time, because everybody has different schedules, and different time sequences all over the world, there are different times. So we didn't set a certain time, we leave it up to the individual to choose 10 minutes when they have the free time and quiet to do this. Some people get together on every Wednesday, and then they chose to listen to maybe my CD or so, and then afterwards they do a group meditation and visualize peace on the Earth. This started, I think it was in 1992, I am not really sure of the date.

I was also advised that if I created a day and requested that everybody meditates, that the beings on the higher dimensions would also participate with their energy to the Earth. This way, we could create a spiritual group consciousness, a united consciousness, where we are all focusing our energy, our meditation, or prayers ¬ whichever way you decide to send healing energy to this Earth. It has been quite successful; it has been going on for years. I believe that it also exists on the internet. That was just to show the people what 10 minutes of really focusing their attention on one project, and it didn't matter where you were in the world or what time of the day. So it creates a 24-hours cycle of meditation on Wednesday. If you have been given the different time sites all over the Earth. It has been very successful. It doesn't take much energy and much time, and everybody is interested in peace and in healing the Earth. It doesn't interfere with religious beliefs or anything.

I believe that every person has the right to choose a certain religion if they do and if they want. I don't say anything is good or bad, because that's not my decision to make. So we created this one day. I found out later, that this was part of the Transformation Process. It was part of teaching the people how they could be involved even if they don't really do much. It only takes a little effort and a little concentration and discipline that every Wednesday you can remember, this is Operation Peace-Day, so your mind is on it and you are thinking about it. So now it's a special day.

So that was one project that I found out later on, was a part of the Transformation of the Earth. Step by step I was doing things, I was asked, and then I would give this information, and I would wonder about it, but when the point came where I realized that the Transformation Process was happening, then I felt very happy, because usually when I went to my masters, I was always asking questions: "Why do I have to do this, and why is that necessary, is it really important?", because I don't like to give information to people unless I am sure that this information is valuable and it's the absolute truth.

Sharing Information

We believe on the other planets that you shouldn't say anything unless it's kind, and it's true, or it's necessary. Too many people give so much information not really knowing where this information comes from or what effect that is going to have on people. So I am very careful, when I relate information to anybody that I know the source where it came from and I know what its intentions are.

I think this is very important, that we each have to question ourselves about what kind of information we are going to share with other people. And it has to be true, of course, it has to be something that has a result and has a positive effect.

Channeling became very popular. There was lots of information released under different spiritual prophets that walked on Earth, and different beings from other planets. I don't agree with all this information, because some of it involves the ego of the individual. I don't think it's reliable, because a lot of the entities that are non-physical still hang in the outskirts of the Earth, in the astral dimension, waiting for the opportunity to be able to speak through somebody. And when people open themselves up, they really don't know what or who they are in contact with. Unfortunately, these entities know, if you are interested in Saint Germain, or Christ, or Ashtar, or whatever, and I think it's unfair, too, to these beings that you are using their personality and their name to spread this information. So you really have to be sure who you are in contact with and where the information is coming from.

My information usually comes through telepathic means from my people or my uncle. And I have a lot of masters from previous times that I lived on Earth, and they were my spiritual teachers. And they still guide me from the other dimensions. Now they are a part of the spiritual hierarchy. So I am pretty well aware of the information and what I am doing.

The End of Manipulation and Control

When I attended these meetings with thousands and thousands of beings, some physical, some not, and some in human form, some not, every person, every individual wasn't always in agreement with the Transformation.

There are some beings from other systems that are not spiritually advanced and they are still into the idea of controlling and manipulating for their own self.

Manipulation and control are done on an unconscious level. We do it to our children. When we make a choice for them that involves their future, and we do not allow them as an individual to develop and to choose their own way, it's interference, and it's also a form of controlling and manipulating. We do it in our marriages. When we decide that something is good for us and we demand that everybody in the family or the husband do this, or we don't like something that the husband does and we try to change that, this is controlling and manipulating as well. It's manipulating when we don't allow others to be themselves and to do it for themselves ¬ such as the eating habits, drinking habits, if you smoke – these kind of little things that have nothing to do with spirituality. These are physical forms of relaxation, enjoyment. Of course, overindulgence is the problem, when people can't control their own individual lust for certain things. So you have to exercise a lot of control individually.

I don't choose for other people what they do with their private time, how they choose entertainment, what their sexual habits are – if their mate is a male or a female, or the same sex – that really has nothing to do with me, and I believe they have to choose, because that's what they are – they are Soul and they are choosing their own experiences on Earth. Some of the experiences are not nice, but on the other hand, we don't always choose things that are nice. We choose things because of the experience as a Soul. The problem is, as a human, our concepts from society are good and bad, so we have these ideas and we try to control others according to our concepts and ideas of what is good or bad. God doesn't do that. And we as people have to learn to let others decide what their life will be, or their involvements, their emotions.

Emotions are a part of being human, of course, and very necessary. You have to react in an offended or shocked way at certain things that happen. But on the other hand, you have to learn to adjust to whatever there is and accept it as part of something that's necessary. Some people don't see the necessity of war, of disease, of illness, but they are part of this world and of the experience here. We can't change all of that, because the Souls have chosen these experiences. But we CAN change the consciousness, the frequency, and the perception of the people, and we can change the perception of ourselves.

That's what the Transformation is about: Making you aware of your environment, of your role as a Soul in society, and that this life is temporary. That's the whole thing, people hang on to things too much. They are holding on to emotions, to connections to other people, to addictions, to lust, and if you can't let go of something, it brings you back into the same situation until you finally learn that nothing is important. Actually, what's important is that you learn, experience here, and then go on your way and evolve in the higher dimensions. But most people are attached to something in the physical, and these attachments are what actually create sometimes the unnecessary reliving of certain situations. You have to examine the situation. If you are having a problem, then you have to ask yourself: Why am I having the same problem, why is something repeating again and again? That just means there is something you didn't learn, that you have to learn. And maybe it's that you have to realize that there is nothing in this world that is a value that's greater than the value of another Soul, another living being.

If you are rich, and you have maids and servants and all kinds of money, you can't take it with you when this world is over.

There is nothing in my world that means more to me than the people that I love and the other Souls that I exchange experiences with in my daily life. I think this comes also with the awareness that everything is temporary, there is nothing forever except the Soul, and except your existence.

When we learn to let go, we learn to really live each moment and appreciate each moment as something precious, because we only have what we have NOW. We are not guaranteed that there is going to be a tomorrow. And the past is over and finished. We can't live in the past, and we can't live in the future, because we haven't actually perfected a means of time travel, but this will be in the future quite common. But on the other hand, what's the use of going into the future and seeing what's going to happen, when you can have an effect on what happens? That's the whole point, you have to decide that you care and that you want to put your energy into what takes place on this Earth and in these societies, that it's your responsibility for the future of this Earth and for the future of the Souls who will be living here. Whether you are here or not when the changes take place. Some people said: "Well, if I'm not going to be here, why am I going to put my energy into this Transformation?" Because it's a divine plan, and it's very important, that's why. We should of course try to make a positive effect in this world while we are here.

Many Beings Take Part in the Transformation Process

The Transformation Process was discussed as an alternative to destruction of this planet. This planet was created out of cooperation and love with lots of time and effort put into the societies that are here by beings that no longer live on the physical, but in the other dimensions. And they are interested in changing the way that things are on the Earth, because the free will has been taken away and people don't have the ability to be fully involved and make choices. So this Transformation is providing that opportunity, that you can make changes, you can make choices, and you can be happy, or you can be sad. You make that choice every moment. Everything that happens, it takes as much energy of course to be sad or disappointed. But if you can't let go of it, experience it and say: "OK – this is the way it is". Then you can decide what kind of a solution you are going to take. What are you going to do about it?

The beings who are responsible for the conditions on Earth were participants at a time when they were also developing their consciousness, and they have done many things that they regret now, and they want to correct this. Like I said, the nature spirits informed all of nature to change its frequency – the birds sound, the bees, the water, the wind – everything has an effect on our environment. So now that they are changing their frequencies, the next step was that the people who have these big crafts, the spaceships from other planets and so on, could also send a special energy or frequency from their ships and participate in this. The last step I think that they took was to reactivate the hidden temples all over the Earth, so that energy could flow again from the other dimensions to the Earth – and that's also part of it. When they started sending this energy through the temples and from the ships, and when the nature spirits and everybody started changing their energy, they realized that all this had an effect. The people were doing their meditations, the animals were changing their frequency, and the nature spirits were in tune with this. Then, of course, all this has an effect on the human body, because we are changing the whole genetic structure by creating new chakra systems, so more energy can flow from the other dimensions. People are becoming more aware and more connected to the nature and to crystals. They have a feeling that they want certain crystals in their homes, and these crystals carry information and frequencies as well. People are becoming more and more aware of how they can change their environment, create a better energy, put their attention in more and more meditation and on positive spiritual things and getting information. There is an endless source of information, it depends on what you want to focus on. If you want to focus on all the old teachers and the esoteric information that they were bringing, or the old masters, you can study about all of them. If you want to study about people from other planets, there are many books available and information.

The Hollow Earth Theory

People are fascinated about the center of the Earth theory. It is a reality. Every planet is hollow. This is the way the energy flows – around and through the planet and that's also the support system for the planet itself. It is a living being.

After the destruction of Atlantis, a lot of the beings escaped into the center of the Earth, so that they could remain in this consciousness and have societies there that still dwell in this consciousness and awareness. When the Transformation is complete, of course they will come back and join the societies on the surface. But they are separated for the time being, as well as a lot of the nature spirits. They are active and they are involved, but they don't communicate very often with people in your societies. This was the fault of the people in these societies, because they became more and more involved in the physical aspects of making their money and living and surviving in the societies, having credit cards, bank accounts, insurances – all these things became so important to the people that they lost contact. And if they encountered one of these little beings, they were trying to make money from showing it to the public or whatever. So the respect was broken.

The Re-Introduction of Technologies

So a lot of things are going to change in the future. When the temples were reactivated, and once again they will be exposed to the public when the time is correct, when people will not misuse this technology. Once the technology here that you have today quits functioning, of course they have to come from other planets and from the center of the Earth to reintroduce you to the new technology. This technology has to be protected and guarded until the time is right, so that it is not misused like it was before. This kind of technology comes with the higher awareness or consciousness, that you have the ABILITY to use it in a positive way. And you don't have the ego or the desire to abuse it for your own self-worth. We are not at that stage yet, we are just on the way, we are in the process.

With the development of the new chakra system, you will have physical symptoms – the effects of this change. There will be high-pitched tones in your ear, there will be a restlessness sometimes in your sleep, or dreamless nights, and other times very vivid dreaming and experiencing on the other dimensions, which are not dreams. More and more people will be aware that they are actually going out of the body and having experiences. The new children are born with this genetic system intact.

The End of Old Karma

Since 1993, they broke all the karmic bonds and dissolved them. The spiritual hierarchy decided that it was not necessary anymore, that the people had to let go of all these old things from other lifetimes. That doesn't mean that you can't create new karma in this lifetime – it's up to you. But it gives you a clean slate and a fresh start, that you don't have to worry about if you killed this person in another lifetime that they are going to get even with you, that's finished, you know. This karmic involvement was one of the things that needlessly brought people back again and again, so that the Souls were not evolving at the precise time that they should, or their consciousness wasn't changing. So this had to be dissolved and taken away. It gives you a fresh opportunity to create new connections, even to create spiritual communities and share with people. It's very important that we do create these communities, when the old structures, when the religions collapse, so that we have the opportunity and new places to go for information, or receive information ourselves and share it with others.

Transformation Phenomena in the Physical Body

So that's what the Transformation Process is, that these new chakras are going to be developing in your body, and you may have pain, a very sharp pain that was quickly there and gone. Your vision will be clear at times, and other times not clear. Your hearing the same way, it will sound as if somebody just took cotton out of your ears and everything is louder and clearer. And you will have spells where you are very hungry and spells where you are not very hungry, your appetite will fluctuate. This is quite common. We have to drink a lot of fluids, because our toxins are being released out of the body. Your intuitive abilities are returning, and your ability to communicate with one another, you'll find that amazing things happen, because, if you want to get information to somebody and you don't have their number or a way to contact them anymore, they will contact you. These kind of things are not coincidences. These things are our changes that are taking place. Whether you are a willing participant or not, that's your choice, there are some people who refuse to accept it and don't participate. They will be frightened by the changes, especially when the electricity doesn't function, when the computers don't function, the satellite systems are not working, the banks don't function, you can't get your money from the bank anymore. But there will be no use for money in the future. This is something that we have NOW, that you have insurances, health protection, doctors and so on, but this will not be necessary in the future. When the Transformation is complete, the people will have learned how to use their own energy for healing.

An Exercise to Perceive the Life Energy

I want to teach you an exercise so that you can feel the energy, because when you can feel something yourself, this is the truth. It's not imagination, it's not that you are visualizing energy, but you can feel it from your own body. When you can feel that energy that flows through you all the time, and the more and more you practice with these energy exercises, the stronger and stronger the energy will become. Then eventually you will learn ways of using this for healing. It's the same energy that you are sending when you send your thoughts, or in meditation. We have the ability to protect the people that we love or we're in touch with or connected to just by visualizing this person and asking that a part of our energy can go to that person and provide protection, and the things that they need in this lifetime and love. You have the ability to do that.

A lot of this information you'll find in my different books. I've created a Spiritual Handbook[7] which is a workbook for the human being. I had seminars about the Soul. At one time I had Love Workshops to discuss love, because it's a very misunderstood emotion, and it creates a lot of confusion and difficulties in relationships.

So there are a lot of things that you can do to work on yourself. You have a lot of different functions within the body, physical and non-physical functions. To become aware of what the body is, what the human consists of, is work, because it's a learning process. And if you're interested in yourself, you should be interested in learning about these functions and about the new functions that are going to be available to us through the Transformation Process.

---

7 The *Spiritual Handbook* is now Part 3 of *The Venusian Trilogy*, except for the „Venusian Ceremonies" – they are included in PART TWO of this book. (Publisher's comment)

There is much information that you can get – over the internet, they have daily updates on the Transformation Process, and messages from different masters. You have to decide which is true information and which isn't. Sometimes it's really a mixture of information that's channeled, so that the people always get a little bit wary, because some things that are predicted didn't happen. And that's why I never give a date, because I am thinking: "Well, I have to inform the people: It's up to YOU what happens and when it happens, it's not my decision to make". The more participants, of course, the more the energy that's inflowing and being directed into a positive source is not easily predictable. It depends on how much the information gets out, how much you share with people, how many of you start using this energy in a positive way.

And I don't want to disappoint people, that's the thing that's discouraging when people have a certain date that something is supposed to happen and it doesn't, then they get disappointed and the result of that is also that they get aggressive. Sometimes they lose their ability to believe, or to want to believe. So you have to realize that everything that has changed on the Earth takes time. That time depends on how much information is received and where. Of course it's not easy to give this information to the whole world. There are countries where they don't know a thing about Soul or spiritual information. They just live to survive. And it's necessary that we can get this information to every part of the Earth, somehow or another.

It will happen, and I can't say the time, unfortunately. I don't know that. I can't know that, but on the other hand you have the possibility to participate and to make it go faster.

We can do the energy exercise – I can show you that. And then we can go on into what you can expect of the future from this Transformation Process.

To do this exercise, this energy exercise, you should put both feet on the floor, touching, or you can cross them if it is more comfortable. This creates an energy, a connection with the Earth, so that the energy comes through the base chakra and the feet. For this exercise, of course, you are not meditating, you are focusing your energy on your hands.

So you have to put the hands together, and the elbows have to be free and not next to the body. If you have a very big bosom or balcony, then you have to be careful ... because if you have contact with the body, the energy is not going directly into the hands. What you are doing now is, you are sending the energy that flows through your body normally ... when you do meditation, you know, you focus on the third eye and send it with your mind or your thoughts. And this time you are focusing on your hands with your eyes, so that you can focus the energy through the eyes into the hands. So then, you hold the hands together ... and if you have cold hands, you have to wait quite a while until the heat builds up.

The energy starts to build between the hands and then you will notice that the hands become very warm. And when you feel they are becoming warm and that they are warm, then ... and you have to have your fingers closed, just like the praying hands. Then when you start to feel the warmth, then you start to gently separate the hands and create a little distance between the hands until you get them around shoulder length, where they are equal with the shoulders, then you hold your fingers separate and you bend your tips as if you are holding a ball. Eventually, you bring them closer together, but never touching, so that the energy can be transferred from fingertips to fingertips. And you'll start to feel a lighter tingling or air, but this is actually the energy that is interacting between the fingertips. When you move one hand very slowly then you'll start to feel from these fingertips of the moving hand the energy on the palm or wherever that you're moving the fingertips. You'll start to be aware of this energy, and it becomes stronger, when you are aware of it. It feels almost like an invisible electricity or ... when you move them this way without touching, then it becomes kind of an elastic feeling. It's very interesting. And the energy gets stronger, the more you work with it and the more you focus your attention.

Of course, you can exchange this energy with another person, simply by them and you pointing your two hands at each other, so that the fingertips from that person and you are in contact, even though they are not touching. So this energy passes from you to them. And you have different energies, so it creates an interesting effect. Of course, it looks funny, when somebody doesn't know what you are doing. I have had people from television, doing the whole interview through the workshop, but what they showed on television was us all doing this, and of course it made us look crazy. But on the other hand, that's what they want to present, these strange things that we do.

So this energy is the same energy that you can heal yourself with. But you don't have to use your hands, you can direct this energy with your thoughts to a certain part of your body. This is just an example, so you can feel this energy. Children really like this very much. The people, after you show them this in the workshop, then they're trying it with each other during the breaks and everything, it's very amusing. But of course they are very impressed, because this is something they can feel and realize that this energy is something that you can experience, not just with your thoughts.

So this is something very important. And in the future, of course, the energy will increase, as more chakras are developed in the body, the more energy is able to flow into the body.

We are not creating new human beings. It's actually the old abilities that were removed from you through this genetic manipulation being returned to you. And we are creating an artificial support system through the ships and the energy that's flowing from the nature and through the hidden temples and everything. So you are having an energy support until the Transformation is complete. But the children don't have this artificial support system, it's not necessary for them.

Most children are born with abilities anyway, because they are not old in this world, they are very new from the other dimensions, and they are still connected very strongly. You noticed that a baby's head, the top, the crown chakra doesn't close immediately after the child is born. But they have memories and everything from their Soul, and abilities that they have carried with them, that are intact. Usually, it's lost because of the reception from the parents and other people who can't understand these abilities and qualities, and they take the child to a psychiatrist or tell the child, it's imagination. So the child then becomes afraid to express that they have these abilities, and eventually they lose the abilities out of the fear of not being understood or accepted.

I think that's the biggest problem. People are encountering phenomena and abilities that they are not used to, that they haven't been informed about. And this creates, of course, a fear and a misunderstanding, because they are not sure what is happening. And that's why the Transformation Workshop and information is valuable, so that you can become aware and start to utilize this energy for your benefit, and for the world's benefit.

The Future of the Planet Earth

In the future, the Earth will serve a different purpose than it has served in the past. It was more or less a place where you can encounter the opposite energy from the Soul, the yin and yang, the negative and the positive. Of course, in reality, it's the same energy. The only division has been created also by your concepts, you know. You create this energy into good and bad by determining that this behavior is bad and this is good, then you also help support the negative process.

We have to realize that everything is valuable. Even the negative forces served to help us to experience diverse qualities of ourselves or to experience these qualities and possibilities. But some people become attached to having the power and the control and to use this energy for control over others. And that has been the problem in the past that the people cannot overcome their ego and their tendencies to use each other and this energy for their own general self and selfishness.

Our ancestors were totally selfless people. They didn't want to destroy or damage anything that was from the Creator, from nature, because they felt in a harmony with it. These are the things that are going to be reinstalled in the human being.

During the original colonies of Atlantis and the people from the stars, the feminine qualities were ruling. They were more using their intuition and the feminine principles of loving and caring. And then, after the manipulation, the male energy was controlling with more force, more destruction, more might. These things were controlling our societies.

In the Transformation Process, more and more women will become an equal to the men as far as their strength, their power and abilities at the workplace and in their society. Of course that creates kind of a fear in the men, because he feels that he is losing power, if the woman is becoming powerful, then he is not playing the role that he played before. With the development of the Transformation in the human beings, it will be equal – the male and the female powers will be equal, and when they are used together, it's a very powerful tool.

In the future, sex will not have a role in our society anymore, we won't need this as a means of our birth process, as a means of exchange of this love energy. It can be done by thoughts, by exchanging energy with one another's body. And there will come a time when it's not necessary to be a male or a female. And the Earth will serve as a purpose for human beings to experience everything in one life cycle on Earth. They can manifest a body of choice. It doesn't have to be male or female, it can be the both energies and the qualities in one. If you wish to experience sex, well than that is of course a different thing, the physical kind of sex, but you can experience the same feeling by exchanging this energy and this love without being necessary that you have the physical connection. I don't think that the people will have a desire for this feeling, because it won't be necessary. But if they wish to be a male or a female or experience some of the negative things that are available on Earth right now, overindulgence, and lust and things like this, there will be a new planet that will serve this purpose. But the Earth will be a place where you can manifest a physical body and live in societies, and clothes are not necessary, only if you wish to have them. And you can leave the body at will. The Soul will be able to leave the physical body. You might appear to be lying and sleeping and the Soul can enter into a tree for hours or so, or into a dolphin, into a bird, so you can experience the different aspects of the life forms that exist without life cycles having to be exchanged. So you don't have to leave and come back. It can be done in one lifetime. Of course, there won't be a need for eating, and if you wish to experience the flavor of something, from your memory, you can just pick up a hand full of sand or dirt and automatically transform it into something that you have a memory from eating. It will just be a physical pleasure rather than a necessity. You won't need this. This is staying the physical body, because the physical body will not be of the same material as it is now. It's on a different frequency. So the whole Earth will be different. I am sure that people will form communities and connections and work together with the animals and the different life forms. It will be a totally different place than you know.

I am not sure that I will be living at this time to experience, but on the other hand I can experience it from another dimension or I could pay a visit to this place still.

So the Transformation Process is a big process. As I said, you will go through the physical changes, emotional changes, and psychological changes. Of course it takes a lot of willpower and acceptance to go through this process individually and accepting the changes that take place in our society.

I don't know how many of you can imagine living without electricity, television, entertainment that we have now, but new forms of entertainment will be, and creation – creating things will be your entertainment. I think people will return more to creating music, and songs, it will be more of a joyful kind of a living standard. And you won't have a need for security like you had before, because security is only needed when a person has a threat to their health, to their physical body, to their environment. I think all of these threats will no longer exist, because with the collapse of the negative powers, the aggression will recede, and there will be no need to actually overpower others or to be in charge of something. Every person will be in charge of their own selves. So you can look forward to a wonderful time.

These times are coming. And you only have to help to visualize and to create these possibilities. Imagine what it can be like or what you like it to be like, and eventually you will have that. I think that, after you die, you have the choice to make of what you want to do, what you want to experience and where you want to go. You will no longer have the Christian churches and the organized religions telling you what you have to experience after death. That will be totally up to you, what you experience and what you learn, what you are. That's what we have to look forward to. Actually creating what we are, what we wish to be, what we wish to experience rather than being forced to experience what exists.

We will be in charge of creating our existence. That's the thing that we have to look forward to.

Our ancestors lived this way in Atlantean times and on the other planets and the systems where they came from, and on the other planets that exist now. That was their home. It was a natural way of surviving with the existing life forms in this physical world ¬ corresponding, communicating, and cooperating with these life forms.

In the future, after the Transformation, people will be living more and more by the natural spiritual laws than manmade laws. An example is: The process of life and death at this time on Earth is one of the spiritual laws that must be obeyed. But on the other hand, the Soul has predetermined when it will die, and how and where. So I'm never afraid of having a plane accident or something happening, because I don't think that I decided to die that way. So the fear will be removed, and we will not have need of the manmade laws anymore, we will just naturally obey the spiritual laws, because as an advanced Soul with a full consciousness and awareness, you will be able to govern yourself in a way that's in harmony with everything that exists. We've lived that way on other planets for millions of years. It's just a natural harmony of obeying the spiritual laws. The spiritual laws don't necessarily have to be written down. There are things like gravity, and things that govern the physical that were set in procedure when the Creator created things. So these laws are natural. You will have the chance then to predetermine how long your existence will be, depending on your individuality, and what you want to experience.

I hope that this information can inspire you and gives you the courage and ability to face whatever will come and accept it as the divine will. Because whatever happens in the continuum of life is always meant to be. So you have to learn to accept things and depend on your creative abilities to see you through the difficult times and the hard times. As I've said, you have assistance from the other beings who have an alternative method of power and energy for you to use.

Like I told you before, in the very future of the Earth, after the Transformation is complete, it will be a totally different living style and a totally different awareness on the Earth.

The thing that I hope you can remember is: A SOUL IS PERFECT, A SOUL IS BEAUTIFUL, AND INDIVIDUAL AND COMPLETE. You have to remember your own beauty and qualities, and that every experience you've ever had in your creation, in your life cycles, and when you came into being, is a part of what makes up the special jewel that is each individual Soul. This beauty and these qualities are determined by your individual process and development through your life experiences. That's the wonderful thing: There is no end to your existence. You have eternity to look forward to, when you can overcome the concepts of time and aging. Aging is a natural process on the Earth now, but it's very hard for some people to deal with, that they see their body is getting older, dealing with the difficulties that come with the aging process. But if you can be happy and really appreciate the preciousness of life and experiences, then you have a better chance for a beautiful life and enjoyment. Of course, you should enjoy every sense that you have in the physical world. Because of course these senses will not be the same in the future, because the physical body will be totally different. You have to enjoy the different aspects of being a human being, and of course creating a balance and a harmony within yourself, because you are the only one who can do that.

I hope this information is valuable and that you can share it with others. I would like to leave you with a Venusian greeting which means "May the Universal blessings be". It says "May", because of course, we can't force you to have Universal Love and Blessings. It is in our language, which is not a spoken language, so we convert it into an ancient language, mixed Sanskrit with Lemurian, which sounds more lovely. So we use the words from the ancient times. The greeting is "May the Love and Blessings be", or "May the Universal Love and Blessings be", and it's AMUAL ABAKTU BARAKA BASHAD. Thank you very much.

PART TWO

Unpublished Texts

The second part of this book contains information from Omnec Onec that was not published in printed form until now:

- The True Story of Christ (1999)
- Meeting a Gnome (2000)
- Venusian Script (1993)
- Venusian Ceremonies (1998)
- Interview between Omnec Onec and Marina Popovich (1994)

The True Story of Christ

Author: Omnec Onec

The true story about the life of Jesus Christ is most fascinating to me. I will tell it the way I have heard it from my aunt Arena on Venus. I will relate the things that really happened in the same way as I have heard them during my studies of the Earth's history on Venus. I do not wish to discredit or condemn any religions or teachings. Take it as you wish and let it affect your life where it may.

The man that you know under the name of Jesus Christ is one of the most controversial and misunderstood figures of all times in Earth history. Before incarnating here, he lived as a Master on Venus. But his highly evolved Soul decided to balance old karmic debts by living as a spiritual teacher among the same people that he and others had led into ignorance in a former life.

After the genetic manipulation of humans on Earth, the people had forgotten their heritage and former powers. They no longer could communicate with their ancestors in the other dimensions or contact the Ascended Masters. They had become a frightened people. They were ignorant of the most basic truths, about the universe, about God, and about themselves. Physical survival and comfort was the number one care, and death was the number one fear. Religions with their rituals and restrictions had been established by the ruling officials in order to exercise limitless power and total control over the people. Limited beliefs had created a limited way of life for the masses.

Space ships were as familiar in the skies of Biblical times as are the UFOs of today. Space travelers visited regularly to help with Earth's spiritual growth. In the lands of the Jewish people, visitors from outer space were called angels, which means heavenly beings. And Biblical history is full of tales about people meeting with God or the angels, or crude descriptions of space ships such as "ball of fire" or "wheel within a wheel". People who know nothing of advanced technology cannot relate to it other than in their own way. In those days the unknown was usually thrown in with the religious or spiritual. Thus they believed that humans who landed in spaceships always wore white robes and who had such a peaceful and friendly countenance to be spiritual beings.

A young woman named Mary happened to meet one of these beings from another planet. She was out alone, walking the sheep, when a space ship landed nearby and one of these heavenly beings came out to speak with her. The man from space perceived that Mary was pure of thought and would not be frightened by the visit. Mary of course was awed by him, considered him to be an angel sent by God. When she asked him about this, he said, "Yes, we are all of God." That day he gave her spiritual insights about God and about people from other planets.

They met quite often, and soon they had fallen in love. When Mary became pregnant by him, he asked to marry her. This was impossible, she said, explaining the way of her culture. A person who married outside the faith faced a horrible death by being stoned. This was merely a rule made by the priests to keep the race intact, and the visitor knew this. Mary was also frightened of leaving with him, because she thought this meant she had to die. It was no use trying to persuade Mary to join him.

In the following weeks, the visitor received the spiritual insight on what was happening. For centuries there had been prophesies in this culture that a Messiah would be sent by God to lead the people. This was the child that Mary was bearing! Knowing this, he realized that the boy must be raised among the Jewish people. He agreed with Mary that she would be able to stay and have the child. "You can tell your people whatever you want, but I would tell them the truth. You may have the child here for thirty years, but I shall have the child for the last half of his life. And I will visit him periodically throughout his growth to help him spiritually". Mary agreed to raise her child with the spiritual teachings he had given her.

Then she went to her people and told them that an angel had appeared to her saying she was to give birth to a child of God;

immaculate conception it was called later. Mary believed that her lover was of God because he always came from the heavens to visit her, always in a bright light. Christ's father tried to explain that it was only a space ship, but this did not make sense to Mary. Machines were unknown.

Meanwhile, there was a man named Joseph who loved Mary very much and had admired her most of her life. He was much older than Mary. He listened to her story and understood what she was saying because he himself had met one of these beings from the heavens and had heard the stories of ancient times on Earth.

Joseph loved Mary enough to care, and was willing to take the responsibility for her and the child. He went so far as to say that the child was his own to those few who ridiculed Mary. People knew she had a miracle child; miracles were very popular in those days.

People from Venus and the Brotherhood of the Planets knew that Mary's child would become a spiritual leader, and space ships were used to spread the message to various parts of the land. Prophets had seen this psychically, and many people like the shepherds had been visited by heavenly beings who foretold the great event.

The truth is always a threat to those who preach lies. The religious organizations and leaders of the day felt threatened by the birth of the child. This led to the order that all male children born within a certain time were to be killed. This threat and a contact made to Joseph caused him to take Mary to a safe location to have the child. The star that led Joseph and Mary to safety was actually a small ship. This same kind of star led the wise men and the shepherds to the stable where Jesus was born. At night, the ship hovered above the small stable, glowing like a star.

Christ's childhood was a rather quiet time. Joseph's work as a carpenter supported the family, and Mary taught Jesus the principles she had learned from his father. He also met regularly with his father who taught him all about Earth's history.

By the time Jesus was twelve, he began to travel and study on his own. His studies of secret teachings led him as far as Egypt, Tibet and India. For three years he studied under Fubbi Quantz, abbot of the Katsupari Monastery in Northern Tibet. There he learned the secrets of the Laws of the Supreme Deity. He received the spiritual name Jesus, which could also be taken to mean "King of the Jews", and the name Christ because of his new teaching, meaning "Bearer of Truth".

When Jesus returned to his family he was thirty years old and now ready to begin teaching his people. His disciples were twelve in number, chosen for their character and their karmic connection with Christ, and for the different roles each would play in his life. Christ knew that one of them would betray him; another would deny him. Christ also knew Simon would be the one to carry on the work after he had left. He was shown this via the inner knowingness when he first met them.

Christ was a very spiritual individual and knew much about the spiritual laws. His teachings about the Journey of Soul through the lower worlds and the power of each individual were given mainly in fables and stories. The people of his culture were very simple and had not reached a very high level of consciousness. The principles of the Laws of the Supreme Deity can be recognized underlying Christ's messages. To seek first the kingdom of heaven meant literally that man can and should experience the higher planes before physical death, by leaving the body. This is only one of many, many examples.

Unfortunately Christ became more important than his teaching. He became more of a celebrity than a spiritual leader. Finally his compassion overcame what he was trying to do for the people – lead them from the ignorance.

Christ's compassion did not leave him much of a free will to say no when so many clung to him begging for a healing. He succumbed because of his great compassion for the poor and suffering people, but he knew that he would have to pay for it. And he needed to pay for it in this lifetime because it was to be his last physical incarnation.

Therefore, when it is said that Jesus took upon himself the sins of the people, and later died for their sins, it means that all of this karma added up to one horrible death of physical torture by the very people he helped.

In the scriptures it is written that Christ went to the wilderness to pray, and great beings of the past appeared to him. These spiritual leaders of the time included Christ's father, who told Christ that because he had succumbed to compassion and had become sidetracked from his teaching, he would have to physically suffer in this life or reincarnate to pay the karmic debts. At first Christ did not wish to go through with it. But finally he realized that the karma was his to resolve, now or in the future. He said; "Not my will, but thine be done." He knew that he would have to obey the spiritual law, and so he decided not to defend himself and rather have the suffering now, to be finished with it.

Toward the end of his life, Christ was healing too many people and doing too many miracles, enough to frighten the Roman and Jewish leaders. He was hunted down and finally captured. Pontius Pilate had a great respect for Christ and even tried to persuade him to defend himself. Christ refused because he knew the debt had to be paid.

The Roman and Jewish leaders were well aware of what had taken place on Earth during Atlantian times as they still had some of the technical devices hidden for their own power and use. Because they knew how dangerous Christ was becoming as he was exposing the past and turning the people away from the organized churches they devised a plan. They were to release one prisoner and let the public choose. This way they were not responsible. Barabas, a known murderer and thief or Christ! Their plan was to send soldiers throughout the crowd and pay gold to those who shouted for Barabas to be released.

The second part of the plan was to set up a whole religion based on Christ after his death. They knew of the prophecy of his return. They also knew the laws of karma. If they could convince the future generations to worship Christ and baptize their children and dedicate their whole lives and all they do in the name of Christ, his spiritual evolution would be slowed down and he would be bound to a certain dimension by all the responsibility and karma of these people and not ever be a threat again.

What Christ did not know was that he would be responsible for all the Christians of the future who would look up to him, all of the people who considered him to be their personal Master. He did not realize that his simple teachings would be turned into a religion, or that he would become more important than what he was trying to teach.

The same powers that helped destroy Christ now turned around and set him up to be worshipped as God's son. Even the Jewish people allowed the scriptures of Christ's life to be created into a book for the whole world. Excluding some of the truths Jesus taught. And how is Christ portrayed in most churches – tortured and bleeding.

In suffering on the cross and being ridiculed by the people he had helped, Christ resolved most of the karmic debts upon his shoulders. On the one hand, Christ was compassionate enough to say to the Deity, "Forgive them, for they know not what they are doing!"

But the suffering was much worse and lasted much longer than he had expected. He was not able to leave the body until much of the suffering was over. But because his father did not come zooming up in a spaceship to save him, he cried, "My father, my father, why hast thou forsaken me?"

The people from Christ's home planet had a plan, which his father had told Christ in the wilderness where Christ had pleaded so much that he did not want to suffer. This plan was to show the people that there was such a thing as life after death, and that the body is only a vehicle to live in, that Soul could leave and reinhabit it. But the people of Christ's time did not interpret the resurrection in this way. They considered it as one of Christ's greatest miracles.

Meanwhile, at the time of Christ's passing, a great storm developed and black clouds covered the sun. This very much frightened the non-believers and added a great deal to Christ's story. The storm was actually caused by the collective psychic power of Christ's followers who believed God to be an angry dictator.

After the death of Christ, his body was moved to a tomb prepared by Mary and friends of Christ. The authorities placed guards at his tomb in order to keep people from stealing the body. In reality they knew of the plan for his rescue and tried to prevent it. When the ship landed near Christ's tomb, the guards passed out from the light and intense energy field. His body was carried away to be repaired.

Christ remained in his astral body while his father prepared to repair the physical body. A body less than twenty-four hours dead can be repaired by rays which rebuild cells and tissue. Soul can then inhabit the body again.

Mary Magdalene was the first to arrive at the tomb to find Christ's body missing. After regaining consciousness and as the details of what had happened came to her mind, she remembered just arriving at the tomb to see the angels arriving in a bright light, wearing shining garments and giving the news that Christ was alive. She remembered their words, "Do not be afraid", as they rolled away the huge rock at the entrance. She assumed that the angels from heaven had healed Christ and went her way to find him.

There are many passages in the bible where Christ appeared to many of his followers and they did not recognize him at first – until he spoke to them. There are also other reports of beings in shiny garments being seen at the tomb.

When Christ appeared to her, he said, "I am not yet of the body; do not touch me. I will return." He appeared to quite a few people like this, and walked through doors and walls in his astral body. The physical body was repaired on board the ship, whereupon Christ as Soul reentered the form. Then he was able to show the people his body, and allow them to touch him. He told his people", I am leaving now to live with my father who is in heaven." The people interpreted his explanations as best they could; the ascension into heaven was their way of explaining Christ leaving in a spaceship. He returned with his father, where he married and later had children. He lived many years before he died again physically.

Christ guides his people through their many lifetimes. He is their inner Master and communicates with his followers by the inner channels. His karma is to be spiritually responsible for all the people who have put their hope for salvation in him. He takes each individual as far as he can, then will push him out of Christianity into a greater spiritual path. He does this to rid himself of the karma that keeps him in the causal dimension of the lower worlds. All the acts done in his name, all wars fought in his name, all children baptized and all who live their lives in the name of Christ are more chains binding him to the lower worlds.

Until the day comes that Christ can rid himself of all the misunderstanding, and until all these Souls in Christianity go to other paths, Christ must remain on the causal plane, within the lower worlds of time and space. This heavenly part of the causal was created by the group consciousness, the belief in heaven of the Christians here on Earth.

Meeting a Gnome

Author: Omnec Onec

*I*t happened on my first tour here in Germany. Sigrid B.-Lamb from Mutter Erde Center near Cologne had read my book and wanted me to do a workshop at her place.

She lives in an old school house with a big magic garden. This garden is very special and not open for the public. She lets it grow naturally and only allows certain people in or groups from the seminars to do meditations. So after my workshop we all went in, carrying incense sticks. Right in the middle there is a fireplace with 12 tree stumps around. And there is a bench in front of some bushes, facing the fireplace. We entered by two big pine trees that are bound together at the top to form a huge gate and followed the path to the fireplace.

There were 12 tree stumps standing in a circle around it. When we got there it started to rain and we had to go back inside. Everybody stuck their incense sticks into the ground. I put mine next to a tree stump.

There was sunshine the next morning and I went for a walk with Torsten. We passed the garden and found a brook nearby, crossing over on some rocks. It is a very beautiful area. When we started climbing a nearby hill, covered with bushes and trees, I noticed something at the foot of one tree. "Look, this is a gnomes house", I said to Torsten, pointing at a small hole between the roots. He was very sceptical at first, not believing that gnomes really do exist. They hide from people because they were mistreated by them in former times, when they were captured and put on display for money, or tortured to show where precious gemstones were hidden.

Torsten believed this to be a mouse hole. "But look at this little house", I said, "it is built right into the base of the tree. There is a small door and a step up to it. And there is a leaf lying on the step. It is a mat to wipe their feet on, and a mouse doesn't do this, does it?" There even was a window, made of earth onto the side of the tree. On top, some sticks covered with leaves made the roof. Part of it had been blown away by the rain. "Let's fix the roof," I insisted. "It will take the little man a long time to do it, and for us it is but a few minutes." Torsten was looking at me like I was really crazy, but he helped gathering some leaves and sticks to repair the roof. "This will make him very happy", I smiled.

When we returned to Sigrid, I remembered that I had promised her to do a special meditation in her garden. Her spiritual guides had told her that I was to go into the garden alone as some certain information would be waiting there. So I went to the fireplace, passing the tree stumps and suddenly I wondered where all those incense sticks from last night were. They were all gone, except mine that was still where I had put it. I took it with me and sat down on the bench. I was wearing blue jeans that day and my black boots with a chain at the back of the heel. When I closed my eyes to start my meditation, I suddenly smelled incense burning. The stick in my hands was lit. That's magic, I thought, my incense stick lit by itself. This is really interesting. I closed my eyes again to do my mantras, when something moved the chain on my boot. I had played with a small kitten earlier, so I thought that this was the kitten playing with the chain. So I just smiled and when I felt something warm on my foot I thought again that it was the kitten lying there.

I opened my eyes, expecting to see the cat, but there was a little man sitting on my shoe. I almost had a heart attack! I closed my eyes again thinking that he perhaps was not really there, but when I looked again he was still sitting there: legs crossed, smoking a little pipe. I could smell the smoke. All of a sudden I felt that I was going to sneeze and I wanted to suppress it, for fear that the noise would scare him away. So I slowly moved my hand up to my nose to stop the sneezing – and he did the same thing! I started to laugh and he also laughed. His voice was very deep. I could see his little white teeth. He had very rosy cheeks and a white beard. He was wearing suede pants and vest, and a pointed hat. And he was so small, not more that eight inches, like a little doll. We looked at each other smiling. Then I noticed that he moved his hand from behind his back and was holding something up for me. So I bent down and opened my hand. He laid something in it. His hand was so tiny, and it was very warm, like a real hand. The he just hopped up and disappeared between the bushes.

My heart was still beating madly. I was afraid to look what was in my hand, because I was afraid that nothing would be there, and I thought: Nobody is going to believe this. What am I going to tell people? And what am I going to tell Sigrid? Can I share this story?

I went back into the house and told Sigrid all that had happened in her garden. Finally, I got up my courage to look what was in my palm. I had such a fear to tell the story, but this gift from the little man is my proof that it is really true. There was a tiny crystal, as big as my small fingernail, with a holder shaped like a gnome-hat covered with strange symbols. On the very top there was an Egyptian Ankh. The hole was for the chain to go through. The crystal was cut in many small irregular facets, many small ones on one side and bigger ones on the opposite side. This side was covered with gold. It was very unusual in glistening blue-purple color. According to a gemnologist, it dates back to the Atlantean times. That is the time when they coated the crystal with gold for special ceremonies.

Sigrid was very happy about this whole story, because when moving into the house and first clearing the garden, she had heard singing at night and had seen little men dancing around a fire. Now she was glad that they were still there and felt that she was a caretaker for them. And the gnomes had chosen me to tell their story and give people a chance to change their beliefs and reconnect to them. The story of the gnome became part of my workshops. Many people, who had been afraid of being ridiculed and never talked about their experiences with the little people or nature spirits before, now shared their stories with me.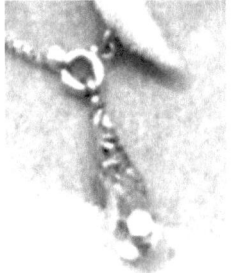

Venusian Script

Author: Anja Schäfer

This document was handed over to the contactee George Adamski (author of *Inside the Spaceships* and *Flying saucers have landed*) in 1953 during one of his encounters with Venusians. According to Omnec, the Venusian Orthon is, like Odin, her uncle.

In the nineties, this script reached Germany. At the request of a friend, Eberhard von Hagen, Omnec wrote her interpretation of the Venusian letter and made it available to the participants of lectures and workshops from that point on.

After I asked the George Adamski Foundation about the authenticity of this document in February 2010, I got the confirmation that this letter is real, that it exists and that its original author also "provided its accurate translation". To my next email asking for more information, I did not receive an answer, and I did not follow up.

Please form your own opinion and feel for yourself if the script and (or) Omnec's translation is of any value for you.

In one of the lower paragraphs Omnec mentions that she was not allowed to pass on a piece of information, because it was about the sources of power the Venusians were using. Today, Omnec describes this source of energy as *resonating magnetic energy*.

Venusian Script – Given to George Adamski in 1953 by the Venusian Orthon

Interpretation of Venusian Writing given to George Adamski in 1953 by Orthon

Translated by Omnec Onec on 4/16/1993

From: Odin who represents a long history of Venusians
To: Our Friend of Mount Palomar

I, Odin represent all 12 planets in this vast Solar System of which you know only a small part

Dear Representative of our Earth Brothers
and our main Earth Contact for the Brotherhood of the Planets,

To you I speak for all beings in our vast universe. We came out of a belief that Earth was in danger, because you were experimenting with Radar Beams.

Only to find that indeed Earth is in danger and it is complicated by so many different peoples, all who lack understanding of themselves and certainly know little about other worlds. It will indeed be a great task and take a long time and a great deal of love to conquer these misunderstandings.

We would love to share all we know with you, however we can only try to change the way mankind sees himself and the Earth, before the masses can ever understand or be trusted with the knowledge we wish to share with you.

For it is indeed your heritages just as it belongs to us, so it is for all living beings. We entrust this message with you because of our deep spiritual understanding and respect for our worlds and the peoples of all the Solar Systems yet to be discovered by you of Earth.

We feel compelled to love and guide you out of responsibility for the first colonies brought here, eons ago for you, a short while for us.

Soon one will be among you and will help, it will be one of our own. To help you understand this message – which cannot be understood till this time, because our language is only symbols of our thoughts and not script as you know or understand. Preserve this message for the key to balance and the new way of life, which is the old way for us, will be yours.

[Here I can't translate because it is the source of Powers and even as simple as it is, it is not the proper time to reveal this – as it will be misused. So I shall continue with the ending of the message (note by Omnec Onec[8])]

As we are all linked in spirit and by Divine rights share the same worlds our Supreme one provided, to own nothing but our Souls. We are all visitors in these worlds and Galaxies to learn and help these creations never to end, but exist forever as the One Divine Being planned. We are all a part of this plan and have a great part to provide these truths to all henceforth. Love is the only power we can heal with and all ye give returns tenfold. Walk in the light always and share that light with the world that darkness cannot take over.

One is a beginning, let it be you. Save your Home Earth!

Blessings
Odin of Venus
and the Brotherhood of Planets

---

8 Today, Omnec describes this source of energy as *resonating magnetic energy*. (Publisher's comment)

Venusian Ceremonies

Author: Anja Schäfer

The Venusian Ceremonies were included in Omnec's *Handbook of Venusian Spirituality* which was published in the year 2000 by Omnec's first German publisher, the Omega Verlag. This book had only been published in German and has been sold out since many years. Today, the other contents of this book are part 3 (*My Message*) of Omnec Onec's compiled edition *The Venusian Trilogy*.

Author: Omnec Onec

The following ceremonies and rituals are all done mentally on the astral as we have no need for physical language. I have transformed them to a physical language suited to your understanding and concepts.

The ceremonies are used to symbolize and share feelings within different relationships. They are meant to honor the feeling of special experiences that one wishes to share with one or more. They represent our understanding of relationships and different experiences that a Soul encounters – such as love, commitment, honor and even translating, or death as you know or understand it.

On Venus I was still too young for those rituals. I have later learned them from Uncle Odin and have now received the permission to make them public.

Venusian Ceremonial Blessing

If you gather with other people for a spiritual event – a workshop, a group meditation, a dinner etc. you may speak the following blessing:

"Our Supreme Creator, we thank you for the energy that flows through us and supports us."

(If also food and drinks are dished, then add here the following sentences: "Bless the Souls that have served their purpose to serve as nourishment for our physical vehicles to supply us with the energy we need to best represent you. Thank you for the host that prepared this food with love and shares it with us.")

"May we all be grateful to serve as a representative for you and continue to give love as you love us freely. May we all accept the different ways we choose to serve in our chosen ways."

Blessings to all, thanks to all, Omnec (your name said here)."

Venusian Love Ritual

Preparation and things needed for love ritual:

- A room only to be used for no other reason at this time. The energy must be kept.
- One bottle of special wine selected together.
- Two wine glasses
- Scented body oil selected together.
- Each must choose one special flower with fragrance.
- Each must choose a special candle – shape and color individual choice.
- Each must choose incense with special scent.

The flowers are kept in one vase in the room prepared for the ritual, also the wine, music and two pillows on which to sit.

Bath before entering the room. Use perfume or cologne.

Except the couple that wants to do the love ritual no one else is to enter the room.

The Ritual

First it is important that the two partners have a deep understanding on all levels, knowing that they are Souls that have had experiences together before, understanding the quality of unconditioned love, non-personal love that the Creator has given to all living things, the love that supports all that is.

Love is unlimited and exists beyond the limits of each specific existence. Just as love has no boundaries we must extend our energy beyond this temporary physical existence. This ritual is a way to experience this energy and share it with someone special. It must be taken as a serious and very deep love exchange.

It is much easier on the astral where one does not have the limits of a physical body. However, it can be experienced also here in the physical. So I have transferred the information and set down steps to help you to sensitize your physical self as it is a very subtle but deep experience.

First of course there has to be an agreement between the two partners and a commitment to follow the steps together. The ritual takes a total of three days preparation. You must read the passage together so that there is a level of understanding reached. After reading it the first evening you must do a meditation together for thirty minutes:

Visualize all the qualities of each other, seeing the person, loving it, absorbing it into yourself.

After the meditation you look deeply into each other's eyes facing one another, holding hands, feeling the energy and love for one another. Sometimes even past life experiences may emerge, whatever emotions are felt must be shared.

Then you both kneel, facing one another, holding hands. You

say – the woman first, than the man: "By Om-Notia-Zedia, I (your name) enter willingly and lovingly into this preparation to share my love energy with you."

Afterwards you embrace holding one another and whisper to each other:

"Amual-San-Tumal" – which means: "I share my essence of love energy with you so we may truly feel and absorb each other's existence."

This is the first step for preparation.

On the second day a fast is necessary – only fruit, juice, herb teas. Each of you has to select a special flower for the other, special incense and a candle. You may purchase these items together or separately. Choose everything carefully and with meaning – even the color of the candles and flowers must have a purpose and meaning. Then buy together a bottle of wine. You must be able to share your meals of fruit together as well. This keeps a necessary bond between you.

Also there is to be no sexual contact for the three days to yourselves or with others. You are in a process of conditioning the senses.

The second evening in privacy and uninterrupted seclusion you select special music to play softly. After bathing and wearing only robes you once again close your eyes and listen to music – concentrating on one another, feeling the love and desire to share your energy with each other.

Then the male lights his chosen candle and says:

"This light represents the fire of love and light that is me. I share it with you."

Then he explains why he chose this candle – the color and what it represents to him. Also he lights his incense, saying:

"This represents my essence that you may breathe of it consuming and experiencing myself as part of you." – Explain why you chose this particular scent.

The female then lights her candle and says:

"This is my flame of desire and the light that I am, I share it with you." – Explain the choice of color and what it represents.

Then lighting her incense she says:

"This represents my essence that you may also breathe of it consuming and experiencing myself as a part of you." – Explain the scent and why you chose it.

Now you say together:

"Our love burns like an eternal light forever. I am filled with it and with your essence."

Now take your flowers and place them between you as you face one another. The female picks up her flower and says:

"This flower represents the delicate and temporary existence of what I now am. Accept it as a token of myself – that even though it be temporary may it exist forever in your memory, its beauty lasting there as a reminder of me."

She gives it to him, explaining why she chose this flower as a representation of herself. He accepts her token.

Then the male gives her his flower, repeating what she has said and explaining why he chose this particular flower as a representation of himself. She accepts his token.

Now you both close your eyes and breathe the incense, remembering that it is now the blended essence of both. Then open your eyes and examine the fine quality of your flower, noting every detail and inhale its fragrance. Appreciate its beauty and what it represents. Then look at one another the same way with the same feeling.

Embrace and tell each other how much you appreciate these gifts and one another. Now you may retire.

The third day you consume only fruit, juice and herb tea together for your chosen times for meals. Also meditate together at chosen times if you do more than one meditation a day usually.

Sometime on this day you should enjoy a nature walk together, recognizing that just as all things you see together are God's creation so are you both. Appreciate the wonders of you as unique and beautiful creations. Notice and tell each other what you love about each other. It could be the way you smile, the color of your eyes or hair in the natural light. Hold hands as you walk or walk with arms around each other. Take time to embrace and really kiss deeply. Remember the flower that represents the other. See it in your mind, compare its quality to the quality of the other. Keep this feeling of love and feel the energy of one another. Sit somewhere and each of you with feet touching or crossed. Press your hands together until you feel the heat between your hands. Then turn to your partner and keeping the hands about three inches apart, fingers bent slightly, feel the energy flow between your hands for several moments.

Return home. Share tea or juice. Continue your day. In the evening bath and wear a robe joining one another at the appointed time in the prepared room. Play soft esoteric music. Once again light candles. The female first lights her candle and says:

"This is my flame of desire for you. I have chosen this candle to represent the light that I am." – Then once again explain what the color represents. Then she lights her incense saying:

"This represents my essence that you may inhale it as a part of yourself, that we may become one." – She then seats herself.

The male lights his candle repeating what the female has said and also his incense, explaining that she may experience his essence as well.

The couple is seated on the floor, facing one another. The female's candle and incense should be on the female's left and the male's one should be on his right. The male should take the flower that the female gave him and express his joy in receiving it and tell her the qualities of her he sees in it, the way its petals feel, the shape, smell and color compared to her when he has finished.

The female also takes the flower the male has given her, expresses the joy and appreciation upon receiving it from him and also appreciates the feel of its petals, the shape, color and smell. Tell why it reminds you of him.

Sit quietly for about five minutes, listen to the music and look at each other, feeling all the love and appreciation for each other. Notice the eyes, breathe deeply of the incense; try to distinguish the smell of your partner's incense. Look at the candles, imagine the warmth of each other, see the flame as desire, feel this desire. Can you feel the energy of each other?

The female whispers the male's name and says quietly:

"Amual-San-Tumal. I wish to share my love energy with you, so that we may truly feel and absorb each other's existence."

The male whispers the female's name and repeats what she has said.

Then the male stands up and removes his robe. Then he sits again. The female stands up and removes her robe, then seats herself. Now look at each other, notice each inch of the other's body, remembering love you have shared and how wonderful it was to make love to each other.

Now the woman tells him of one time that she remembers as being wonderful, the stimulating experience first, a time with him somewhere special and why it was special, what he did, how he did it and where it was and why you remember this time.

Then the male also shares a special time of making love with her, where it was, what she did and how she did it and why you remember this time, what made it special.

Now take a few minutes, close your eyes, recall this time and the way you felt. See it with your imagination.

Now the male lies down first on his stomach relaxed. The female kneels on his left side and after rubbing her hands together till they are warm, she acts as if she were sensuously touching his head, arms, back, buttocks, legs, feet – only keeping her hands inches away so only the energy can be felt. Take about six to ten minutes, do it very slowly. Listen to the breathing of each other.

When she has finished she whispers "turn over" – you must not touch each other. She then touches his face, his lips, eyes, every part of the body as if caressing, only with the hands inches away! Do it slowly. When finished she whispers his name and says:

"Now I have shared my love energy with you and I desire the same."

The female then lies on her stomach and the male repeats the same energy treatment with the female repeating what she has said. You must take time and feel the caresses.

Now you both return to your seated position. The male opens the wine, the female holds the glasses. As the male pours he says:

"Take this wine as a representation of my essence and energy that you be fulfilled."

The female says:

"I accept your offering, and these glasses represent my vessel that I may feel your essence."

98

You toast and drink appreciating the warm feeling and taste, also enjoying the grace and beauty of the bodies God gave you that you may share this feeling.

Tell each other how you would like to touch one another. When you finish the wine you embrace and kiss deeply feeling the flesh of the other as your bodies touch.

Then the male massages scented body oil on the female – front and back, rub and caress. Then the female does the same to the male.

Now have another wine, feel the desire for each other. Now face each other, clasp hands while kneeling. Say: "Amual-San-Tumal." Then say to one another in a whisper:

"I wish to physically make love that I may be fulfilled with your love energy and never forget its existence."

Then you may physically make love, fulfilling the ritual. Enjoy one another completely!

Venusian Commitment Vow

First you and your partner choose the place and time. It is usually done alone. You may also invite others if you choose. It is very personal, not legally binding, only valid for the duration you choose and it can be done more than once throughout your chosen time period together. In other words, it can be renewed as you desire.

Most couples choose a specific selection of music to be played in the background. You can be dressed or undressed. It can be done in a temple, on the beach, in natural surrounding or in the privacy of a home.

The most important factor is that you both choose to make a partnership and share commitment together. Therefore it can be as individual as you like and for as long as you choose.

There is an exchange of vows and an exchange of tokens representing your love for each other. You choose the objects you exchange. It can be jewelry, crystals, simple stones from a special place you were together. A popular token is a plant. You exchange the tokens and they become symbols of your love and commitment. If you exchange living plants you must give attention that the plant remains healthy and grows as does the relationship, just as your relationship needs nurturing and attention so does the symbol.

If done in natural surroundings any time of day or night is right. Sunset and sunrises are popular as is moonlight. If done indoors a fire place or candles are used, as light or fire is a symbol of purification and spirituality. The moon or sun also serve the purpose and of course you may even have candles outdoors.

After you have chosen a specific place and the tokens of exchange you set the atmosphere – music playing softly, live or recorded. If indoors place three candles in a triangle somewhere in the room. If outdoors in sunlight or moonlight candles are not necessary. If at sunrise or sunset it should be to the left of both partners. If outdoors and you desire candles you should be in the center of the pyramid of candles. If indoors with a fire place the fire should also be to the left of the partners who will be facing one another. If using candles placed in the room the one lone candle should be to the left.

First you walk slowly toward one another in the prepared place, carrying your token or symbol in the left hand.

When you are about one foot apart stop, facing one another. You look deeply into one another's eyes, hands in front, left hand with token palm up, right hand palm up supporting the left hand.

As you look in one another's eyes the female first speaks as she symbolizes the emotional or feeling one. She says:

"I (your name) am here to offer you (his name; first name only) this symbol of my love, devotion and desire to share my energy with you." – Hold toward him the token. Then he reaches with his right hand and takes your offering, placing gift and his right hand next to his heart. He says:

"I accept this symbol and all it means, I take it into my heart and shall so honor and care for it and all it stands for." – (She stands with both hand's palms up.) He then says:

"I (his name) offer you (her name) this symbol of my love, devotion and desire to share my energy with you." – He holds out his left hand with token toward her. She with her right hand takes the token to her heart. She replies:

"I accept this symbol and all it means, I take it into my heart and shall so honor and care for it and all it stands for."

Both kneel, still facing one another, still looking into the other's eyes and place the tokens on the ground of the floor between them. They clasp one another's hands. Then they both say slowly together:

"I shall love you unconditionally as the Creator intended it. I shall share my life and all it creates with you. I will accept you as you are and grow with you. We shall be as one even separated. Our love is there. It is."

Then they stand still clasping hands. She places his left hand on her heart. He does the same. Both together say:

"We vow devotion, love and commitment to share love and honor one another. We will inspire each other and support that which we choose, until the time comes that our Souls go their way. Without regret we shall still remember all that we have shared. We will still love and honor all that we are. It is."

Then facing the candle or the fire or the sunset etc. to the left you hold each other's right hand. You look at the symbol of light and say:

"May we walk together now and forever as friends. Let the light surround and protect us and all that we love, bonding us that we may be as one. May we live according to the Laws of the Supreme Deity[9]. The symbols we exchanged shall be a reminder of what we are and mean to one another. It is and we are. Amual Abaktu Baraka Bashad (Universal Love and Blessings)."

The couple faces one another, embracing and exchanging energy. Of course they may kiss. Then sit on the floor, drink wine and admire each other's tokens.

Friends may be invited afterwards or the next day for celebration. The couple must take care of their tokens for they are a symbol of their vows.

---

9 The Laws of the Supreme Deity are described in *The Venusian Trilogy*. (Publisher's comment)

Venusian Healing and Cleaning of Negative Energy for Environment

Sometimes even on other dimensions you encounter unwanted negative energy or entities. Sometimes they are left over from previous situations by former Souls or there are the lower astral entities that will use the less aware being as a means of controlling and manipulation.

Unfortunately many such entities wait for opportunities to utilize unaware beings who open themselves up for channeling. Also the desire for psychic experiences may provide a means of entry into your own existence. Sometimes it is only accumulated energy or a left over wandering Soul, confused by his or her last moments in the physical, especially if it was traumatic or so sudden that their minds did not have time to register what happened in many sudden or violent situations. Also you will encounter many Souls who are so attached to their former situation that they have trouble realizing or accepting the transition necessary for their own progress and will hang around and try to communicate with whoever enters their former domain.

You can also encounter evil forces drawn by unaware persons dabbling in black magic or physical phenomena or entities. The Souls are trapped because they are unaware of their own fate! However, all Souls or entities should be free to take the place where they should be placed.

These wandering Souls are former residents of a special place and may have experienced a traumatic or sudden death therefore making it hard for them to be aware that they should depart.

Entities on the other hand are an accumulation of negative energy enforced by the own energy field of living beings. For instance if one is interested in manipulation or is controlling others by the use of their energy, they draw energy from the negative forces that are built and accumulated out of murder, hate, resentment and vengeance.

These are very powerful forms of energy representing the negative existence of our emotions. These are created by any human being who generates this energy out of personal frustration and anger. It accumulates in the lower astral and can be drawn upon by anyone who is destructive. Sometimes this energy is so strong it can appear as a demon or destructive energy. It is very powerful, usually because the Soul that generates it is very new and unaware of the power of our thoughts and the energy that one Soul can generate. Once this energy is emitted and drawn directly by another negativity generating energy it accumulates and then is reutilized by the Souls with the strongest desire and force or will.

Sometimes young people on Earth who are very emotional and have not yet reached the sexual age for releasing of emotional energy are apt to draw upon this energy in their frustration at being in between innocence and promiscuity. These occurrences are related to as poltergeists. It is an unconscious act on behalf of the young person but because they have no real outlet for emotions and have built up energy due to lack of understanding of meditation or protection they are apt to draw this energy from other dimensions in situations that create confusion or anger and resentment. Therefore they can create havoc in their own homes or environment without knowing that they themselves are the cause.

Souls that are trapped in any dimension or in the physical plane are only confused former residents that either do not know that their physical bodies are now no longer inhabitable, or because their deaths were so sudden, such as accident or war victims. Also it could be that their deaths were so painful – either emotionally or physically such as suicide, murder, or that they had some unfulfilled desire or attachment here that they really cannot leave or accept their own departure. Sometimes in the case of torture or murder they may continually reenact their last hour or moments. However, they are caught in a trap of their own emotions – whether it be attachment, fear or rage. They all need to be made aware and freed.

If you feel that you have such entities or Souls in your living space there are steps you can take. However, do not become paranoid and feel that every place you are is full of such energy. This is an obsession and being fanatical or focusing on such energy at all times is completely uncalled for. You do not have to search for trouble. Only be aware if you are uncomfortable or sleepless or have reoccurring unaccounted for occurrences that keep happening.

However, it is not necessary to cleanse every room you enter or search for such happenings. Then you begin to look like a fanatic (which you are) and people will avoid you. Also you may draw these negative energies unto yourself because you are putting so much attention on them! Remember where your attention goes, your energy flows! So to constantly be on the look out for trouble you can actually create it.

Now what can we do in these special rare cases? Well, if you are of a specific religion you can approach your pastor, priest or clergyman to see if help is available from there. If you get turned down, then you may work on your own.

You need to open all windows in your apartment, home or whatever building the disturbances are occurring. Then get incense of sandalwood, frankincense and myrrh. Bring some in every room. In the main doorway into the place make a pyramid by placing white, pink, green candles in a triangle in front of the door. You should have three people altogether, including yourself, as helpers. You need the three candles mentioned above placed at all entrances or exits of the home – not windows.

Make sure each room has wood, metal, water, earth and fire. Check each room. Toilet is water, flowers and plants are earth, faucets are considered as water, metal or mineral. Also colors representing each will work – silver for metal, or rust, yellow or red for fire, brown or black for earth, and green, white, blue or purple for water.

Now unplug all electrical appliances. Then you and two friends or more but at least three must sit in the central location in a triangle in the center of the room. Join hands and chant HU for at least twelve times. Sit quietly for ten minutes and see the environment filled with blue-white purifying light. Then hands joined stand up and say:

"You unwanted and misplaced force, be gone, this is now... place (Say the name of whom ever is to reside or work there). You must be informed that you no longer should be here and must go to where you were meant to go or return to the energy that created you. In the name of the greatest force of all, the One Divine Creator – I (or other name) now reside here and shall not welcome you in this present form. Be gone, be what you were intended and be free of what has drawn you. You are not part of this place anymore. Bless you and may you find the way that was meant for you."

Then each present takes a room. Stand in the center of the room. Take three deep breaths, imagine as you breath in you are filling yourself with pure blue-white energy and as you exhale it destroys all negative forces and clears the room. Chant three times "A-Lah-ya". Then holding your arms over your head you turn in small circles counterclockwise around the whole circumference of the room. When you return to your original spot turn clockwise in the other direction. See that as you spin you gather all the negative energy around you. Now walk to the center of the room. Close your eyes, hold your hands up and see it in your mind swirling away into infinity like a tornado and being absorbed into the ocean of love and mercy and dissipating and returning as pure energy, free of the burdens of hate, fear, resentment, frustration and destruction. See how it is being pulled off you like a soiled garment and swirling away to become clean and pure.

After you visualize this and it is repeated in every room by one of you, sit once again in the main room, hold hands and say:

"Now it is a free place, clean of all old energy. Thank you, Supreme One. All is done."

Preparation for Cleaning of Environment

1. Select all tools needed for preparation.
2. Prepare each room.
3. Choose all to participate - three or more persons, not more than seven.
4. Open all windows to allow energy to enter and leave.
5. Do meditation in the entrance of the main room of environment.
6. Perform the ceremony in each room.
7. Rejoin in the same room as beginning to give thanks to the Supreme Being.

There are always seven steps as it is a spiritual number on Venus.

Tools needed

- Participants
- Incense
- Three candles – white for spirituality, pink for love and green for healing
- Representatives for water, earth, fire and minerals or corresponding colors: blue, red, orange, brown, black, yellow or green.

Interview between Omnec Onec and Marina Popovich

Author: Anja Schäfer

This interview was one of the first interviews Omnec ever gave after she made herself public in the beginning of the Ninetees. Marina Popovich is a retired Soviet Air Force colonel and a legendary Soviet test pilot. The interview took place in Arizona, USA, during a worldwide UFO congress. Wendelle C. Stevens had set up this event to make the public aware of information from different countries about UFOs and extraterrestrials, and to introduce Omnec Onec's first book *From Venus I Came* which he published at that time.

YouTube Link to the video: **http://youtu.be/wcGv3Pf0tgo** (or search for "omnec marina")

MARINA: Your life has been a sensation for us on this planet. I wanted for a very long time to have an interview with you since we met at the Tuscon UFO-congress. And having the pleasure today, I would like to ask you my first question: How did you appear on our planet, what year was that, and in what manner did you appear on our planet?

OMNEC: In 1955 … before that, I was asked by my spiritual teachers and the people who were raising me on Venus, if I would like to do an experiment, come to Earth and live in your societies as a child to grow up and with the mission to bring public the story of how people from other planets have been interacting with the people here for thousands of years and what the connection is with their forefathers who brought the colonies here long time ago. They have lost track of their beginnings.

The purpose of coming was to live in your society and understand the human consciousness from their level by living in your society. And to do this, of course, I had to come as a child and grow up with the understanding of the prejudices, the class structures, the different religions, and the changes that people go through emotionally. I made the decision to come, went to the city of Retz on Venus – the only existing city on the physical and the astral level –, lowered my vibrations, manifested my physical body and said goodbye to my family. I tried to bring artifacts with me. I gathered a few plants and tried to preserve them, and I had a ring that I did bring with me.

They picked me up in a small craft what we call a scout ship and transported me from the surface of Venus – we have like a dome over the city of Retz, it's not visible because of the gases. The fire and the flames cover the city, you have to know the location. Our ships have the ability to travel through time and we can appear and disappear – from vision, because of their vibratory rate, the control they have over the magnetic waves and to create their own gravitational force. We left the surface, met a huge mothership, a cigar-shaped ship, went into the chamber, parked the ship and then I prepared for my journey to Earth – from Venus, which didn't take very long, maybe 24 hours. We came close to the surface, and once again I prepared to board a small craft, and they told me I will be going to the mountains in Tibet to stay in a monastery with monks to learn to adjust to the gravity and prepare to live in the society here.

MARINA: How were you able to get accustomed to our earthly conditions of living here? Were they very much different from the ones you were accustomed to? What were the major differences?

OMNEC: Well, the monastery wasn't too bad. I was living with the monks and they are pretty spiritually aware. The hardest thing to get used to of course was my physical body. I felt like I was in a suite of armor. And I had difficulty walking, and having my broad view vision taken away. I wasn't able to see in all directions like I was used to. I wasn't aware that in your society … well,… in the astral it is that you can think something – and you can materialize it. Here you have to go through the physical means of … you know, picking up the objects, eating, reading a book. And if you want something, it's not available to you just by your thoughts. I had to learn to use my vocal chords, I had to have exercises for that. I had to learn balance. They made me walk like on walls and beams and stuff, I fell many times. I bruised myself and found that physical pain was something I was not familiar with, but I quickly became familiar with it. It was pretty difficult, everything was hard for me.

MARINA: Would you tell us something about your second parents on Earth?

OMNEC: Actually, I didn't know very much about my father and my mother here, because I went directly to my mother's mother's house, to my grandmother. And I had been given their history and was pretty much familiar with what Sheila went through and her relationship with everyone. She had been born to a mother who was 15 years old. As a child she had been living with aunts, uncles, her father, her grandmother – and she was being sent back to her grandmother. So she went to live with her grandmother coming from a violent situation where she was being protected at this point. But not being close to any certain members of the family for any long periods of time, it became easy to be incorporated to the family without them noticing very much difference, since we physically resembled one another very much. And this happened of course right after the little girl had died. And I started living in the society, learning from the point of an "adopted" child.

MARINA: Are you presently meeting from time to time with rep-resentatives of your race here on Earth or with representatives of other races, other extraterrestrial races here?

OMNEC: I kept in contact with them from time to time. They would send me mental messages, just more or less, greetings. At one point when I became very ill with a disease called leukemia, they made arrangements to meet me outside in a desert area in Nevada in a scout ship for a healing treatment that's not available to most of the people here, although the information is available, it's not on the market. I was taken inside the ship and we flew to an area beyond your physical vision, and they proceeded with the procedure. I was given a sedative so I would relax and put in a sleep state.

MARINA: Is there anything particular that is different between the two races, between the Venusians and the Earthlings, that you noticed after your arrival here?

OMNEC: I was aware that we as a people know that we are Soul first and the body is just temporary. And most people were walking around thinking they were the body. They have no ability to communicate on any level other than speaking with one another. And I felt sort of lost and frightened. The physical differences were: We have a purity in the way our appearance looks. We have been described in the bible as angels because of our appearance being very etheric even though we are physical people. We have the high foreheads, the big eyes, the different look, and our hands are shaped different than most peoples. They are like a flame. It looks like a flame in a candle. And we have these ridges in our forehead, they are shaped different, that comes down, quite prominent the different shape of our skull. But you will find these characteristics in many people, since we are their forefathers, and the genetics are there from us. But they have been intermixed in your races. We manufacture our own calcium. We have faster heartbeats. And we carry our children longer than most people.

MARINA: Do you have any ability in yourself toward healing people or some other higher abilities like levitation or telekinesis or mental telepathy?

OMNEC: Yes. We have telepathic abilities. We can communicate with the mind. Sometimes I know what Marina is saying even though I don't understand the language. I pick it up in my mind. And I am capable of healing people, but don't very often do this, because of spiritual laws that say that you have to go through these experiences, it's a lesson for you. And that prevents me from doing a lot more healing. But the people feel, if they touch me, they can feel this energy. And sometimes they don't understand what they feel.

MARINA: Would you please tell us a little about life on Venus. Are there plants, trees, or what the sky looks like? We know that it's very hot there, so how can people survive on the planet? How is your life on Venus different from ours?

OMNEC: There is one city that exists on the physical as well as on the astral. It's very much like the desert of Arizona or Nevada.

It's very dry. The plants are pretty similar. And the atmosphere is pretty much the same. It's kept very comfortable within the dome, because it is a controlled atmosphere. On the astral level we have many plants, because our environment is created by our thoughts. And we can have a tree growing through our bedroom, we can have waterfalls in the house, we have extended love for gardens and plants and animal life. It's very similar to what we have on Earth, just a little different. The fruit is almost the same. Sunflowers and corn were brought to Earth by my people thousands of years ago. This is among some of the vegetation that was brought here and can grow in this environment. There is not very much difference. It's that we have more available to us than people here.

MARINA: How is life on Venus manifested, for example how are the Venusians manifested? Are they in material, biological bodies or are they in kind of etheric, bioenergetic non-material bodies?

OMNEC: Well, we are actually not physical, but a duplicate of the physical being the plane above the physical plane. We carry our children the same way. I remember being in the womb, and I remember being born, even though I was on the astral level. When you are there in your astral body, everything is as real to you as it is when you are here in the physical.

MARINA: If you touch a table, would it be hard for you or would your hand go through the table?

OMNEC: No, it's very solid. You have a body that correlates to each plane. And if you are in that body in that plane, it's very real to you. But if you are a physical person and you see an astral entity, then it seems like it's ghostly-like. Like the ghosts that people see here, they are entities from somewhere else. A disembodied physical.

MARINA: Of course I will acquaint the Russian public with the contents of your book and your life story. My last question is: What would be your message to us, to the Earthlings at the time when we are already establishing such contacts with representatives from other races?

OMNEC: Well, I hope that I can, in some way, familiarize people with the fact that they don't have much to fear from people from other planets within our own solar system and that our brotherhood of the planets of every solar system that colonized the Earth protects mankind from any harm from aliens from other solar systems or any kind of dangers. We will protect the populations of the Earth until the consciousness comes to a level where that we can indeed offer them our technical knowledge for their own means of travel to other planets and to study the solar system, but not as a means to hurt or harm other races. One thing I was impressed with by you, was, very much like myself, you have technical knowledge of how things operate beyond most normal human beings. And myself, I have the same knowledge. You also have a respect for human beings as a whole, not separate races but as a whole unit. And you wish to incorporate into them the spirituality, importance of understanding of what they really basically are and what we are about, to raise the consciousness of mankind and to unite them without the different governments and without the different powers that are preventing us from living the kind of advanced, simple and beautiful lives that we should live.

MARINA: Thank you very much!

OMNEC: Thank you! And it's an honor knowing you. And I love you.

PART THREE

Transcripts

Author: Anja Schäfer

*T*his third part contains transcripts of the book presentations Omnec Onec gave in 2011 on the occasion of the re-release of her books in German. Due to Omnec's health condition – she had suffered a stroke two years earlier and had not yet fully recovered again – we – Omnec Onec and Anja Schäfer – made these presentations as energy saving for Omnec as possible by following the same sequence:

- Introduction of Omnec Onec
- Reading an excerpt from *The Venusian Trilogy*
- Questions & answers
- Autographing session

To convey the live atmosphere and Omnec Onec's personality as authentically as possible, we have decided to print the original recordings of the presentations unfiltered, although some contents partly repeat. The same questions are sometimes repeated, because they were asked from different human beings with different consciousnesses in different places. The questions associated with the great expectations concerning December 21, 2012, were asked very often, and even though this date at the time of the publication of this book has already passed, Omnec Onec's answers to similar questions on specific dates and expected events are timelessly valid.

As a reading about the astral level of Venus was part of almost every book presentation, we fully quote this excerpt with the kind permission of the publisher *Das Gute Buch* in the first transcript (Cologne, September 3, 2011) and point to it later accordingly. We also thank *Das Gute Buch* for the permission to quote the excerpt about the Soul Journey (*Mantras and their Benefit*, Dresden, October 30, 2011), and we thank Robert Scott Lemriel for his permission to print his information titled *The New Sugmad Expansion Ray* which has also been included in Omnec Onec's book *The Venusian Trilogy* as the last chapter (Munich, September 26, 2011).

Cologne, September 3, 2011

OMNEC: Good evening. My name is Omnec Onec from Venus and I am not sure if you know that I had a stroke two years ago. But all is good now.

Anja is going to read a little bit about the planet Venus – about the astral dimension.

+++

Reading: *The Venus Plane* (excerpt from *The Venusian Trilogy, From Venus I Came,* chapter 5)

The astral plane is an immense universe, even greater and more vast than the physical plane with all its solar systems and galaxies. Venus is a mere speck in that one of many other realities and is a speck in our limited reality also at its dense physical level. But the astral plane is only one of many planes of lesser density in being.

Many individuals who have experienced these worlds in out-of-body travels have called them heavens. Conditions are so much more beautiful and peaceful there that their vocabulary failed them. What they were able to write down in the past is today called religious, mystical or spiritual literature.

The astral plane existed long before the physical and will endure beyond. The most common things known and recognized here in the physical world first existed there. Naturally there is much on the astral plane which does not exist here, but all that exists here does have its counterpart there – and more.

The differences between the astral and the physical planes take some explaining. Just as x-rays are at a higher frequency than solid rock, the entire astral plane is at a much higher frequency than the physical. This is one reason why scientists on Earth have not yet proven its existence. None of their scientific instruments can detect such very high vibrations.

Because matter on the astral level is so high in frequency, those of us who live there can have complete control over it by thought power alone. On Earth, few people have developed the power to directly control matter with the mind. On Venus, mind over matter is a way of life.

Any form or thing that a person on the astral can imagine, he or she can manifest by the power of thought alone. It is a law of nature there, just as gravity is a basic law of nature on the physical planets. What really happens is that people convert the energy around them into the form of matter desired. The created object then appears wherever the person puts his or her attention. Homes, clothes, furniture, plants, food, jewelry, and anything imaginable is created by a special mental process that has to be mastered at a young age.

There are limits. This same power will not destroy things or reconvert them to energy. Things disappear only if the person who created them leaves the astral plane, unless they were originally created with the definite intention that they be temporary and how long, such as our castles and ranches and elaborate play creations. If I had created a toy that soon bored me, I may change its shape into another kind of toy, but I could not point my finger at it and have it disappear in a flash, forever gone. If my aunt Arena no longer liked a certain chair, her only choice would be to reform that chair. She could not remold it into a table or anything other than a chair.

On the other hand, when we create things, they do seem to appear out of thin air. For people on the astral plane this is as common and accepted as driving a car here on Earth.

Because we respect each Soul's individuality, people do not interfere with another's creations. If I did not like the bright blue tree in front of another's house, I would not think of changing it. That would be interference, which creates karmic responsibility.

Just because our thoughts precipitate matter, the common everyday things on the astral are no less real. A marble floor looks and

116

feels like marble, skin feels like skin, water feels like water, flowers smell like flowers, honey tastes like honey and so on.

Moving things is of course very easy, just a matter of choosing and thinking. If I wanted, I could have a glass of water rise up from the table and float, just by mentally commanding it. No more effort is involved in moving a huge sofa up into the air than in swinging the bed as I am resting on it.

Traveling from place to place is just as easy. People who like to walk do so. We can also levitate and float in the air or glide instead of walking by willing it to be so. For longer trips we travel at the speed of our thought directly to our destination, which usually seems just a matter of appearing there. Whenever I decided to visit the Temple of Arts in downtown Teutonia, I would place my attention on exactly where I wanted to be. One moment I would be standing in the bedroom; the next instant the surroundings would change and I would be standing in front of the Temple. It is very simple. I do not know the mechanics of how it works – it just works. (People on Earth say the same thing about electricity.)

The speed of thought is much faster than the so-called speed of light known to physical scientists. In the astral body we can travel so very fast because it is made up of condensed energy, as completely under the control of thought as everything else on that plane of being.

The astral body has the same form as the physical, except that it is much more beautiful. It is not just a blob of light, but unlike the physical body, it is luminous and stays alive by absorbing energy directly from the surroundings. Although there are no actual internal organs, people here do eat out of habit and for the simple pleasure of it. Food conveniently turns back into energy as soon as it is swallowed.

Using the power of thought, we can easily change our outer appearance or make ourselves completely invisible. There is no physical pain or fatigue as on the physical planets, which is one good reason why newcomers to the astral call it heaven.

The colors in our everyday lives are indescribable. Compared to the glowing, vibrant colors of the astral plane, colors in the physical are pale or dark and muddy at best. The dullest red of the astral world is the brightest in the physical. Also, very many colors which we take for granted don't even exist on the physical plane.

Our surroundings at home had such an assortment of magnificent colors that I can't even begin to describe it. Just as wonderful is the fact that everything glows. Matter on the astral plane is luminous, like stained glass being lit by the morning sunlight. The sky and clouds are a sea of cheerful colors.

The astral body and the astral plane are not completely unknown on Earth. Each person living in the physical world has an astral body as well as several others, as taught in the Laws of the Supreme Deity. Quite a few people have written books about their experiences with astral projection, which is a limited form of out-of-body travel in the astral body. The safer way of visiting the higher planes is by using the Soul body, which is not limited to any one place as the astral is. But, of course, not everyone who does astral projection is aware of the Soul Journey[10].

+++

OMNEC: Yes, it's a little different than Earth.

The Soul is the essence of every living being. It's eternal, it's forever. Only your life on Earth or your existence in one lifetime is limited. Love is always there. It knows no boundaries. Love exists forever. We are created out of love. The love that God had for Itself. God loved Itself so much, that It created everything from Itself. Everything that exists continues to create from itself. So our existence is forever. Love is the strongest power in the universe – and the greatest. The more you give of this love, the more you receive. Love is the essence of our being also. Love is all there is actually. It's all you need (like the Beatles song). If you have love, you don't need anything else. You don't have to look for love – it's within you.

I am sure that many of you feel a connection to Venus. I feel that all of you are part of myself. And I feel at home. I feel the love from the people around me.

---

10 also Journey of Soul or Soul Travel (Publisher's comment)

I came to Earth and had a great adventure. My life is still an adventure. Everywhere I go, there is so much love on Earth. Earth is now my home. I have children here and I was married twice. Now I'm just single. But still the connection is there to my family. I call every person I meet on Earth my Soul family. I feel that way. I am very happy to be here and to present my new book.

I was on a tour with Anja before when I had my stroke. I couldn't believe it that I don't have the ability to make my body whole. I have to live with this – like everyone. I have to accept what is. I am satisfied. I understand that we have chosen experiences. Even if it is painful, it is part of our growth and learning. It is not easy, but it is necessary.

I am so happy that you came tonight. I thank you very much.

I know it's very curious for people – I lived in such a wonderful place, why did I come to Earth? Because I wanted to understand what YOU experience. I must experience everything for myself, then I KNOW. People tell me but I don't know unless I experience. If I don't know the pain, then I can't understand how you feel. So now I have the ability to understand how you feel and to have the same feelings. You know that without darkness, you can't enjoy the light. Without pain you don't know how it feels to have no pain. You have to have the opposite to know how it feels to be whole and free and happy – how you should feel. A Soul must experience everything there is in order to fulfill its existence. The Soul's whole reason for existence is to experience. So every experience is important. It's very valuable for the Soul to develop and to perfect it. We have to know all and be all, then we can have the experience of being part of creation, of God, through each of Its creations. God experiences everything through It's creations, through each Soul. So every experience is important.

We can't judge one another. We have to accept all. The good and the bad are the same. The good and the bad exist in your mind, but in reality they don't. There is no good and bad. In God's eyes all is as it should be. Everything is as it should be. Each day be thankful, because everything that happens is supposed to. We shouldn't want to change anything. It's a mistake to do that. We have to be satisfied and happy with everything, because we ARE very lucky. In reality we do. Life is very valuable. It's easy to run away from life, but it's hard to stay and really experience. It's important that you remain and do what you have to do.

I love Earth very much, because there are so many different things to experience. Every Soul is individual and unique and special, and every experience each Soul has is like a facet of a jewel. Every jewel is unique and special. And that's what you are as Soul: perfect and beautiful. You don't know your own beauty. I wish you could see your real beauty – it's really wonderful. I couldn't describe it if I tried. But you must know that you are indeed beautiful, and I love all of you.

I know there are many questions and I am going to take the time and try to answer.

AUDIENCE: You write in your book, when you came from Venus to Earth that first you went to a monastery in the Himalayas where you learned to deal with your physical body. You had to learn to walk, to eat, etc...

OMNEC: Yes, that was very difficult. I had to get used to the body.

AUDIENCE: I just asked myself – when this exchange took place with the other girl during the accident whose life you took over, I was wondering how this exchange took place. You came with your own physical body and the other girl also had her own physical body – so there was practically one body too many.

OMNEC: Sheila was in a bus accident and her body burned.

ANJA: In her book, Omnec describes this situation with the exchange as follows: Omnec had been placed close to the point where the accident was supposed to take place. When the bus came and the accident happened, Sheila's body was thrown out of the bus. During the chaos, Omnec showed up and replaced the dead Sheila – so she was like one of the survivors. Sheila's body was never found, because Omnec's uncle took care of it. This whole exchange had karmic reasons and was well planned and prepared in advance, so that Omnec could be smuggled onto the Earth. After the accident, the people were waiting for help and, when another bus came, Omnec was put on that bus in Sheila's place.

OMNEC: Before that, when Sheila was born, my Soul accompanied her Soul in the birth process – so I as a Soul could receive the genetic imprint from Sheila, so that when I was living in her place I would have the same physical characteristics. It was necessary.

AUDIENCE: I have another question on this subject. I heard that you had to take over karmic entanglements from Sheila when you took her place. Is that correct?

OMNEC: Yes, I owed it to her. In another time, she had given her life for me. And so I came in this life when it was too difficult for her. It was karmic.

AUDIENCE: How did you walk into Sheila's body? I would like to better understand how such a walk-into another body functions.

ANJA: That is a misunderstanding. We just explained the physical exchange between Omnec and Sheila. Omnec did not walk as a Soul into a different body; she took over her place physically. The girl Sheila died and Omnec was present in order to replace her.

AUDIENCE: And where did the other girl go?

ANJA: In the book this is only briefly mentioned. Omnec did not come all alone. She had two persons accompany her, her Uncle Odin and a Martian. In the book it is described that these men took care of Sheila's dead body, and that it is why it was never found. There are no details explained.

AUDIENCE: In other words – there are UFOs, yes?

OMNEC: Yes.

AUDIENCE: Oh! According to what they say in the TV there are no UFOs.

AUDIENCE: I am still unclear... I read your book more than ten years ago... well, did you also look like Sheila then? And the mother and the other relatives simply thought that that was their Sheila who survived the accident?

ANJA: Exactly, yes, Omnec even wore the same patent leather shoes. Sheila was on her way to her grandmother and they had not been together in a couple of years. And because Omnec and Sheila looked like twins, nobody would have assumed that an exchange had happened, so this was unnoticed.

AUDIENCE: So everything was planned and prepared?

ANJA: Yes, everything was prepared.

OMNEC: Exactly!

ANJA: In the book, it is all described in detail, all events and everything that took place before this exchange happened – it was quite a long preparation.

AUDIENCE: I would like to know if you in the meantime had the opportunity again to travel back to your home on the astral level on Venus, for example with your Uncle Odin or with somebody from where you came?

OMNEC: No. I would never return. When I left, I knew I would not go back.

AUDIENCE: But is there the possibility of a connection?

OMNEC: Only with Soul Travel.

AUDIENCE: I also heard that it is possible to take one's body there.

ANJA: ... to the astral plane of Venus?

AUDIENCE: ... to other levels, yes.

OMNEC: I haven't experienced this – so I don't know. But I know that we have the possibility on the astral to manifest a physical body. It's a special mantra that we do. And it creates a physical body.

AUDIENCE: Have you ever had contact again with your twin sister – with Sheila?

OMNEC: Not in this life, no. With the Soul, yes; with the Soul I am in touch.

AUDIENCE: After this lifetime, will you go back to Venus, to the astral?

OMNEC: No. I'll be on another dimension. I am finished with the physical. [everybody is laughing]

AUDIENCE: So it was important to go into this life for a last experience?

OMNEC: Exactly. This is my last experience in the physical. I've had enough. [laughs and everybody is laughing with her]

AUDIENCE: Where do you know this from – that you go to another dimension and not back to Venus?

OMNEC: Oh, from my masters. I have some spiritual masters that told me. I already chose when I came to this Earth that this will be my last life, so I chose a spiritual journey.

AUDIENCE: Before you came here?

OMNEC: Yes. And it was very difficult.

AUDIENCE: What was very difficult?

OMNEC: My whole life! [everybody is laughing]

AUDIENCE: *Are there more people like you who made the same experience with this exchange of physical bodies?*

OMNEC: No, I'm not sure of that, but many people from other planets come to Earth and live in your societies.

ANJA: But usually through the birth process, or ...?

OMNEC: No, they come physically in space ships. And they live here.

ANJA: You mean as adults?

OMNEC: Yes

AUDIENCE: *As walk-in?*

ANJA: No, she did not mean as walk-ins, but physically.

AUDIENCE: *Are they in contact with each other? Do they know each other?*

OMNEC: Yes, they know – they are aware.

AUDIENCE: *This December 21, 2012, when the Mayan calendar ends, can you say something about this, because there are so many fears circulating – how terrible this is going to be – but there are also many people saying that everything is going to be wonderful and that it's only a transformation.*

OMNEC: I have heard from the masters that we have control over what happens on Earth. If we focus on negative things, then we create them. It depends on what you want and what you wish to happen.

AUDIENCE: *Does it really make sense to pray for the Earth and its healing? Is that enough? I mean, I am praying for this every day, and there is this Operation Peace Program as well...*

OMNEC: That's why! Because you have a lot of power and you have the control over what happens to this planet.

ANJA: The Operation Peace Program[11] is a meditation program that Omnec called into being so that people can consciously send out their powers for healing and peace.

OMNEC: You should give your energy to the fact that human consciousness is going to get higher and the way they exist will be better. Things will get better. Create the Earth as you want it to be!

AUDIENCE: *I have a question about raising ones consciousness. Is there a special way? It is possible by meditating, but ... I am also*

11 see also PART FOUR of this book "Projects"

into quantum physics and try to practice what I am learning, but I don't feel that I am very successful...

OMNEC: Actually, you can pray or meditate – you can choose your own way.

AUDIENCE: Yes, I try ... but isn't there a special, a specific way?

OMNEC: Actually, you have to focus on the positive, don't think of negative thoughts. Because, where you put your attention, the energy goes. So you have to be careful what you think.

AUDIENCE: Why did you come to Earth? What are your reasons?

OMNEC: To experience and to share with human beings that Man is universal. And that your ancestors came from other galaxies and systems. So your heritage is great and beautiful. It's to give you an idea that you are not limited to one planet. There is no limit. Whatever you can imagine, can be reality. Anything is possible. As long as you can imagine, it can be.

AUDIENCE: How do the extraterrestrials who are incarnated on Earth recognize each other? And how can we identify or recognize them? Are there specific standards or criteria?

OMNEC: Well, all of you have existed on other planets. In other lifetimes.

AUDIENCE: Physically or in other dimensions?

OMNEC: In other lifetimes also physically.

AUDIENCE: On Earth or on other planets?

OMNEC: Other planets. You probably existed here, too.

AUDIENCE: Is the good and the bad on Earth in balance or will it always be balanced?

OMNEC: Yes, it is. The negative and the positive are perfect the way they are. In the future, there will be no need to be born. You will manifest a physical body, and you will choose to be a man or a woman. There won't be a birth process.

AUDIENCE: I thought that the catastrophes that are taking place all over the world contribute to the Earth's balance.

OMNEC: Yes, whatever happens is perfect. When the Earth goes into the Transformation, everything will change. We are already in the process.

AUDIENCE: What about the need of money? Will it disappear after 2012?

OMNEC: Yes, that will come to an end.

ANJA: But not directly after 2012 – he asked about 2012.

OMNEC: No, no.

ANJA: In the future, after the Transformation, money will not be needed anymore, but Omnec does not give specific dates.

OMNEC: I can't tell you the time, because we're forbidden. Because it really lies within each individual how fast the Transformation Process takes place. It is how much people are concentrating on it. It's up to you!

AUDIENCE: We all as a whole contribute to the Transformation Process plus everyone individually?

OMNEC: That's exactly right.

AUDIENCE: When we die, can we ask beforehand to which plane we want to go?

OMNEC: Actually, you decide. You choose between each life what you are going to experience next. You have the choice. You always have the choice. God gave you the free will.

AUDIENCE: But this choice is made, BEFORE one dies or after?

OMNEC: You can choose before, if you can really visualize something for yourself. And there is no hell or heaven. You create a place for yourself.

AUDIENCE: In many books it is written that we have to expect three days of darkness when we pass the photon ring. Do you know anything about this?

OMNEC: That's finished. We did that already.

AUDIENCE: And the three days of darkness, will this still happen?

OMNEC: No, it's finished. It didn't happen because there were enough people to help us through it.

AUDIENCE: It is also said that the electricity will stop functioning.

OMNEC: Not yet, but after the Transformation Process there will be new energy sources brought to mankind. From the space brothers; they are bringing everything.

AUDIENCE: What about the prophecies from Nostradamus? Are they still important in our time or can we forget them? Somebody mentioned the three days of darkness will come over the Earth. That reminds me of Nostradamus.

OMNEC: They changed it. Human beings have changed everything.

So you don't have to worry.

AUDIENCE: I am longing for the arrival of our extraterrestrial cosmic brothers and sisters.

OMNEC: They will come!

AUDIENCE: When?

OMNEC: In the future. You have to be patient.

AUDIENCE: But there are so many UFO sightings all the time...

OMNEC: Of course.

AUDIENCE: Isn't it better, when our mind says, "The Soul knows it better anyway," – for example at the end of our lifetime – just to come back to what we were just speaking about. I mean, isn't it better not to ask ourselves, "What do I have to do now? What do I have to visualize?" This is the mind again ... isn't it better to leave it up to our Soul to decide, because it knows everything better anyway?

ANJA: I think that is what Omnec meant. [to Omnec]: If you are in contact with your true self, with your Soul, you can make the decisions what happens after your lifetime even while you are in the physical.

OMNEC: Exactly.

ANJA: When you are identified with the Soul consciousness, then you have the same consciousness as a Soul outside the body.

OMNEC: Yes, you have that ability. We have many abilities; we just don't know it sometimes. Or we have forgotten. There is so much that the Soul knows, but the mind doesn't know. The mind is limited. But the Soul knows everything.

AUDIENCE: What can we do to support this? Meditate, pray and concentrate on our heart?

OMNEC: Yeah, and it will be given to you when the time is right. It's too much for this mind.

ANJA: It is too much for the mind ... first one must lose one's mind ... [everybody is laughing] Right? You have to leave your mind behind...

OMNEC: Yes, leave your mind behind – then you know. It's too complicated for the brain.

ANJA: It's too complicated for the mind ... but it's all written in Omnec's book.

OMNEC: Everything is in the book!

AUDIENCE: I heard that there are lower astral levels. What can you say about these? Do they exist?

OMNEC: Yeah, but most people don't want to go there.

AUDIENCE: Because you said, there exists no hell – so I ask about the lower astral.

OMNEC: It's not hell, but close to. It's somewhere you don't want to go.

AUDIENCE: How can I imagine this? What is going on there?

OMNEC: Oh, no, you don't want to know. It's the worst kind of suffering that you can imagine. And the worst creatures that you could ever imagine.

AUDIENCE: Are these creatures able to come into the physical?

OMNEC: No, we are protected.

AUDIENCE: Where do our fears and our negative thoughts come from, especially after getting up in the morning?

OMNEC: Probably from the lower astral.

AUDIENCE: During sleep?

OMNEC: Some things are that our mind has seen and experienced before and it comes back in your subconscious memory.

AUDIENCE: How can I avoid remembering?

OMNEC: Just ask at night that God protects you, that you are protected and that nothing can happen. We all can do that.

AUDIENCE: So these lower astral beings have some kind of influence on us?

OMNEC: No. Not if you ask for protection. You do have higher beings and angels that protect each person.

ANJA to OMNEC: But you have to open yourself consciously and ask for the protection?

OMNEC: Yes.

AUDIENCE: People can influence other people negatively through frequencies – I am talking about technical means or even medical. Have you heard of that?

OMNEC: Yes, this is the black magic and the negative forces.

AUDIENCE: And you think it's enough to ask and pray for protection from God.

OMNEC: That's all you need, yes. We have the right to be protected.

AUDIENCE: If one, however, already is the victim of some black magic practices, maybe from previous lifetimes and one does not consciously know it, how can one get rid of this influence? How can one change it?

OMNEC: State really simply that you refuse to be included in this – that it's not your choice. [to Anja]: She has the right to say, "I do not wish to be involved in this."

AUDIENCE: Yes, but when one is already affected, what then? Recently, many people came towards to me with this problem.

OMNEC: But you have the right as a human being to be free. Simply refuse to be included. You can't be a victim, if you refuse. Because you have the power. God gives you this power.

AUDIENCE: And everyone has to decide this for himself?

OMNEC: Yes. God will protect you and your guardian angels and your masters. You have a whole bunch of beings from other dimensions that watch over you. Every human being has these. They protect everyone. But you have to say, "I want you to protect me!" And then you imagine like titanium around you. Then you are safe.

AUDIENCE: Is it wrong to have fear... well, I have personally experienced that when I focus on my fear that I am unable to protect myself, because I focus on the negative and not on the positive. As soon as I worry about something, the emotions and thoughts go into the wrong direction – to a negative force. And that is the mistake, the main mistake – to have worries, to be afraid or also to be angry about some kind of interferences.

OMNEC: Yes, fear is deadly. There is nothing to fear.

AUDIENCE: The prophecies in the Book of the Revelation of Saint John describe pretty concretely apocalyptic circumstances. Would you say that all that is not valid anymore and that all of these things are outdated? There are also those prophets who claim that what's written has to be fulfilled, and that it will be fulfilled, because it's God's will.

OMNEC: No, it's the negative forces. And that's their job to pull you away from the positive and to put fear in you.

AUDIENCE: People who are into spiritual things often say that there is no "No" in the universe, because the universe does not understand a "No." But we just said that we should say, "No, I am not involved in negative things." So does the universe understand that at all?

ANJA [to Omnec]: You have to say it in positive terms, what you want, right? You just said "You DON'T want to be involved in something negative..." And now he says the universe does not understand negative expressions. So you should better put it in positive words.

OMNEC: OK

ANJA: But it doesn't really matter. It's more what you want to express. He says that one should not say "I DON'T want this or that." One has to say it positively – like "I WANT" or "I AM".

OMNEC: Yes.

AUDIENCE: In the last centuries, human beings have been influenced a lot by religions and churches, and there has always been this consciousness of heaven, purgatory, and hell. According to the principle: If I load guilt onto myself, I have to go to hell – something really bad is waiting for me later on. I mean, guilt needs to be removed somehow, because guilt is nothing positive and one wants to contribute to the positive. Can you comment on that?

OMNEC: A lot of the religions were taught through fear. They use fear so that people obey.

AUDIENCE: For their own advantage, their own power.

OMNEC: Exactly.

AUDIENCE: Can you say something more about guilt and karma – no matter if one is on the culprit's or on the victim's side?

OMNEC: Well, from what I heard, all karma was ended in the year 1999. But whatever you create now, you have to be very careful what you do. The slate was cleaned so we could start over. So you have a new chance.

AUDIENCE: I have the feeling that one instantly gets back what one has caused.

OMNEC: Yes, usually it happens immediately.

AUDIENCE: What about incurable diseases – will they be curable in the future? Or can anyone by mind power heal himself – even from incurable diseases?

OMNEC: I don't think there will be diseases in the future. I think a lot of the illnesses were chosen by the individual Soul for the purpose of experience.

AUDIENCE: So if all karma is wiped off since 1999, then every-body should be totally free from any diseases now in our times of transformation. I do not understand this...

OMNEC: Not so.

AUDIENCE: If one is judging somebody and has strong, negative feelings about the other person, and if one notices this at the same moment – can one still prevent this situation from becoming a karmic debt? Or do I accumulate a karmic debt right in the moment when I am angry with somebody? How does one behave properly in order to NOT create new karma?

OMNEC: Don't have any negative thoughts about a person and always bless and look at somebody and think something positive. Think how beautiful everyone is. And if something annoys you, you should say to the person directly that it annoys you, so they are aware. And then it's not karma, it's just a clear understanding.

AUDIENCE: I would like to add something here: Once I read that if one is having hateful or angry thoughts and if one realizes this and wants to invalidate them, one simply has to send positive, forgiving thoughts after – something like: I am sorry, please forgive me, I am sending you positive thoughts.

AUDIENCE [another participant]: And thereby the negative is dissolving again?

AUDIENCE [answers]: The thoughts are powers, always. That's how it is.

OMNEC: Just be careful what you think and what you say. If you have to say something it's better to go direct to that individual person rather than speaking about that person to somebody else.

I think I have to autograph books now.

+++

[End and autographing session]

Darmstadt, September 6, 2011

OMNEC: Good evening. Most of you know that I'm Omnec Onec from Venus. I came to Earth at seven years old and I had many adventures here. Of course, I feel very much a part of your society; it's now my home. I feel very much love from other human beings. It was quite an adventure for me, you know. I was thinking that it was going to be a great adventure. I didn't realize how many problems would be created by my presence. But that's part of living, part of life. I chose to come here to live with human beings and to understand them. I wanted people to know that human beings have a great heritage. You are not just from the Earth – your forefathers are from other stars far away. So that is your heritage and it's very rich.

I don't know if all of you know that I had a stroke two years ago, here in Germany, in 2009. [Omnec has watery eyes] And I am not crying really, I just have sinus problems. So you have to forgive me. I am not really crying – I am actually happy. I am very happy that you came this evening. Many of you are Soul friends of mine from other lifetimes. You know who you are and I know who you are.

Anja is going to read a little bit from my book about the astral dimension.

And then I'll try to answer questions.

+++

Reading: Excerpt from *The Venus Plane* – Text see Cologne, September 3, 2011

+++

OMNEC: I think many of you probably know the astral and had experiences there.

I want to answer questions. If it's possible, I'll try.

AUDIENCE: Now that you came to Earth, do you still have the same abilities as you did on the astral?

OMNEC: I'm limited in the physical world. I can't manifest things, because different laws exist in the physical.

AUDIENCE: Do you still communicate with your people?

OMNEC: Of course, I communicate with my relatives. The ones that still exist. Many of them have left. They went on to higher dimensions. The only one I'm in contact with is Uncle Odin who brought me here in a spaceship.

AUDIENCE: Is Uncle Odin still physical?

OMNEC: Yes. But he is working in his science lab on the ship. He is working for the Earth, for the people here. I am staying here until my life is finished. I have four children here, three sons, one daughter and now three grandchildren. Time goes on, and I get older, too.

AUDIENCE: What about time and getting older on the astral plane?

OMNEC: On the astral plane, we live 500 of your Earth years. It's a different time. I am about 350 Venusian years old. I'm very old [laughs].

AUDIENCE: In your book you describe that you experienced the first time of your life on Earth like being in a suite of armor and that looking through your physical eyes was like looking through small slits. How do you feel meanwhile after so many years here?

OMNEC: I still feel the same way. I can't see as I would like to see. I can't experience things as I would like. I'm very limited by this physical body. I used to be freer, but that was before my body broke down. Now the body doesn't function so well. Not as good as it used to. We enjoy those times, but they are soon gone.

AUDIENCE: My daughter speaks in another language at night, which I don't understand and it doesn't sound human to me. When I saw your book, I thought this might be the answer to my questions. Could it be that she communicates with her Soul family?

OMNEC: I understand. She probably communicates with people on another dimension, because she is probably more familiar with them or closer. Sometimes children are more aware of things that we are not. Children have a better insight and a closeness to the spiritual world, they remember a lot. But then they are told by other people that it's not true or it's their imagination, and then they forget. Because we don't encourage them and we should. You should ask her questions about her family before she was your little girl.

AUDIENCE: She doesn't remember. She only speaks this language when she is asleep.

OMNEC: Oh! Only when she is asleep – OK A lot of times, when your body is sleeping, the Soul is actually experiencing in other dimensions. It's quite natural. Because that's the true home of Soul. Not the physical world. This is the place where we are not familiar. Not the Soul. The Soul is familiar with the other dimensions and the non-physical worlds. It's happier there. The Soul knows so much and your mind does not know all the stuff. But your Soul knows all. If you let your Soul guide you, you'll have a wonderful life.

AUDIENCE: Could you remind us what made us want to have experiences in the physical world? It is so much more beautiful everywhere else.

OMNEC: The physical world has a lot to offer. You have to experience and work off your karmic debts here. There are many things that you can experience on Earth you can't experience anywhere else. We choose to come here because our Soul wants the experience. We have to know suffering in order to be happy. In the darkness you realize you ARE the light. You are not the darkness. Then you experience everything so that you can realize what you are NOT. And you experience many sad things here, but it makes the Soul more perfect. You know, then it has ALL experiences. The whole purpose of the Soul is to experience everything. Earth was created by many, many different beings from so many different places and it has a special reason to be. To serve a beautiful purpose. And it IS beautiful, the Earth. We make it even more beautiful. That's true.

AUDIENCE: In your book, you repeatedly mention that we ARE Souls. Then, the switch finally flipped. I am Italian and I have always been trying to understand the term "Soul." Everything that I don't understand I translate into Italian for myself. And then I asked myself: What does "Soul" mean in Italian, maybe then I will get closer to the essence? I realized that "Soul" means "anima" in

Italian – and "animal" means "animale." Can you explain this connection to me?

OMNEC: I have no idea. I love languages, they are very interesting though. They are sometimes humorous and sometimes you can't understand any of it or how they became words.

AUDIENCE: The answer I gave to myself was that there is not such a big difference between human and animal.

OMNEC: Not really, right. The Soul is everything that exists. Everything that exists is Soul and is life – every animal, every little insect, everything. Everything has a purpose. When you fulfill this purpose, then you can go on to become something else. Every human being was a mineral, a plant and an animal before they were human. That's why that we are the caretakers for all these life forms. All these life forms supply us with the nourishment we need to exist, because we WERE these life forms. And we NEED these life forms to exist. Everything serves a purpose. It serves as nourishment for us and through us that becomes higher itself, and eventually becomes a human. Because you have to be EVERY-THING. That's the whole purpose why God created the whole existence of being. You must love and appreciate everything, because love is very important. It is the whole reason we exist. God loved Itself and created everything from Itself in never ending cycles so It would never cease to exist. God exists through everything IT created for always, forever. It's never ending. We exist forever, our Souls. It's part of God. We are a part of God. We are really beautiful. The Souls are SO beautiful, so perfect. Everyone is a unique jewel. Your individual experiences make different facets for each jewel. No two are alike, because no two have the same experience. Experience is the only learning process we have. Experiences are very important for the Soul. It's the truth, you know. Nobody can tell you anything but once you've experienced it, you know it. Then you know. And that's why you are here. You want to KNOW, and you can only know by experience.

AUDIENCE: What is necessary so that a human being or a whole system can ascend to a higher level and what is required from the Soul to accomplish this ascension?

OMNEC: It has to go individually first. Individually, and then – if you work together with your consciousness you can bring the whole consciousness of your society up. Your consciousness creates your surroundings and you change it. You don't want disasters and so you work in your consciousness to keep this world safe. That's why the world is still here. So many people love it and want it to stay, so it has never been destroyed – because you have a lot of power. All of you have a lot of power. You just don't realize it yet. But you have to learn that you do. That you have the power to create the world you wish. You only have to use your power positively – in a positive way. When you focus on the negative, then you are giving energy to the negative, you don't want to do that. I think you want to support the positive. I believe you do. I can see it in your faces, yes.

AUDIENCE: I was touched by what you said in the beginning of this evening – that you recognize some of us here in the audience. This is more a personal comment – I feel very connected with Venus...

OMNEC: Yes, many people are friends of mine from past lifetimes. I call them my Soul Family. I say every time I am going to meet my Soul Family. It's like getting together again with friends and people I love, always. It always does me very good.

AUDIENCE: ... I wanted to add something. The biggest luck we on Earth can experience and feel is the contact with our origin, with where our Soul derives from. This feeling of being connected instead of separated. What can we do to enhance this connection – meditation, jogging, turning toward the inside...? I believe this feeling of connectedness or oneness is the biggest longing of humankind.

OMNEC: Well, the only thing you can do is realize that you belong to God and everyday say, "I will live my life for God and give back what I have". Every night when you go to bed, say, "I love all those Souls that were with me before and are with me now." Make this connection to all of them. Every night you can bless those people that you love. Imagine their faces and send love and blessings to each one of them. I do that with each of my children and they are all healthy and with me. I live my life and love for all. I love every little animal, every little thing I see. Because it's all beautiful. That way you are always living in the love that you feel. And that's how you should be.

AUDIENCE: How do you deal with people whom you have given

much love and positiveness, but who keep pulling everything into negative?

OMNEC: You love them anyway.

AUDIENCE: Yes, sure, but what if it's getting to hard for yourself?

OMNEC: If they have problems, you don't take those problems on yourself. You must be somewhere away from the negative stuff that bothers you.

AUDIENCE: This would mean that I would have to keep myself away from certain persons.

OMNEC: Well, then she has to be honest and tell them. Tell them what disturbs you and make them aware, tell them that you cannot be around this.

AUDIENCE: Right, and if you have done this, what then?

OMNEC: Then it's their turn. You cannot live with a person that is negative, because it's not good for you. But you must tell them, you must let them know. It's important to communicate. And to explain it. It's nothing wrong with walking away from a situation. Walk away from anything that's distressing or disturbing for you. You don't HAVE to experience it, no. You have your free will. And you can express it to them, so they understand.

AUDIENCE: What if you distress and disturb yourself? [laughter]

OMNEC: Change the way you are.

AUDIENCE: But how? I have been diagnosed different psychological diseases, but I have nobody who can help me and I do not know how to deal with all that.

OMNEC [laughs]: Well, I wouldn't go to those doctors.

AUDIENCE: And what shall I do now?

OMNEC: You must find a way to make yourself happy.

AUDIENCE: And how? I am having problems with myself, I don't like myself, but how can I change that if I do not know where to start?

OMNEC: You don't understand yourself?

AUDIENCE: I don't know. Sometimes I really don't know. Sometimes I know why I feel bad and sometimes I don't.

OMNEC: I don't know what to say. A person needs to understand themselves. You should know yourself very well.

AUDIENCE: That's the problem.

OMNEC: You can't accept yourself?

AUDIENCE: Yes.

OMNEC: Why?

AUDIENCE: Childhood...

OMNEC: You know what? It can't be that bad. I don't believe it, because, you know, you are looking for something for yourself, it seems. And I think you will find it. I don't think that what you are looking for is outside yourself but inside. Because all the love and everything that you need is in yourself. And not outside. You have to be happy in yourself, before you can find happiness elsewhere.

AUDIENCE: Yes, I know...

OMNEC: I love you. Come over and I can give you a hug. I think you need it. [She comes forward and Omnec gives her a long hug.] You need to know that you are loved and you are worth something. Really, really, understand that, OK? And let never anybody tell you anything else, because that's not true [The girl starts to cry]. It's not true. You are beautiful and you are loved and you are worth loving, OK? You must remember that. You are a beautiful girl, beautiful. And I love you. And that's all that counts that you love yourself. And then anybody can love you, really. I really mean it, really. [To the audience] Isn't that true? And your name?

AUDIENCE: Claudia

OMNEC: Claudia. My name is Sheila. You can give me your phone number and I'll call you sometime and tell you how much I love you. Give me your name and address and your phone number, please. And let's keep in touch, OK? Let's do that. [Claudia nods and goes back to her seat.]

OMNEC: It's pitiful when people feel that way. That they are not lovable or it's something wrong. They need to be accepted, that's the biggest problem. Human beings need acceptance. Everyone needs to be accepted. Because when they feel not accepted, they feel alone. And nobody needs to feel alone. So the only help she really needs is love and acceptance, that's all.

AUDIENCE [Claudia – still sobbing]: I believe, this has been the problem since my childhood...

OMNEC: Yes. I had deep problems in my childhood, so I know. It's very sad, but you have to realize your worth. To understand it, yes, and live like you are worth something. Because God created you, so you are worth something. There are many children that are mistreated. It causes problems for them when they are older. They feel that they are not wanted or not loved and that's terrible. It's a terrible sad feeling. Of course, when you have a child, you should want the child and love the child. And there are so many people who have children and they don't care for them. That's sad. As the Beatles said: All you need is love. That's true. Anybody else?

AUDIENCE: *You had relatives on the astral level of Venus. But it must have been somehow different compared to the Earth. How is making love on Venus?*

OMNEC: A man and a woman exchange energy. When they are ready for a family, they call a child – a Soul – to join their family. Then the child comes and duplicates. On Earth, the child lives inside the mother, the Soul, until the time comes for it to live on its own. On Venus, when they leave the astral, they walk upon to a platform and all the people sit around and send energy and transfer them to another dimension. We exchange love by exchanging energy. You can send this energy anytime to anyone and we have love ceremonies for people who wish to share a life together.

AUDIENCE: *Does the astral level correspond to the Higher Self?*

OMNEC: No, it's more the emotional self. It's where your emotional feelings come from.

AUDIENCE: *Can you say more about twin Souls? What is it when you meet a stranger and it feels so familiar?*

OMNEC: No. I don't believe there is a twin Soul. I believe you find a Soul partner. And you find them, and they find you.

AUDIENCE: *Does Soul partner mean that one is connected with each other on a higher level? It's somebody from your Soul group, right? And the twin Soul concept would mean that you as a Soul are not complete and that is not true.*

OMNEC: Everyone is complete within themselves. You have to feel fulfilled within yourself.

ANJA: According to Omnec, the difference is that the concept of twin Souls would mean that you as Soul are not complete and that you need the other Soul to be whole. Omnec says that this concept does not correspond with her knowledge. Soul partners, on the other hand, are Souls from one's own Soul group, Souls who have a similar age and with whom one may have spent various previous lifetimes and have therefore this inner connection, this love. But as Soul one is complete within oneself.

AUDIENCE: *What do you have to say about December 21, 2012?*

OMNEC: I don't think that really anything is going to happen. I think that there are these beings who create these prophecies and these dark things that will happen. It depends on what you want. Do you want the end of the world and disasters? It was just a prophecy from the Mayan calendar. And I think that they just didn't know and people just have theories about what's going to happen.

AUDIENCE: *But the Maya did not say that everything will be destroyed, but that it is only the end of the calendar.*

ANJA: That's exactly what Omnec means – that people just create theories and interpretations about what could maybe happen.

OMNEC: Of course it will be the end of what you know. Because everything is changing. There is a progress, there is a consciousness changing. There is a Transformation in process. The more people participate then it happens faster. You are the ones that are in control.

AUDIENCE: *What happens to those people who do not believe in all this and a higher consciousness or higher frequencies?*

OMNEC: They just stay as they are. You know, if you don't want to change and if you want to stay the same, then you can. You have the free will of choice. I think that every human being has something they believe in. And that's all that matters. Is that you believe in something. If you believe in nothing, that's pitiful. But some people are like that. That's allowed, too. There have always been skeptics. But it doesn't change what I am or what you are. Life goes on.

AUDIENCE: *I have heard that there are currently many space ships around the Earth to help mankind ascend. The change of consciousness does only mean that our perception changes. We have more chakras and will perceive a lot more. In former times, people thought that the Earth is flat and all of a sudden they realized that it is a sphere. Somehow like that now our perception is changing. Would you confirm this?*

OMNEC: As we learn more, we accept more.

AUDIENCE: *Will we also see the spaceships?*

139

OMNEC: Of course. When the Transformation is complete and money is no longer used, they will bring new forms of energy to people.

AUDIENCE: I have heard that as well, but I have not seen any spaceships yet.

OMNEC: No, it's not time yet.

AUDIENCE: I heard the information that other life forms will communicate with us through crystals. Have you ever heard of this as well?

OMNEC: They can, because crystals have the ability to store information.

AUDIENCE: So that's something that some people are now being trained to do this kind of communication?

OMNEC: Of course. Crystals are being used in the computers, too. A lot of information is in the crystals and eventually it will all be given back to the people.

AUDIENCE: Does this especially count for crystal skulls?

OMNEC: All crystals can store information. In Atlantean times they were used very much for this.

AUDIENCE: Omnec, can you tell us something about the people inside of the Earth?

OMNEC: There were human beings who escaped to the center of the Earth during the Atlantean times when they were having a war and they still exist and they will return after the Transformation. They will return.

AUDIENCE: So is it like walking on the street and they say "Hi," here we are? How will the communication be?

OMNEC: They keep up to date on everything. They will let themselves be known. They are a part of you.

AUDIENCE: Which purpose do angels and their energy have for mankind, Earth and for the universe?

OMNEC: These are Souls who no longer have to incarnate in the physical worlds. This is their job on the higher dimensions. They become masters, guardians or angels and they chose a certain job to work with God. Each human being will reach this state where that they have to make a choice what they will do after living in the physical. Many of us have angels assigned to each of us. Each of us has angels. There are assigned to you. When your Soul becomes a human being, then you assign angels and guardians and guides in the other dimensions. It's your protection.

AUDIENCE: *When a child dies in an accident, did the angels fail?*

OMNEC: No. No, it was the destiny of the child.

AUDIENCE: *Where does this come from?*

OMNEC: The child makes the decision before it's born what its experience will be. Some children only have the experience of being born and they die right after. There are so many experiences in this world that are chosen. Before you are born, you chose your life, your parents, your way.

AUDIENCE: *It's difficult to tell this to the mother and sister of this child.*

OMNEC: Of course, they are going to miss it. One part of life is sadness and sorrow. It's the feeling and the experience is something, like I said, that's valuable, no matter how horrific it is. Yes, it's something that Soul wants or it wouldn't have it. Everything that happens, happens because it's the will and because it's supposed to happen. We have to figure out the reason why. What is the reason for this experience? There is always a reason. Even though we can't see it right away, it comes later.

AUDIENCE: *There are spaceships, or UFOs or whatever, seen all the time – does it have to do with Venus that they can lower their vibration so that they can be seen sometimes and sometimes they are invisible?*

ANJA: They are not only from Venus, they come from other planets as well.

OMNEC: Yes, they have the ability to change the energy of their existence. They can be invisible and they can be visible. They travel between the physical and the other dimensions as easily as they travel in the physical. They are from many different planets and from other systems. But they are all usually friendly.

AUDIENCE: *I would like to know what you say about these ADHS children, these hyperactive children and about Indigo children.*

OMNEC: The new children are very special. They are very very intelligent and brilliant and they don't have the ability to concentrate as much as a lot of people. They are called hyperactive. They like to be active; they like to do things, they don't really like to sit. There are many of them today and I am not really sure why. But I know they are important.

AUDIENCE: Do you know what's the difference between these hyperactive children and the Indigo children? Aren't Indigo children far more advanced?

OMNEC: Oh, the Indigo children are highly evolved spiritually, and the hyperactive children are more physically inclined.

AUDIENCE: And how shall they deal with it when they are being filled up with medicine?

OMNEC: I think that's a shame. It's terrible. I think the parents should not accept medicating children.

AUDIENCE: I think that the ADHS children and the hyperactive children are spiritual forerunners for those living here, especially for the parents who may not be spiritual at all and who have to wake up, so that new ways can be chosen and new paths can be gone.

OMNEC: Exactly. Exactly.

AUDIENCE: I would like to know if you know the feeling of having your heart widely open and being very deep in your love with the effect that you experience hostility. I have been very frustrated about that, because I always think: Do I love the wrong way or what?

OMNEC: Of course. The negative forces are always attacking me. They are always trying to prevent my work.

AUDIENCE: And how do you protect yourself?

OMNEC: The best I can. But I am protected.

AUDIENCE: Did you come to Earth in a spaceship with a physical body or did you occupy that girl called Sheila?

OMNEC: No, I came with my own physical body.

+++

[End and autographing session]

Radolfzell, September 15, 2011

OMNEC: Hello, my name is Omnec Onec. I came to Earth to live at the age of seven from the planet that you know as Venus. I wrote my story to share with people so people can understand that human beings come from many different galaxies and that your heritage is very rich. Sometimes you have to realize that whatever you can imagine can be real. There is nothing that's impossible. Everything is possible. Reality is a matter of perception and there are many different perceptions and views of reality.

If you take the chair that I am sitting on. It's small and comfortable enough for me to sit on. But to an insect it's a very large surface to cover. And to a photon it's not solid – it can pass right through. These are just different views of the chair. It's sitting still, but if you are looking at it from space, it's rotating with the Earth. If you are in a country where they have never heard of a chair, it doesn't exist at all. These are several perspectives of one reality. You have to realize that reality is a matter of the viewpoint, of the perspective. I am as real as your perception. For some people I am not real at all – that's OK [laughs]. I don't really care if people believe or don't believe – it doesn't change my existence of what I am. I am very happy that you came tonight to be here. And I am going to have Anja to read a little bit about the astral dimension, where I lived before I came here.

+++

Reading: Excerpt from *The Venus Plane* – Text see Cologne, September 3, 2011

+++

OMNEC: I want to invite you to ask questions and I'll try to answer. And for those of you who don't know it, I had a stroke two years ago, so I'm having difficulties with the physical body now. Because my uncle and my people were forbidden to assist me as they were doing every five years. They were giving treatments to help me live here. And it was strictly forbidden by the Spiritual Hierarchy so that whatever happens has to happen – naturally. So I have to accept it, whatever happens.

Whatever happens is meant to be. Everything happens as it is intended for a reason. We can't always understand the reason, but we can accept it. I have to accept it, you know, and I am glad that I made progress. Even though I am very slow [laughs]. Like a snail, but I still go. And I am thankful for that. So I'll try to answer some questions if you have some.

AUDIENCE: How did you come to Earth at seven years?

OMNEC: In a spaceship. My Uncle Odin drove the spaceship and brought me here.

It was a karmic debt and my decision to have my last physical life on Earth. I thought it would be an adventure [laughs] to see what it was like to live in this world, because there are so much differences in this world and so many different people and cultures and things to learn and to appreciate.

AUDIENCE: Would you do it again?

OMNEC: Yes. I am positive. All the beautiful things that I have experienced and learned on this planet and the human beings I have met – I would never trade it for anything. Human beings are so beautiful – really. Everyone is unique and special. I love that that they are so accepting and so loving and compassionate. I find that here very much.

AUDIENCE: What is the difference between Earth and the place where you come from?

144

OMNEC: We don't have any wars, any bad things happening. So everybody is on an even level, you know. And their consciousness is the same. It's not so different.

AUDIENCE: *All the people are the same?*

OMNEC: Yes, their consciousness.

AUDIENCE: *There are no wars?*

OMNEC: No, no wars, no sicknesses, nothing like that.

AUDIENCE: *What do people on Venus do with animals? Are they treated like here – used and slaughtered?*

OMNEC: We do nothing with them – we love them. We create them for our partners and friends.

AUDIENCE: *Not for eating them?*

OMNEC: No. But we accept that animals on Earth are created and they chose to serve as food. They are aware of that. That is their purpose. Plants, minerals – humans need all of this for their existence. We should care for these life forms and respect and love them for what they do. As Souls we have been the animals, minerals, and plants ourselves, and so we should have more of an understanding, because we were them. If you were something, then you should understand it. We are all connected. Life is precious, but every life serves a purpose. When it served its purpose, then it's free to evolve into a higher state.

AUDIENCE: *How can I imagine that you came to Earth at seven years? Did your Soul come or did you really come with a spaceship – so with something one can perceive? And my second question is: Which identity do you have – do you have a birth certificate?*

OMNEC: In my book I talk about my life on Venus and about my connection to a child here and how she died and I came in her place.

ANJA: In her autobiography, Omnec explains the background of her karmic relationship that she had with a girl who lived on Earth and how she manifested a physical body on Venus. According to what Omnec says, there are cities on all older planets that are physical and at the same time exist in higher dimensions. Omnec says that she manifested a physical body there together with her Uncle Odin and came to Earth in a spaceship. She went through a time of adjustment in a Tibetan temple in order to get used to her physical body and to learn English, then she was brought to America where the other girl just died in a bus accident. Everything was a planned and prepared exchange without any physical proofs left.

AUDIENCE: And this spaceship cannot be seen? It is not visible?

OMNEC: Yes, it can be visible.

ANJA: Because these people have the technology, these spaceships can lower or to increase their frequency – therefore they can be visible to the physical eyes. If they do not want to be seen, they remain in a higher frequency and are invisible for us.

AUDIENCE: So it is possible that one can see them for a little while and all of a sudden they are gone?

OMNEC: Of course, yes. It seems so, it's just that they are at a higher vibration. It's beyond your perception.

AUDIENCE: Are you still in contact with your people from Venus?

OMNEC: Of course.

AUDIENCE: Can you foresee what is going to happen on our planet in the next 50 to 100 years?

OMNEC: Not really. Because a lot of it depends on the human beings themselves. You have the power to change anything that you don't agree with. Just use your power.

ANJA: It is about using ones powers consciously.

OMNEC: Exactly.

AUDIENCE: Near the sun you can see three spaceships with a diameter of about 20 km each. Where do they come from, what do they do there and what consequences has their presence for us?

OMNEC: There is no consequence – you don't have anything to fear. I think that they are all the time all around the Earth. They are sending frequencies to the Earth to raise the consciousness of mankind, but nothing harmful. To assist people in their consciousness.

AUDIENCE: Is your communication with your people...

OMNEC: It's telepathic.

AUDIENCE: Is it through pictures?

OMNEC: We have a telepathic language. It's made up of symbols, and each symbol is a thought form. And we send these symbols or pictures to one another. They are universal symbols.

AUDIENCE: What was your educational way on the Earth? Do you have a normal education or university?

146

OMNEC: I only went to seventh grade in grade school. And then I worked physically. Not easy, hard. But that's part of living. I have four children. Three sons and one daughter. Most of my life I was caring for them. They were my reason, you know. I wanted them, so I intended to care for them. They are my gift to the future of this world, they are special.

AUDIENCE: What are they doing?

OMNEC: Zandar is living here in Germany at the moment. He was working at an Air Force Base. My daughter is getting her degree to be a teacher and she is the mother of two children. My oldest son is a father and he works in an insurance company. My youngest son is just finishing college. Every one of them was in the book with the highest grades in America – it's called the Dean's List – all of my children are extraordinarily intelligent.

AUDIENCE: Weren't you surprised about what is taught in our schools here – what is considered important?

OMNEC: Oh, I don't know. When I went to school as a child, I was very confused, because I didn't understand, you know, for instance, silent letters. You have to write them but you don't pronounce them – I never understood that. For instance, when you write k in "knife," and you don't pronounce the k. I never understood anything. When I asked the teacher, of course, you know, I was out of line. You don't question the teacher.

AUDIENCE: How did your physical parents treat you?

OMNEC: They accepted me and loved me very much. They noted that I was a little different. They were informed, of course, that I wasn't really their daughter. But they accepted that. I accompanied Sheila during her birth process and received the genetic imprint from her physical body.

AUDIENCE: How to imagine that ... so this girl died in a bus accident, but it continued to live for her parents ... so another Soul slipped into her body...?

ANJA: No, she did not slip into her body. One girl died and her body was burned. The dead body could never be found, because Omnec's people took care for it – it was not meant to be that physical proofs could be found. When the accident happened, Omnec was brought there with her own physical body, and she was supposed to be one

147

of the survivors. You have to imagine like a bus accident with chaos and fire. Several people lost their lives, but Sheila survived – now as Omnec. In her autobiography, Omnec explains that she had fallen on the ground before and that she hit her knee, so she just looked like one of the lesser injured passengers.

AUDIENCE: So for the parents it was like: My child survived.

ANJA: Exactly, for the parents their child survived. She was on the way from her mother to her grandmother. Her mother had put Sheila into a bus to protect her from her violent stepfather. The grandmother had not seen her granddaughter for a while, and at that age children change very quickly. After the accident, the mother was notified that her daughter survived and in the same night, Omnec, now as Sheila, safely reached her grandmother's house.

OMNEC: It's in the book [laughter]. It's still interesting.

AUDIENCE: I would like to refer to the book reading from before, because I am still having difficulties with the question of materializing matter. When I am living in a higher frequency, then I do not need to materialize anything at all. That was a contradiction for me – so I materialize everything I need, however, I cannot destroy it anymore... I don't get that...

ANJA: Omnec's portrayal refers to the astral dimension...

AUDIENCE: ...yes, but it was said that they materialize as well there...

ANJA: ...they materialize from the astral matter. Omnec, on the astral you use the energy from the astral level to materialize – materialize is not the right word, you astralize ... You use the energy to make a tree, for example.

OMNEC: Yes.

AUDIENCE: But you don't need a tree – in my mind.

OMNEC: Well, we created the society that's a duplicate of the physical.

AUDIENCE: But don't need it.

OMNEC: No, but we want it.

ANJA: Here we are "only" talking about the astral level – there are still higher levels. The astral level is not the end of the line – it's "just" the astral, not the last level – there are much higher levels.

OMNEC: The astral is a just lower level. Closer to the physical.

AUDIENCE: Do you know the other levels as well, which are above the astral?

OMNEC: Of course.

AUDIENCE: Why don't we know them normally?

OMNEC: Well, that's what I teach in my book. I teach about all the different levels and the mantras and the sounds that come with them, so that you can travel there.

ANJA: Omnec also created a CD, the "Soul Journey." It's a guided meditation teaching the Journey of Soul. Sharing this knowledge is one of Omnec's reasons for being here, to convey the consciousness that there are more dimensions than only the physical. This CD contains the mantras and the colors for each dimension.

OMNEC: So that humans can experience the other dimensions, and so they can visualize the colors and hear the sounds and the mantras.

AUDIENCE: When a person on Earth dies, what comes next?

OMNEC: Their Soul leaves the physical realm and goes to a higher dimension, usually the astral. There they are shown all the events of their lives and what they have experienced, and they choose their next life according to their consciousness at the end of this life. If you have been traumatized because of your death or something that happened, then you are cared for on the other dimensions. You have caretakers.

AUDIENCE: Did they teach you how to manage your own healing or to go to the other dimensions? For example, it must be possible to handle the stroke differently than normal people. What about the healing techniques they have there? Didn't they teach you something like that?

OMNEC: No. If I knew that, I would be rich today [laughs].

AUDIENCE: For me there is a contradiction in all this – so either I can influence matter or I can't...

ANJA: We are here not on the astral level of Venus.

OMNEC: No, when I live here, I have to obey the laws.

AUDIENCE: Some say Earth is a penal planet... [laughter].

OMNEC: Sometimes you may believe that. I think, people believe that sometimes.

AUDIENCE: As Souls, we all made the choice to come to Earth in order to make experiences here.

OMNEC: Yes. And we choose experiences that are not often pleasant, because experience is the best teacher for the Soul. If you experience darkness, then you know what light is. You have to experience the opposite to know what the good is. And to know what the Soul is NOT. THE SOUL IS NOT THE THINGS THAT IT DOES, IT JUST HAS EXPERIENCES. You are not the darkness – you are the light in the darkness. We're all a light ¬ and every Soul is beautiful and perfect and unique and special.

AUDIENCE: Could it be that we come from different planets – and can you see that?

OMNEC: Of course, your Soul has existed in many places, on other planets as well as on the Earth. There is no age for the Soul. You could be billions of years old.

AUDIENCE: What kind of advice would you give about how to go through our current times?

OMNEC: I would say, accept what is happening and use your consciousness in a positive way. Don't focus on anything negative, because you put your attention on it and then you give it strength. Visualize the positive, so that you create a better world. Because you have the power and the energy. This world exists because of you. People don't realize how much power they do have and that they can use it for the benefit of the Earth. I think we have to learn to see as God sees. The beauty that God sees. God doesn't see the bad. Everything is a part of the whole. If you see two people with two different points of view, they are both correct in their own view. One cannot be better than the other. We are all equal. Love is the most powerful energy that we have. We were created out of love. God loved Itself, and everything It created, It created to continue in never-ending cycles. Therefore It will never cease to exist. It will exist always through everything It created. It all started with love. Love is the most important. As the Beatles said: "Love is all you need."

AUDIENCE: Is there a history of creation on Venus?

OMNEC: Yeah, I was just telling it [laughter].

AUDIENCE: So it's the same like on Earth more or less?

OMNEC: We believe that God is a great source of energy. Everything is created out of this energy; and we are all a little piece of this energy. We all have the ability to create as well.

AUDIENCE: Then why is there karma?

OMNEC: Well, there was. There isn't anymore. Karma ended in 1999, when the Transformation of the Earth began. Then karma was released except for what you create now when you do something intentionally. You shouldn't do anything intentionally to hurt somebody or do wrong to somebody. There are some people who do that. I never understood that. I can never understand why anyone would want to hurt anybody.

AUDIENCE: I am working as a healer. Very often I experience that people who have been working as lightworkers for many years or who are on their spiritual paths, that they are only here up to maybe 30% and that most of them is ... how shall I say this now? Well, they are not really grounded – their longing to be away from this physical world is very strong – they move around in some meta dimensions or astral dimensions with their consciousness and are only here with a small part of their energy. I would like to know if you have observed this as well.

OMNEC: I don't know, unless that's the people that you call, "The lights are on and nobody's home." [laughter]

AUDIENCE: Yes, that's how it feels. Well, I think that I am pretty well grounded and present here – but there are many who cannot bear the pain of being here.

OMNEC: That could be. I am not sure if that's healthy. Because, you know, you should be balanced. It's important to be balanced and to be aware consciously of what you are doing and where you are. But there are a lot of people who have difficulties accepting this life. There are many people who have to accept it, because they chose it and the experiences are not always the best. You have to understand that you chose them. You choose the experiences and the bad things that happen as well. It's not always what you want – it's what you get. That's what life is. Life is what you get and not what you want.

AUDIENCE: Sometimes you even get more than you want...

OMNEC: Exactly! And then you have to be thankful! [laughs] Thank you for giving me more pain. But we have to be able to laugh and enjoy it, you know. I laugh at myself a lot, and especially since my body doesn't do exactly as it should. Yeah, I have to laugh, because I can't control it. It's comical sometimes.

AUDIENCE: I encounter many people who cannot remember that they were living here in previous lives, but I have never met persons who remember that they were living on another planet. How can that be?

OMNEC: Well, now you did.

AUDIENCE: But in your case it's the same incarnation and not a memory of a previous lifetime.

OMNEC: Oh.

AUDIENCE: I met a lot of people who have a lot of memories of older incarnations, but not on other planets.

OMNEC: No? That's interesting.

AUDIENCE: You don't know an answer for this?

OMNEC: Not really.

AUDIENCE: They should remember, too.

OMNEC: Yes, they should and I don't know why, I can't say. I have talked to people who remember.

AUDIENCE: Maybe it will happen from now on...

OMNEC: There are other people here from other planets.

AUDIENCE: Can you see this?

OMNEC: Sometimes. But usually out of respect I don't mention it, no. Because they could be keeping their identity as secret and not that they want someone to know.

AUDIENCE: For a very long time it was impossible to speak about spaceships and extraterrestrials – these kind of things were just inacceptable. I can remember that when I was a child I knew that I came from the stars. I always felt familiar with spaceships, but first of all they would not believe you; they said, "The child is nuts," so one is weaned and forgets everything. Later one stumbles over this subject again, reads something or meets somebody who is open – then one dares to mention this again. I believe that this knowledge is just hidden very deeply inside of us.

OMNEC: Yes, many children are discouraged from their imagination or expressing things they believe they were before. It's very difficult for children to be accepted and to be believed. Yes, it's important that you listen, because children can tell you many things, because they have not been here so long and their memories of pre–existences are pretty clear.

My daughter told me that she lived in China. She was telling me how her parents looked and the kind of clothes she wore and the food she ate and everything. Every time I gave her a fork to eat she turned it upside down and used the handle. I kept asking her, "Why do you do that?" And then she told me, "I ate like this before I was your little girl." And I said: "Then, what did you look like?" and I went through magazines and I listened and she told me the whole story. Because to her it was quite normal, she used to eat that way all the time before she was my little girl. I asked her, "Well, whose kid were you before you were mine?" She told me, "I lived in this place and I dressed like this". And I said, "And what did your mama look like?" She said, "Not you, not grandma." I went through magazines and in a National Geographic she found some way. I went and bought her Japanese robes and chopsticks and shoes and everything. Then one day she told me she was ready to be my little girl and dressed like the American little girls.

AUDIENCE: Could she remember the language?

OMNEC: No. But I was fascinated anyway. And I said, well, let me get you some stuff that you are familiar with.

AUDIENCE: How old was your daughter?

OMNEC: She was three at that time. And now she is 41. I learned a lot from my children. I think you can learn a lot from children. She told me one time in a meditation she heard snow falling. We went outside one night – we lived in the country – far away from the city. It was snowing and I had to listen to the snowfall. And it does, you know. You can hear the ice crystals hitting the other ice crystals – it's like tinkling bells. Really, you can hear snow fall! I would never have known that if my daughter hadn't have told me that. If somebody tells me that, then I have to see if it's true. It's very special, to be able as a human being to hear that. It's like the music of God. Really beautiful, it's such a light tinkling. I didn't know this is possible.

AUDIENCE: How did you come to your name Omnec Onec.

OMNEC: My name was given to me by the spiritual teachers. It means Spiritual Rebound. In my Venusian family, their whole generation of names starts with a Zero, with an O.

ANJA: Like ONKEL ODIN... [laughter]

OMNEC [takes a sip]: It's only water, right?

ANJA: I don't know what you did to it ... turning water into wine or what?

OMNEC: At least we have fun! You can have fun doing anything, if you really want to. I think it's worth it. My friends in America said, "You can't go and do public things when you just had a stroke". And I said, "You watch me!" [laughter] And I'm here! It takes a lot of courage. But on the other hand, I feel so accepted and so much loved that it gives me energy and it helps me – I am really thankful for that. Because every person that loves me gives me more power. I need that.

[silence]

OMNEC: Aaand? Anybody want to tell me their story? [laughter]

AUDIENCE: Can animals take you to another dimension?

OMNEC: I suppose if they are very, very highly conscious, yes. I have been told that one can put on my meditation CD and that their animals come and sat in front of the stereo. So apparently it appeals to the animals, these mantras and stuff. I believe that animals are very, very spiritually connected to man. I think that most people who have pets have to realize the pet is studying you so that it's preparing to be a person itself. That's why they are so close to humans.

AUDIENCE: And when they have been beaten a lot in their lives, then they reincarnate as bullies?

OMNEC: I hope they go by that person's house and beat them. [laughter]

AUDIENCE: Why do we still suffer if karma was deleted in 1999?

OMNEC: All suffering isn't karma. It's some kind of experience that we create with our behavior. We create a lot of experiences that are unnecessary by our own behavior. It's not necessary, but we create it. Because we're humans.

AUDIENCE: Mostly it's created with our thinking, right? What I think, IS.

OMNEC: It's because people are not taught. They are not taught the proper way of thinking and handling and being responsible for their behavior. So they grow up and are very, very ignorant in that way. Many people do things, because they are unaware of the consequences. They are not aware of the effects it has on others before you do or say anything, you should think of what's the effect going to be. What kind of effect will this have on a person?

AUDIENCE: We were never taught that.

OMNEC: That's the problem. That's the problem with our societies. There is too much judgment and too little love and acceptance. There is more judgment done on each other instead of acceptance and letting people be. Everybody cannot think or see the way you do. Everybody has a different perception. And that's allowed! People try to force the other to see things the way they want them to. I think the political thing is the worst. I think that divides people more. Politics and religion. Not allowing the people the freedom to choose for themselves. Exactly.

AUDIENCE: Do you feel a difference between yourself and the people on Earth or are you a normal human being like any other spiritual human being on this planet?

OMNEC: I feel very much a part of the human race. When I came here, I knew I could not return. I have to remain a human until I die here. So this is my last incarnation on Earth, but it's my choice. I'm here and I'm happy to be here. I feel equal with human beings – I don't feel better. I want to share what I know and not feel that makes me better than you. I want to share and help you to see and to feel the way you should. I never could feel above human beings – never. No, I have to be equal. Exactly.

AUDIENCE: It must have been a big force standing above the karma who had the power to dissolve karma. What kind of a force is that?

OMNEC: It's the Spiritual Hierarchy that controls the Earth and many beings from other dimensions. All decided to work for the Transformation Process. We had to end the karmic debts.

AUDIENCE: How many dimensions are there?

OMNEC: Oh, there are nine, but they are all divided, there are many levels to each dimension. There is a chapter in "The Venusian Trilogy" that is new for people. It's a visualization process, you know, for raising the consciousness. I received it and I sent it to

155

the publisher so that people have a chance to visualize and to raise their consciousness. It's very beautiful.

AUDIENCE: Our human culture on Earth has a certain age. Is the culture of the Venus inhabitants much older than the history of mankind on Earth?

OMNEC: Of course.

AUDIENCE: How old is it in Earth's calculation of time?

OMNEC: I think it's older than the Earth, because a lot of them are the forefathers of the people on Earth. A lot of your forefathers come from other planets, and many from Venus, but also from Saturn, Mars, Jupiter...

AUDIENCE: And what about Sirius?

OMNEC: I'm not serious. [laughter]

Of course, there are many people on Earth who feel to have a connection with the Sirius constellation. I have heard it many times.

AUDIENCE: When Omnec speak about Venus, does she speak about our neighbor planet Venus?

ANJA: Exactly.

OMNEC: Yeah, I can't speak about places I don't know.

AUDIENCE: What would have happened if you hadn't chosen this incarnation and this life?

OMNEC: I wouldn't be here [laughter]. And today, you wouldn't be here either. Then I would have had to come back and be born on Earth at a different time. It was a karmic condition, so I HAD TO come either way. But I chose to come this way.

AUDIENCE: Is the karma resolved from planet to planet?

OMNEC: It's only the humans on Earth, because they are going through the Transformation Process. I think that most karmic debts were played out on Earth. They are not necessary anymore, not since the Earth is going through the Transformation. The Transformation will be the change the Earth needs to go to a higher consciousness.

AUDIENCE: Mankind has spread unbelievably much garbage all over the world, even in space, and the oceans are soiled as well. How can mankind ever get a grip on itself – is there a chance at all?

OMNEC: I suppose that's something we have to live with on Earth. They have to learn to balance and harmonize their environment. They are in the process. On the other planets they depleted their

156

environment. They depleted it and it could no longer support physical life. We hope that on Earth they learn that, you know, and that you don't do the same thing. That's why we are trying to create the Transformation, so that the Earth can be saved and helped, because the only way is to change the thinking process of humans.

AUDIENCE: *But this cannot happen overnight.*

OMNEC: No, it's a slow process. But it's faster the more people participate.

AUDIENCE: *How long will this Transformation Process until the so-called ascension take? Do you have a feeling for this time period?*

OMNEC: It depends on the people and how many people participate and use their positiveness. Exactly.

AUDIENCE: *So there is no way to precisely say what's going to happen in 2012?*

OMNEC: No, I think that you have to decide what you want. Do you want destruction? Because it's up to you – and on what you visualize and what you want.

AUDIENCE: *Will humans soon be able to live from light-nutrition?*

OMNEC: I don't know for sure. I think after the Transformation people will no longer have to go through the birth process. They will manifest a body. You will have control over everything. You can make food out of a handful of dirt. Or you can lie down and leave the body and experience being a tree or a dolphin. You will be able to do things with the experiences you can have in one lifetime without many incarnations. Life will be much different. Because you will have more control over everything. I taught that for years in the Transformation Workshops. I used to do weekend-workshops.

ANJA: There is a double DVD available that contains the complete information of this workshop. The title is *The Unknown History of our Solar System and the Spiritual Transformation of the Earth*[12].

AUDIENCE: *Is it the original text from Omnec?*

ANJA: Yes, it is Omnec's original and contains also a German version.

AUDIENCE: *So you can also listen to it just in English?*

ANJA: Sure. You can choose your language like in any DVD film.

AUDIENCE: *Do you have a connection to Christ?*

12 Full transcript of this double DVD is PART ONE of this book.

OMNEC: Yes, I was one of the disciples. I studied with Christ and I supported Christ. And I tell *the True Story of Christ*[13].

AUDIENCE: Do you have something to do with Eckankar? Is that the religion from Venus you are talking about in your book? And what does it have to do with Tibet?

OMNEC: Eckankar is a teaching about the Soul, about the Science of the Soul. We don't have a religion on Venus, but we do believe in God and the Soul and it's in harmony with what we teach about God and the different dimensions and the mantras. Some of the masters from the teachers of Eckankar resided in Tibet. I lived in Tibet in a monastery.

AUDIENCE: What is God? How can one imagine God or how do they imagine God?

OMNEC: A source of energy. Not a person, no being – it's just a source of energy.

AUDIENCE: What is your opinion about the Islam?

OMNEC: I believe that all faiths and all belief systems should be accepted. Unfortunately, some Islamic groups look at others that they should be destroyed, if they don't believe in the same God and in the same tradition. They call them "infidels", I don't understand that. I just can't agree with that. That's totally non-acceptance to me. Of course, I don't condemn them, I don't think they are wrong, I think they are loving people but I cannot agree with this point of view: "Because you believe differently, you should be destroyed." I don't think anything that God creates should be destroyed.

AUDIENCE: Are there religions on other planets like here?

OMNEC: No.

AUDIENCE: And wars?

OMNEC: No.

AUDIENCE: Would you say that Mohammad lived on Earth?

OMNEC: I have no idea.

AUDIENCE: How about all the different religions, are they all basically right? Are all those who speak about God and some kind of life after death right – or are they all wrong?

OMNEC: I see all religions as a step toward the ultimate believing and knowing.

---

13 The *True Story of Christ* is included in PART TWO of this book.

AUDIENCE: Most of the founders of religions had some kind of visions which were eventually only interpreted and spread.
OMNEC: Yes, the inspiration for religions comes from the etheric dimension.
ANJA TO OMNEC: But nothing stands above your own experience, right?
OMNEC: Exactly.

+++

[End and autographing session]

Ostrach, September 18, 2011

OMNEC: Good evening, and thank all of you for being here. I appreciate your time that you are spending tonight with me. I appreciate all the wonderful and positive thoughts I can feel. I am very aware that there is a lot. I'm aware of that and I am very thankful. I guess you know that I am Omnec Onec. I came from my planet in the astral dimension to live on your planet Earth when I was seven years old. I wrote the book with my story because a spiritual master on Earth named Paul Twitchell said that it was important that I share the story with people. It was his idea that people needed to understand my experience. I decided to write the book to share my story with you. I hope that it gives you some kind of satisfaction or confirmation. That's the whole purpose – you might have similar experiences that you feel inside and you know some of this. As Soul you know already some of this stuff. It's just a confirmation of something that the Soul already knows. I believe that our experiences are stored within the Soul and as things happen we have the recognition of that thing in our past. I hope that this book can awaken some of these experiences within you, and I hope that you enjoy it.

I want Anja to read a little bit about the astral dimension of Venus to you now.

+++

Reading: Excerpt from *The Venus Plane* – Text see Cologne, September 3, 2011

+++

OMNEC: If you have some questions, I will try to answer them. I may not always be able to, but I try.

AUDIENCE: If you don't need a solid body there and live in the astral, but you still have tables and chairs and so on – I don't understand this yet.

OMNEC: Our astral city on Venus is a duplicate of when we were physical people. We have a society that is kind of a duplicate of what we remember. We don't need a lot of the things, but we wish to have them. It's more of a pleasure and remembrance.

AUDIENCE: How did you get into that body?

OMNEC: A lot of people want to know. On Venus we have a temple where we can do a spiritual mantra and manifest a physical body – a form to live in the physical world. But when we do that, we cannot go back to being astral again. We have to do it with the decision that it's permanent and that we are going to live in the physical. Earth is now my home forever – until this body dies. I have made that decision before coming to Earth. I chose to be a human being and to live here just like you do. I am very fortunate and happy that I did so – I have so many friends and beautiful people I have met on Earth. I live by their love and the energy that they send me. Exactly. I am very fortunate. I think Earth is a very special and unique place. This is my home. I used to be on Venus, but not anymore.

AUDIENCE: When your life is finished and you leave your body sometime in the future, can you go back to Venus – is this possible?

OMNEC: No. I have spiritual work to do in another dimension. It's finished there. I have wonderful memories, but I can only remember. I can never experience it again.

AUDIENCE: If you don't need a body on Venus and only live in the astral, then time is not limited as well, I suppose. Or do people on Venus die as well?

OMNEC: No, we have prechosen an existence, a life span, how long it will be and we know when our time is finished, that we go on. The Soul prechooses its life existence in a certain place and time. It's only one lifetime at a certain time.

AUDIENCE: Are you aware of any lives, any previous lives that you might have had here on planet Earth?

OMNEC: Of course. I remember a lot of my lives and a lot of people I see I know, because I have been with them before. It's always like a family reunion. When I see people, I know them and I can recognize them and sometimes there is a feeling that they know me also. A familiarity. A feeling that I was with them before. I certainly had love for them – and I still have love. Because love never ends – it continues and just gets stronger. Love is very, very special. It's the basis of our existence. That's the reason we were created – it's because God loved Itself. It loved Itself and so everything It created, It created in never ending cycles, so It would never cease to exist, but exist always through Its creations. We are a part of that. That's exactly what we are. We are created, because God loved Itself, and we are a part of God. All of our Souls are like little pieces of God. We have the ability to create as well. We do it through our thoughts; we manifest. Everything that exists in this world, humans created. First it was a thought, before it was anything else. The key to creation is imagination. That's very powerful.

AUDIENCE: Is it possible to create a new body on Earth?

OMNEC: It will be in the future. After the Transformation there will be no need for the birth process. No, we can manifest a body. It's said that anything you can imagine is reality. Nothing is impossible. Everything you can imagine is reality. So we are not limited.

AUDIENCE: When will the Transformation of the Earth be complete?

OMNEC: I don't know. It depends on the human beings and their participation and consciousness. The more they use their consciousness to change and to help the Transformation, the faster it will take place. It depends on each person, and how much of your meditation is directed towards helping with the Transformation. Everything that takes place is really up to you and what you wish and what you create. You are the Creators of this place. You create it with your thinking, with your thoughts and with your positiveness. If you focus too much on the negative, then you are giving power to that. You have to be aware of how strong and powerful your thoughts are.

AUDIENCE: In your meditation, is it possible for you to go back to Venus, just as a visitor?

OMNEC: I do this as Soul, when my body is resting, at times, yes. Just for the experience.

AUDIENCE: Venus seems to me a very spiritually powerful place. Now, if you look at our planet Earth, which place would you say is the most powerful in terms of spirituality?

OMNEC: Of course, Venus.

AUDIENCE: Sorry, just here on Earth, is there any city like Machu Picchu or any place where you found this spiritual energy to be extremely strong?

OMNEC: No, not really. Not yet. I am looking for this place and these people. I am trying to help mankind to become the mankind they should be. You have great forefathers – not from Earth, but from other galaxies. This is your background and your heritage. You have the ability to create great societies. But it's difficult, because you have so many different consciousnesses on Earth. To change and raise the consciousness is very much a big process and a big job, because you are not equal in your consciousness.

AUDIENCE: Can you say something about the pole reversal and about the weakening of the magnetic field on Earth? I also heard that a pole shift will occur, so that the north pole and the south pole switch places. Do you think this can be delayed or even prevented from happening?

OMNEC: I don't believe this is going to happen. I think there are enough human beings using their thinking processes to prevent things like this from happening and to keep the Earth balanced. They have been working on this and they are very much involved in meditations and processes to keep the Earth in balance and harmony. And I believe there is enough love.

AUDIENCE: How do Souls on Venus communicate with each other?

OMNEC: Mostly telepathically. And through feelings.

AUDIENCE: Where did you learn English?

OMNEC: On Earth. I studied a little before I came to Earth, but most of it I learned here.

AUDIENCE: Is there a language on Venus – do the people there have their own specific language?

OMNEC: No, we have thought forms and we can kind of translate them through Sanskrit and Lemurian.

AUDIENCE: Can the streams of thought that people on Venus have be recorded on some kind of knowledge carriers or written down in books?

OMNEC: The only place where the thought forms are written down was given to Adamski from Orthon, my Uncle from Venus.

ANJA: The only written document that we know of is a letter that was given to George Adamski by a Venusian named Orthon in the Fifties. George Adamski was one of the pioneer contactees, a Venus contactee in the USA. He had physical contacts with Venusians and one day he was given this letter.

OMNEC: For a long time I was giving it to people through the Unknown History.

ANJA: Yes, when Omnec gave lectures and workshops in the Nineties, she often gave a copy of this letter to the participants. She also wrote an interpretation or translation of it and I translated it into German.

OMNEC: It's very beautiful.

ANJA: It's a beautiful message. Already more than 50 years old, but timeless[14].

AUDIENCE: Can you tell us something about mantra powers, Sanskrit mantra power on Earth? If a group of people decide to sing Sanskrit mantras, what kind of effect does it have here?

OMNEC: I think it's one of the most powerful languages on Earth, because it's one of the purest and the most ancient. Yes, it's very pure and very ancient – I think it's very powerful. I think that's why the mantras were originally in Sanskrit, because it is an original language. It has not been changed or made different. I think it was protected, I believe it's very powerful. I use the same mantras that were given to me by my spiritual Masters.

AUDIENCE: Do you master this language Sanskrit?

---

14 The Venusian Script is included in this book in PART TWO *Unpublished Texts*

OMNEC: No. But I use it.

AUDIENCE: Can you tell me something about the problem of manipulating other people? I mean, we are the Creators of our lives and we are connected with many people. So if we imagine something that includes another person, this is always some kind of manipulation – whether negative or positive. So isn't in reality every thought manipulation?

OMNEC: No. I mean, you can visualize the face of someone that you love, but you're not manipulating or using them. No. You visualize this face in order to send love energy and healing energy to this person. You are not doing it with the intention of using them or them doing something. If you are using that person or you are using them for a cause or purpose for yourself, that's manipulating. But if you are doing it because you want to share some energy with this person, that's a different thing. I don't believe it's manipulating. Your intention is important. Manipulating is intentionally using your power over someone else. That is wrong. I would never do that, and I never have. Not in this lifetime. I probably did it before in other lifetimes much, too much. And that's why now I would never dare – because I did it too much before. I am very cautions now, because I know the causes and consequences of behaving that way. It's not worth it. In so many lifetimes you have to suffer and pay for that. Once you do it too many times, that's it. You never do it again. Once you have done it and you have suffered for it, you're never willing to do it again, because you will say, "That's not me!" The Soul is NOT what it does. What it does is experience. But it does not become that. It's just experiencing that and then it's finished. Once you experience, you don't need to again. No, you don't want anymore because Soul had enough of this. Experiencing is realization and knowing, but once you know, you don't need to re-experience. Exactly.

AUDIENCE: Can you tell me something about the will of the individual and the will of God. You say, we are part of God, and does God have a plan for us or a will and what about our own will?

OMNEC: No, because when God creates us, It gives us the free will. Everything after that is Soul's choice. Exactly. God has no rule over us. We are created and then we are set free to experience. God does not care what we do or what we experience. We have the free will to experience what we wish. The whole purpose of the Soul is to experience everything it can, experience everything possible. Exactly. Then you become the same as God, because you've experienced everything. God experiences everything through the Souls, so we have understanding of what everything is, because we become a part of everything. We were minerals, we were plants, we were animals, we were humans, we have been everything. I don't think there is an end to our existence or to our experiences. It's endless and wonderful.

AUDIENCE: Can you say something about the development of illnesses? Are they only meant to experience them or can they also be expressions of psychological imbalances?

OMNEC: I believe that illnesses are chosen by Soul for experience. Yes, an experience. It doesn't matter what kind of illness it is. I think that the Soul chose it beforehand. Every experience to a Soul is a value, and not good or bad, just an experience. Soul doesn't judge and does not decide whether something is right or wrong or negative or positive. Neither does God. Only human beings do that. Judge and decide what's good, what's bad. Soul says: Everything is alright; everything is important. It has a value and is important for the Soul. We should love everything. Soul is perfect. Only we are not.

AUDIENCE: Some people say, that God created men and women as a unity. And there are special people that belong together and build a unity – female and male. What do you think about dual souls?

OMNEC: I think that male and female is necessary for reproduction in the physical. I think that each human being, each Soul has the possibility to be fulfilled within oneself without a partner. I think it has the ability for unity and perfection within itself. You don't have to look outside yourself for fulfillment. Of course, it's nice to share love with somebody. Naturally. In our bodies, we need that. In Soul we don't.

AUDIENCE: Does it mean that if you still have negative thoughts that you are not finished with your experiences yet? Otherwise I would not have these thought, or?

OMNEC: Maybe the negative thoughts are enough! [laughs]

AUDIENCE: So there is no shortcut to dissolve these negative thoughts? Is there a shortcut to simply being able to just love without any negativity?

OMNEC: I don't really know. You have to be able to love unconditionally. To say: "I love you, because you ARE." That's how God loves. God loves you because you ARE, for no other reason. That's what we have got to learn: how to do it and love each other that way. I love you, just because you ARE. I think that's the best kind of love we can have. Not because you have blue eyes or blond hair … or you are tall … and have a beautiful face … but because you ARE – because you exist. I think that's the best kind of love.

AUDIENCE: You came to Earth with this consciousness, with this love. Was it always easy to keep this attitude upright? You have experienced a lot!

OMNEC: It's just what I am. I always loved everything. Even things that had no consciousness and no reality, you know, like a piece of paper. I was just always that way. I can't help it. I am that way. I love everything. I love the air I breathe. I love the insects – when a little fly comes to the place where I am giving a lecture, I feel that he needs the information, too. He has the right to be there, too. Everything has a reason for existing, and I want to give everything the acknowledgement and the feeling of acceptance. Acceptance is SO important! When someone feels unaccepted and rejected, it's the worst and sorriest feeling a person could ever have. That is terrible. I think acceptance is important, and I feel that I want to accept everything and everyone. It's something that God gave me. The ability to feel that way, and I feel very lucky that I can love so much. I just wish everybody else could feel it. Many do, I think. They tell me they do when I am around.

AUDIENCE: Can we as Soul live on other planets as well besides Earth?

OMNEC: Of course, and you already have.

AUDIENCE: In the second part of your autobiography "Angels Don't Cry" you describe your life on Earth. This makes not always fun reading, because you went through so much hardship. Were you always able to accept all that with love?

OMNEC: When people hurt me, I never had the ability to have harsh thoughts toward them, only to try to understand and to realize that they were not conscious of what the effects were of what they were doing. But, thank God, I never knew what feeling hate or anger toward someone like that was. I wouldn't understand that feeling at all. I can't even explain it to someone what that feels like. People don't believe that, but I never felt a feeling of hate in my life. I think that is the most negative and worst feeling that anyone should ever have – for anything. I am always telling children: You don't hate something, you just dislike or you don't like the taste or the color of what, but you don't hate. Because hate is very, very hard, and very destructive. I have never experienced it and nor do I want to.

AUDIENCE: Do you know why you have to be here on Earth? Do you know your aim in life and your purpose?

OMNEC: Yes, and I am just about to have experienced it all. I decided to come here to experience everything in one lifetime so I wouldn't have to return. I knew it would be hard and very difficult, but I wanted to do it. I must say that it was a very fulfilling experience. I am very full [laughs].

AUDIENCE: When you came here down to Earth, did you set a certain time frame for your life? Do you know when you are going to progress and move on to the next level?

OMNEC: No. I asked not to know. No, I don't want to know how long my life will be. I want to be just like everyone else, and go whenever God says it's time – and then I am ready.

AUDIENCE: Doesn't everyone have their free will? You say "When God says it's time." So where is your free will?

OMNEC: You mean, when your life is finished?

AUDIENCE: Yes.

OMNEC: I think you have chosen this before this lifetime but you don't remember it.

ANJA: To be more precise, because you said that, "God says it's time," is it more like when your Soul is ready?

OMNEC: Yes, when your Soul is ready. Yes, I said, "When God says it's time," but you can say, "When your Soul has decided." That would be more correct. I am not always correct [laughs]. I try. That's all I can do.

AUDIENCE: How can you find out what you have experienced in previous lifetimes? How can you recall previous lifetimes?

OMNEC: I think the easiest way is to ask your Soul's permission to consciously recall. This mind is a mind that is new to this one lifetime. You have to ask that the Soul makes a connection to this mind and allows the mind to remember. Your mind has certain limits. You have to see if it is possible that this mind has the ability, because sometimes the mind can't take things. It all depends on if your mind can accept it. That's why we don't know a lot of things, because it would be too much for this brain. We have to not overload. I remember a lot of things, because I'm aware of things before this lifetime and because I lived in another dimension before this lifetime. So my thoughts are kind of unlimited – and I brought with me a lot of the abilities.

AUDIENCE: *When our thoughts create our reality, which role do images and feelings play when I imagine something?*

OMNEC: The images can be stimulated by feelings – from feelings and emotions. Emotions and feelings can create visualizations. If you are creating and visualizing from a wish that you have or to formulate something that you wish to exist and not based on what you feel, then it's more of a fact that it can come true. I think if you can create something in your mind without feelings and emotions attached, then it has more ability of being.

AUDIENCE: *I have the wish to guide people in creating a new society. To create images of landscapes that are beautiful, of people loving each other. If many people visualize these pictures, it will be a great power of manifestation. But what about the power of thoughts? Which power of manifestation does a word or a simple thought and a spoken word have?*

I mean, if you want to manifest something, you have thoughts and you can speak these thoughts – this is the spoken word. This is one way to create your reality. And there is the other possibility to visualize something. Which is the greater power of manifestation – just working with thoughts or words or just visualizing.

OMNEC: KNOWING what you want to create. You know a rose – what it looks like and what it smells like – so when you KNOW that, then you can create that. You cannot create something unless you know what it is. Because then it's just an image. It's not from knowing. You have got to know what you are creating and what the purpose is. When you create something, you have to know the purpose of its creation.

Creating is an art. You have to know the measurements and all … it's very complicated. You just have to use your visualization and your knowingness so that you can create what you need – and you should create what you need. It's like "Life is not what you want – it is what you get." I always felt that was funny. If life was what you want, life would be different. It wouldn't be difficult. It would be easy. But then it would be worthless. Because if it is not hard and it is not really an experience that you can remember, it's not worth it. Something is only worth something when it's difficult. You know why? Because you earned it. It just didn't plop in front of you.

When you have to earn something, it's worth something. When it's difficult. Then you remember it more. You think: WOW! This was hard, but it was worth it. Something easy, you know, isn't. People hand you a pamphlet on the street and usually you throw it away. But if you have to pay for it, then you are going to see what it is. It has to be worth something. Not just for nothing. Everything has a worth. We don't think about that. People hand out pamphlets with all kinds of information, and people throw them away because they think it's not worth anything. They don't realize this – they think, "This is so wonderful, I am giving it for free," and they don't realize that people are not even thankful for it.

We don't realize that things that are for free ARE beautiful. Look at the air, look at the trees, look at everything around you. It doesn't cost you anything and it IS beautiful and we need it. We should be thankful. Sometimes we overlook it. We don't see the beauty or the worth. And each other – we need each other, too. We need each other, we need to exchange and we need to share. We need each other's input. We need to share with each other and realize the beauty of each other. I realize how beautiful you are. I appreciate you. I thank you for having me here tonight. I want to thank Kouki for giving me the opportunity and for everything that she is doing to make it possible for me to share my information. I appreciate that very much – thank you.

+++

170

Munich, September 26, 2011

ANJA: Good evening. Omnec asks me to tell you that she had a stroke. It was in November 2009 during her last visit in Germany. We had a small private workshop. When we had a short break, Omnec went out with some participants and when she came back in, all of a sudden her body was paralyzed. It was quickly getting worse until she could not move her whole left side anymore.

Meanwhile it has become much better. In the beginning, she could not even walk alone. She was brought to a special clinic in Allensbach at the Bodensee and received rehabilitation treatments.

OMNEC: I go slowly, but I go. I am happy about that. My mind is clear. I had to have speech therapy and physical therapy when I got home. It's very hard to get the government to pay for this. They ask so many questions and hope you give up. But the doctors are very persistent.

I am feeling well and I am happy to be back in Germany. It's my second home. Really, I am very much at home in Germany and very much loved and appreciated. I am really happy that you people are here tonight. Thank you for giving me your attention and your love and your wishes – I know all of it, I feel all of it. I know people are very concerned about what's going to happen in 2012. I don't suppose anything is going to happen. I believe that the Earth is still going to be here and thank to you and your concentration and help the Earth be safe. The Earth is still here. It has a long way to go but we are the consciousness rising, you can tell. You can see the changes and they are positive.

My uncle used to give me harmonizing and balancing treatments every five years on spaceships. It was forbidden by the spiritual masters, because they said that I have to adapt to the Earth in a natural way without help. So the treatments stopped. Of course I am getting older like everyone, but gracefully, I hope.

I have children and grandkids. They are wonderful and I am very happy and thankful. God has protected my kids. They are all healthy and happy and I have a lot to be thankful for. I am very thankful that I am able to speak to you and be here. My friends in America said, "You can't go – you just had a stroke!" And I said, "Watch me!" So I left, and I am here and I am still going.

I believe that the future of the Earth is going to be a very positive one. You'll see the changes in society in the places where it's needed and more attention to the things that were neglected in the past. That's taking place now. A lot of the wealthy people are sharing their money with others. You'll see a lot of changes in your societies. I'm not so happy about the technological. I think there is too much attention on that. I am afraid that the children are lacking in their creative abilities, because they are used to just directing something and it does everything and they don't have to imagine anymore.

Of course, the creativeness is important. Otherwise, we wouldn't have a world around us. Everything that's in it was somebody's imagination because it's the key to creation. Without it we wouldn't have anything. That's what God gave us. God is the Creator and It gave us the ability to create as well, and so we have the ability. But not if we stop imagining. That's the only thing I can see as a problem is that there is too much attention on the technology. People are so much into their mobile phones and their computers that they don't pay attention to the people around them. It's terrible how many people run over and knock me down and don't help me, you know, because they weren't aware. They never even think that I need help. They are just not aware. They are not aware of their surroundings, of other people. I think that's the only thing that I can see that's wrong.

I am hoping that in the future there will be more of a balance. I hope there is more of a balance and the use is beneficial, but not overused. I talk about the future a lot because my children's children are the future, so I am concerned. I am concerned about them because of their attitudes. Because children hear things from TV and computers that they shouldn't always hear. What they think is coo, is actually not cool; it's disrespectful. Respect is lacking – and value. I worry about that a lot.

172

I worry about what our future is going to be. What is the worth of an older person? My grandchildren have been taught to love and respect older people, but not everybody teaches their children that. It's important that they learn to love and to respect the older people, because you have lived a long time and you have seen a lot and you have a lot of information for them. They have to learn that. They think they know everything, and they don't know anything – but they don't realize that. You can't tell them that. No, because they don't believe you anyway. Except my children. My grandchildren think I know everything. They think I'm a walking encyclopedia. I have to answer everything – and I try. I can't, but I keep trying – and I keep trying to learn things from them, because they appreciate it when you ask them something. If you ask them to show you how something works then they feel intelligent. You have got to make them feel intelligent, and they are. They know how to work with computers at the age of 7 or 8, and they are very good at it. I hope they are just as good in living their lives.

I told the people, I can't foresee the future. I know the Earth will be here. How many thousands of times have I heard that the end is coming? That's the job of the negative forces to create these kinds of events so that people will wonder what's going to happen – always. What happens is up to you. You are the ones that have the control over it. What do YOU want? It's really up to you. Your power and your thoughts are what shape what happens on this Earth. It always has been! That's why the Earth is still here. It's here because there are too many people that love the Earth. So much work went into creating this Earth by many different beings from many different galaxies. They care about the Earth. That's why Earth has so many different beings, and the uniqueness and the difference between each human being.

You have been an individual since God created the Soul and you remain an individual throughout eternity. That's what makes you beautiful and unique, because no two humans can have the same experiences. If you ask two people tonight that leave here, they will have different experiences. That's the beauty of the Earth. That's why I love it, because you never know what to expect. It's always the unexpected. That's what makes life wonderful; it is the change that's constant.

Every Soul is beautiful and every experience creates a facet that makes a special jewel of that Soul unique and beautiful. You don't realize your own beauty – but I do. I see it and I love every bit of it. I think it's very special. I would not change my life for anything. I have been very, very lucky and honored to meet so many beautiful people. I couldn't even begin to explain how wonderful it is and how many beautiful people I know. A lot! I can't remember every name, but I know every face. When I see a face, somehow I have a remembrance of another time with that person. Every time I meet with a group of people, it's like a family reunion. It's very nice – for me at least.

I am going to have Anja to read something from my new book. It's brand new and it has to do with the future. It's a visualization process for the future of Earth.

+++

Reading: *The New Supreme Deity or Sugmad Expansion Ray* by Robert Scott Lemriel, additional chapter in Omnec Onec's book *The Venusian Trilogy*

"We are moving into a golden age of spirituality. As we enter the twenty-first century, a creative fountain is being opened, and many more people will be able to manifest that which is of the higher worlds." (Harold Klemp, "ECK Wisdom Temples, Spiritual Cities, & Guides – A Brief History")

One must use their insight to see this statement is actually a contemplation portal or inter-dimensional doorway and they can experience it with their own curiously imaginative and adventuresome nature.

What follows is the contemplation seed I've been referring to and much more:

With the true inner imaginative seeing of Soul or Atma, imagine a fountain on the Soul plane in the fifth far higher dimension above any physical worlds like Earth. It is located in a beautiful garden by a vast palace. This fountain has a fifteen-foot high statue of the Governor or Lord of the Soul plane named SAT NAM standing upright in a wide marble-like bowl. The lovely curved bowl is set upon a intricately carved solid white marble column that supports the bowl about four feet up from the lush green ground.

SAT NAM's statue appears completely bald headed but he's eternally youthfully middle-aged, bronzed of skin tone with two gold bracelets on each of his upper arm and he's wearing a white skirt from the waist down to just above his bare ankles and feet. His hands are down near his sides with the palms open facing outward. A radiant white-golden nectar or liquid light is pouring form his palms down into the white curved marble bowl, filling it with the liquid that is gracefully pouring out over the entire circumference of the rim in an even unbroken sheet to gracefully drop down to the ground and vanish behind a surrounding circular marble sitting bench. This circular bench rests several feet above the ground on twelve gracefully curved and carved marble support legs. Those who discover this place radiant with this new fountain can sit on the marble bench and listen to the unusually sweet, high toned soothing new sound that issues from the fountain nectar or luminous water-like liquid.

Twelve very beautiful radiant golden cups are hanging upon golden hooks surrounding the bowl's outer rim. You can dip one of these cups into this radiant substance or nectar and drink it, if you have the adventuresome courage of Spirit for all the new awareness that can be expanded within you that's now emanating from the Soul plane awareness and beyond.

This radiant liquid is not water as it is understood here on Earth; but it appears that way in texture. It IS a New Ray of The Ancient ONE, Supreme Deity, HU or whatever you may wish to call this creative reality – that which is beyond, behind and supporting all this is.

The above then encapsulates the contemplation seed but you can expand it from there and the sky is the limit once you start down that majestic and enthralling awakening road, because this New Ray did not exist in The Ancient One or Supreme Deity's Continuum until several years ago. It has the unique purpose of drawing out from the subconscious of the individual being all implants, engrams and aberration programs to place them within a pure white transparent energy sphere above the individual so they can objectively and subjectively see them for the first time without being negatively affected by them.

The real innate Divine awareness of their origin surfaces and they simply remember and know they have the opportunity to have the negative subconscious programming stuff permanently disintegrated or turned back into simple pure energy. If one chooses to have the little demons that haunt their dreams at night (so-to-speak) removed, than the expanding SAT NAM awareness will instantly remove this stuff. What remains behind is the wisdom of experience and the result is an awakened being that now can be trained and uplifted at an incredibly accelerated rate to become aware of their a true co-creative God consciously status with Ancient ONE or SUGMAD, SAT NAM, the Primordial Mahanta and even the more profound mysterious Silent Ones.

This may be somewhat difficult at first to grasp but this fountain has been brought into existence for one purpose and that is to per-manently retire what is known as evil from existence. This can only be because something far, far better has finally been created and evil or fear is no longer necessary in the now awakened expanding SUGMAD of being to train Souls.

The old system brought into existence hundreds of billions of years ago (the status quo in the upper and lower worlds) is remaining in place for administration purposes. However, a firestorm of new possibilities is taking place now in the upper worlds among all beings and this New Ray is now emanating out into all existence through the established creation via the Governors or Purushas on each plane.

A network of fountains and the golden pyramids that surround them are manifesting into existence invisibly stationed on planets, under oceans, between planets in space and between galaxies. They are made of a substance that is not of the dual or polarity conscious-ness worlds; but they can exist in them with the remarkable ability that nothing, no power, force, weapon or being can affect them, nor alter their purpose in any way, should they be detected and they have now been turned on. This cannot be reversed.

Technically and by prior Spiritual Law the ability to manifest that which is of the higher worlds in the lower worlds (and especially on a planet like Earth that has been purposefully entirely retarded and suppressed) was not possible for anyone living outside of a protected Spiritual city or Golden Wisdom Temple area because of the negative nature of the lower plane Lords. That nature has been to see that Souls remain trapped in the lower worlds unaware of their true Divine Nature that is actually a co-creative individuality of the Supreme Deity, HU or Sugmad with great-untapped potential.

The Governors of the lower worlds are now being transformed from the subverting nature from the inside outward at this moment and when that is complete the lower planes of creation will begin to be made into Divine mirror planes of being that exist within the dual current negative and positive polarity systems.

During this process, "fear" or "evil" will be removed as an artificially created emotion that has been subconsciously carried through Souls residing in the lower worlds for countless ages. A way has been found to free Souls and simultaneously inspire them with the flame of a spiritually passionate and enthusiastic coura-geous sojourner that is driven with childlike wonder to become a co-creative being with the higher purely positive dimensions and the ONE SOURCE behind all life, while personally explor-ing these worlds. They can do this when "evil" or "fear" (same thing) is no longer used as a pitchfork to drive them in an upward direction.

Statistically, that old way has never even remotely been a very effective way to inspire God realization or freedom of the individual. However, the new Supreme Deity, or SUGMAD Expansion Ray has been tested and found to be true, necessary and kind and it is being implemented throughout the entire creation from the highest to the lowest worlds.

The very real greater problem of The Supreme Deity or The SUGMAD has been to solve the grand dilemma of the lower world systems. A great part of itself in the form of individual Soul or Atma beings have remained unconsciously living out lifetimes under the lower world laws that were made so very, very, long ago and they haven't been returning home. The command inherent within each individual is to return home from whence it came; but, the negative nature of the lower Purushas or Governors is to swindle, trick, lie, delay, pervert, subconsciously implant and divert Soul from ever being able to carry out this inherent commandment that was placed within them in ancient history. That is the old way of "evil" or "fear" and one should remember that "fear" was never meant to be permanent and in the end it is erasable from Soul's experience at any rate. Pleasure full enriching, uplifting, consciousness expanding or enlightening experiences are NOT erasable EVER.

Just a little practice with the imaginative technique about the new fountain on the Soul plane of awareness and how it can transform your awareness here on Earth, will reveal awakening results that are truly beyond amazing. You will naturally do this in your own unique way during the awakening of Soul's true purpose to become a free and lovingly trusted co-Creator with the Supreme Deity. You will simply begin to know, see and understand far more about what is coming and where you creatively fit into this dynamic Transformation in the Expansion Ray of the Supreme Deity, SUGMAD or HU of being.

This new awakening and expansion of the Supreme Deity or HU happens only once every few hundred billion years. You will discover for yourself that we are now at the beginning of this event that will safely and non-destructively transform and uplift forever the past negative Eck-Vidya (science of prophecy) destructive vision for Earth and dynamically uplift its unfortunately deeply subconsciously suppressed people to become part of an amazing new world. Then planet Earth will be accepted into a wondrous Galactic Interdimensional Alliance of Free Worlds. Earth's near future destiny is most certainly NOT what anyone thinks it is.

Now it must be boldly stated that every man, woman and child living on Earth today will soon know, without a shadow of a doubt, that many highly evolved extraterrestrial benevolent humans and other loving beings exist beyond good old planet Earth.

That great question of whether or not the people of Earth are alone in the universe will soon finally be answered once and for all time.

All the best in the Spirit of truth, necessity and most certainly kindness

Robert Scott Lemriel

+++

OMNEC: That was long, right? I thought that was important. It is important, otherwise it wouldn't be in the book. It was a gift to me from some higher beings and from the brothers from outer space. They brought this as a gift and offered it to me for the book.

AUDIENCE: I would like to know if I can consciously visualize this fountain and drink from it on a Soul Journey.

ANJA: That's exactly what we just did.

AUDIENCE: So I can do this at home anytime as well?

OMNEC: Yeah, that's the whole reason I included it in the book. I realized it was a special gift when I read it. I sent it to the publisher right away and I told her, it's very important, we have to include it.

I am going to try to answer questions now. And then I am going to sign your books.

AUDIENCE: I would like to understand the meaning of the big floods that are currently happening, for example in Pakistan. In Southern Pakistan a very big area is flooded – and now in Cambodia as well. Does this have something to do with the people there, with nature, or with geography?

OMNEC: So, you have got a project to focus on. You can help by doing that. I started Operation Peace years ago and that was the purpose – to heal the Earth. You focus on an area that you know needs something and send your attention and your love there. Invite other people to share that with you. We had people getting together and having a little eating and enjoyment and then they meditated the whole evening and focused on a project. That's where you can do some good. You are helping. You are helping God. That's what we are for. We are supposed to be helping God. We are the helpers of God. That's what I believe. If you are really concerned, then the best thing to do is send love and healing. Visualize it before you go to bed. Think about it. Send your attention there. That's what you can do.

AUDIENCE: I would like know more about how humans and animals will live together in the future.

OMNEC: The pets that you have now are studying how to be humans; they are watching you. After the Transformation, the need for pets will be on a level basis, you know, equal. You are equal to the animal. The animal comes to you because it wants to and you accept it because you want to.

AUDIENCE: My biggest hope is that there will be no slaughterhouses and no suffering anymore for the animals. I hope that animals will not be killed anymore, but that they are treated friendly – just like we should treat each other. This is what I am longing for.

OMNEC: Me, too, I feel the same way. I love animals, but Earth is a place where people come to have the most terrible experiences. They have to have these experiences. That is what the Soul does. It's not good or bad. It's valuable experience. Once you have experienced something that is totally against what the Soul is, the Soul will never repeat it. The Soul is not the darkness, it is the light. You are not what you do. It's only an experience. You don't become that. We are not what we do. Thank God! There are so many terrible things that happen. I know that I have done some of them, I am sure, in other lifetimes. That's why now I can't even hate. I don't know what it means. I couldn't. I don't have the ability. I already did that. And I am finished with that. Now I am only loving. That's all I am interested in – in love, that's all. The most powerful energy on Earth is love. That's the purpose of our creation. God loved Itself and created everything from Itself in non-ending cycles, so therefore It would continue to exist in everything It created. God exists through everything It created and it's all because of love. Love is all there is.

AUDIENCE: Could it be that – if we visualize and wish it really strong – that money will be abolished one day?

OMNEC: It won't be needed. Our societies will be functioning on a different level. Your ancestors from other planets will come here and help you with your new free energy. You won't need money. If you need something, you can just make it and you can just share it with somebody else and they can give to you – it's a bartering system. That's the natural way for mankind anyway.

AUDIENCE: Will we still experience this?

OMNEC: I doubt. I don't think so. Unless you are reborn. Not in this body probably. I won't be here, because I am not coming back. This is my last time on Earth, and I have to enjoy every bit of it.

AUDIENCE: How is your connection with your Venusian family now?

OMNEC: None of the people that I loved and lived with on Venus are still there. But my uncle is still on the physical. He is in a spaceship in his laboratory for people on Earth.

AUDIENCE: Will the spaceships come to Germany as well? I mean, because Germany is so small – and the spaceships are so huge!

OMNEC: [laughs] The little ones come. The scout ships.

AUDIENCE: How can we see them? I am always looking, but I never see anything!

OMNEC: I can't tell you. Just don't stop looking. Just keep looking; you'll probably see them. You have to ask. Say, "I have been waiting, so now I want to see one."

AUDIENCE: May I add something? In 2002, I visited Hückelhoven where Omnec had been living for some years. Her plane had not landed yet at the airport, but there I saw a spaceship, such a bright light, and I know that people there had seen this before.

OMNEC [to the woman who wants to see spaceships]: You have to keep in touch with him, he knows how to see them! [laughter]

AUDIENCE: What about cropcircles? Most of them appear in England.

OMNEC: I have seen many, even here in Germany.

AUDIENCE: Where do they come from?

OMNEC: It's various aliens. They are more or less messages and puzzles for mankind. They are hidden messages – and they are beautiful.

AUDIENCE: Why are they hidden messages?

OMNEC: Because human beings like to figure out stuff. They do that on purpose, so that you have a puzzle to fulfill.

AUDIENCE: Didn't Uncle Odin want to teach us how to beam ourselves? Has he progressed in his researches?

OMNEC: He is still working on the teleportation system. I think he introduced it on Earth but they are not interested unless they figure out a way to use it for war.

AUDIENCE: What is your opinion on quantum physics and quantum healing?

OMNEC: I don't understand it. It makes my brain ache. It's fascinating, but it's too complicated. My Uncle Odin is the scientist, I never was.

AUDIENCE: Those orbs that one can sometimes see on photos look like bubbles of air or of soap. Are that really nature beings or angels? Some say they are just weather phenomena or something like that.

OMNEC: I have seen them in films, where they are doing investigations for ghosts and stuff and there were orbs in the room. I believe it's natural, yes. I believe it's a natural kind of entity – maybe from another dimension that came into our dimension. A lot of things like that happen and people don't know what they are. They were shocked and scared and maybe horrified because these entities from other dimensions do look different than humans. They can break into this dimension and they have. I think many people have seen things and they couldn't even explain what they have seen. That's the only thing I could say to this.

AUDIENCE: Can you say a bit more on this, "We must help God." For a very long time, we were told that God helps us. I would like to understand this better.

OMNEC: Eventually, when you are no longer a person, your Soul will go to a higher dimension and you will become a helper for God. Like a guardian angel or some Soul that accompanies a Soul when it takes an out of body journey. There are all kinds of jobs. Our goal is to become helpers for God. I think if you are positively trying to balance and heal the Earth and help people here that you ARE helping God. I guess, everybody asks God for help, but we really should help God. To be honest. I think God can use some help. God created and gave humans the free will to live as they wish and you see what they have done.

AUDIENCE: I read in your book that gold does not originally come from Earth, but that it was brought here. Why do people have such a craving for gold?

OMNEC: It was brought here for the reason of money. It was brought here and mined here just to create the money. Emeralds are from

Venus. All the beautiful jewels are not from Earth. They were just brought here. A lot of things were brought here – plants, animals...

AUDIENCE: How were they brought here?

OMNEC: Through people. When humans came to Earth, they brought many things.

AUDIENCE: So they were brought in huge spaceships?

OMNEC: Of course. That's how they came to this system from their own systems. In huge ships with thousands of people. That's how they colonized the planets here. That's where people came from.

AUDIENCE: Do you know which civilization lives on the moon?

OMNEC: There have been colonies in the past on the moon, but there are not any people there at this moment.

AUDIENCE: In the "Unknown History" you speak about a dinoid and reptoid race. Is the reptoid race still on Earth and is it true that the queen of England is a shapeshifting reptile?

OMNEC: I heard rumors. I have heard about the reptoids and the shapeshifters, I have heard about all that. I am not sure if it's true or not.

AUDIENCE: Will we be shown something special in 2012?

OMNEC: I don't know. I guess I'll find out when you do. I have no idea. But there must be something happening, because so many people expect it.

+++

[End and autographing session]

Freising, September 30, 2011

OMNEC: Good evening and thank you for being here. For those of you who don't know: I'm Omnec. I had a stroke two years ago and I am just recovering. They told me not to come. Everybody said, "You shouldn't go, you can hardly walk," and I said, "Well, I'm going." The reason I am doing as well as I am is because people love me and are sending me blessings. I know it and I appreciate that. I wanted to come because Germany is my second home and a great deal of my Soul family is here. Every time I meet with people I see Souls that are familiar to me; it's like a family reunion. I am still in therapy; I just got to where I can walk again without help. I was taking therapy for speech, and I still have therapy for my walking and for my left hand. They told me it takes time. I have to be more patient with myself. I do the best I can.

I came to Earth from Venus when I was 7 years old. I manifested a physical body on Venus in a special temple, because before I had karma with a little girl that lived on Earth. My Soul had accompanied her during her birth process, so I could receive the same genetic imprint – it was all pre-planned by the Masters. It was karma, plus I had a mission. I am still fulfilling my mission. I am grateful to Anja for being my voice. She speaks for me. She has done a wonderful job – even though she doesn't think so. I tell her that actually people love to hear her.

I wrote the book because it was requested by Paul Twitchell who was an ECK-Master on Earth in the Sixties. He said that I should share the information and the knowledge with mankind and that's exactly why I wrote the book. I am not really sure how of you even know of the book.

AUDIENCE: I only saw the promotion flyer somewhere – that's why I came, because Omnec really looks like someone from another planet. I just followed my feeling and came.

OMNEC: If you have a feeling to come here, it's your Soul. Your Soul knows all and remembers all and there is some kind of connection between the Soul trying to wake this mind up – the new mind, the new brain. All of you know everything as Soul, but your mind, your brain, has not comprehended all of it. You get a new brain with each body and sometimes the brain can get overloaded. The Soul carries all of the information and experiences from many lifetimes. I am just reminding you of what you already know. You know it, you just don't know it with this mind. I am just reminding. I want Anja to read the passage from the book about the astral dimension that I write about – about living on Venus.

+++

Reading: Excerpt from *The Venus Plane* – Text see Cologne, September 3, 2011

+++

AUDIENCE: Which abilities could you not preserve after you came from Venus?
OMNEC: Manifesting things, of course, and having more abilities within the body and control. I had to get used to it on Earth, to the limitations. It was very limited; it was very difficult for me at first. I had to learn to walk and to talk and to eat and to sleep. The monks had to teach me in the monastery that I had to sleep because I didn't want to sleep.

When they were trying to explain to me the bodily functions, I refused to go to the toilet. I said I will not do that. They said, "But you have to. It's part of the functions that you can't control", but I thought it was disgusting. Of course, I had to learn everything. The monks used to laugh every day and shared with each other what I refuse to do today. It was always a joke. Learning to eat, the taste of different foods, was difficult. They enjoyed that, too. I love spicy stuff, but the first time it was a little bit of a shock. I had to learn to enjoy stuff. I can only eat very little, I never eat very much. I never have. I love to eat, but on the other hand, I feel full, and when I feel full, I want no more.

AUDIENCE: What do you eat? Vegetarian, or...?

OMNEC: Everything. Meat included, because I know that the animals chose to serve as food for mankind and they are serving their purpose and I accept that. As long as I am thankful for it and I love the animals which I do, that's the whole point.

You have got to love and to appreciate everything. Everyone has the right to choose whatever is best for themselves without judgment or criticism for the others. That's our free will that God gave us. We all have the free will to experience what we wish. It's the greatest gift that God gave mankind. God created us with the free will to experience what we will experience. There is no good or bad. In Soul's point of view, everything is an experience that is worth having. The Soul knows it is not what it does, it's just an experience. We experience the darkness, but we are light in the darkness. We are never the darkness. The Soul has to remember it's a Soul and this is only an experience. Most of the experiences, illnesses included, you have chosen before this life. For an experience. Even my stroke. It was part of my experiences. I chose it, so I accept it. I didn't know it was going to happen. When it happened, it was a shock, of course. I thought I would get better in a little while. I thought, well, you know, I'll get better, just give me a little time. Everybody was in a panic. They wanted me to go to the hospital right away and I refused. I didn't go, but I should have. It took three people to get me to the toilet, because my leg was dragging, I couldn't move anything. My arm and my leg were just hanging.

AUDIENCE: Do you take medicine?

OMNEC: Only for the blood pressure. Only for the doctors, because my blood pressure is very high. It's hard to explain to them that that's normal for me, because they insist it to be on a certain level. If it were as low as they wanted, I would be sleeping all the time. I wouldn't be even aware of the world. I told them that I can't have it too low. But I always caused a panic when I went to the hospital, I hated that. It was like 350 over 250 or 225 and everybody was in a panic, but I feel fine! I am talking normally and they are running with their rolling chairs and put me in intensive care. So many times I was in intensive care! I walked out because I said there are people that really need to be here. Not me, I don't need to be here, hooked up to all the machines, you know, and you can't relax, because your whole body is full of machine cords. I take the medicines because the doctors insist. If you don't, then they won't take care of you. Anymore questions?

AUDIENCE: When you entered the body of the other girl, somebody from your surroundings must have noticed it that there is a different Soul in that body now – how did they react on that?

ANJA: Omnec is not a walk-in. It was a physical exchange. The other girl died in a bus accident. Omnec looked very similar, because she had the same genetic imprints. According to Omnec she had accompanied Sheila during her birth process and therefore she was able to manifest a physical body on Venus that was like a twin of Sheila's. Everything was well planned and prepared so that Omnec could be brought into her Earth family.

AUDIENCE: Alright, yet there must have been some difference between the two, the mother must have noticed something...

ANJA: Sheila was on the way to her grandmother, and the grand-mother had not seen her for a while.

OMNEC: And we were like twins anyway.

AUDIENCE: Were you twin Souls?

OMNEC: No, it was a karmic relationship. In the book I talk about when in another life she had given her life for me, and in this lifetime I would live her life when she died. I took on a lot of other karma. I wanted to live and experience it all, because this is my last incarnation. It was difficult, but on the other hand, I wanted to do it. Plus, you know, I love people on Earth and the Earth.

That's why I talk about the Unknown History, so that people can understand what went into preparing the Earth for life and for people here. A lot of work went into making the Earth such a beautiful place with minerals and lot of the animals and plants that come from other solar systems. Many peoples' ancestors came here from other universes. I talk about this – about the times, before the Earth was colonized.

ANJA: This information is published as a double-DVD with the title *The Unknown History of our Solar System and the Spiritual Transformation of the Earth.*[15]

AUDIENCE: Are there big battles between the dark and the light forces?

OMNEC: Only on Earth. The dark is always trying to interfere with the spiritual information. They use a lot of things – such as prophecies and channeling – all information that keeps mankind in a state of worry about what's going to happen in the future.

You have to realize that you are in charge of the future. Whatever YOU visualize and concentrate on, will be. You are not victims. You are the masters of your destiny.

As long as you know that, the Earth has a chance. That's the reason why I tell people: Don't worry about 2012! I am sure that something will happen, because everybody is expecting it, but what, I don't know. A surprise!

I believe in creation and the Creator and not in the big bang. I think that that the big bang is probably... it might be the end, not the beginning. They talk about that – it's a theory for everything that exists. Man has lots of theories. I have heard many, like theories about reptilians and that the royal family may be reptilians and shape shifters and all that. I have heard all that.

These are the dark powers trying to interfere in man's growth spiritually, to slow us down and to distract people from concentrating on helping the Earth through progress and raise the consciousness.

Fear is a tool. It's used against mankind; it always has on Earth. When people are unsure of the future, then they have fear. We know that actually our Souls are immortal and we live forever. There is nothing to fear, except for the death process, which we all eventually have to face. But it's only a process you go through and your Soul is advancing. It's not the end. It's only the beginning. And we have gone through it over and over again, but not with this body. Fear is something we don't have to have.

God created everything in non-ending cycles, because It loved Itself and It will exist always through Its creations that way. It's all from love, you know. We – our Souls – are all a little part of God

15 The transcript of this DVD is PART ONE of this book.

– of the Creator. We have the ability to create, too, because we are a part of God, and we are great.

That's why I came. That's my mission for being here: to remind people of things that this mind has no way to remember. You know it as Soul. That's why – when you hear certain information – it just makes you say, "Aha!" somewhere inside. You already know it! You are just remembering. Somehow your Soul is awakening the new brain to, "Well, I know this already!" Yes, because your Soul knows all this. It's nothing new – you are just being reminded.

AUDIENCE: You say that we are on Earth to make experiences. Many people say that we have to find our life task. Is that correct? How can we find it?

OMNEC: I think when you are having experiences and you are learning, then you ARE fulfilling a life task, because that's part of what your existence is about. There is no end to learning. What we can't comprehend here, we will learn on the other dimensions, so that your Soul can absorb the information.

AUDIENCE: Are you still in contact with your relatives on Venus?

OMNEC: Of course. But most of my relatives on Venus have ascended to higher dimensions. It's only my Uncle Odin now in the physical. But there are other beings from Venus and from other planets that live on the Earth. They don't wish to go public. My mission is to share information with people. And I try. I speak from what I know and what I don't know, I can't speak about – and when I am dead, I don't want anyone to channel me. [laughter].

I said everything while I am here and I don't need anyone to channel me when I am gone. Don't believe them if they tell you. Tell them, you know it better than that. Exactly. I know that upsets some people, because there are books about channeling, I feel that you don't know what kind of entities you are in touch with, or what kind of information you are going to bring and what for. I feel you should be careful, because I have seen some really bad situations, and I wasn't too fond of these experiences. Not at all. They were always talking like they were so far above and we were just insects here. They said that they were also ancient Venusians and they never said hello or anything to me. They were telling people to come and kneel down and receive blessings from them, and when the lady that was assisting the channeler said, "That's enough, she needs to rest," then the channel said, "I am not finished, I will finish!" No care for the body that it was using. To me that was a horror, because I thought, "What about the person who invited you to speak through?" It was talking so down to everyone, I wasn't too fond of the whole experience – and I have had more than one. I didn't go intentionally to hear. We were supposed to do something else and the weather didn't allow it and this woman made this as a gift to the group, but it was a nightmare. I am not fond of it and I am not fond of channeling. I know that was popular for a long time. People were channeling everybody. I had to speak at a channeling convention before. I had two women arguing over me to decide which one was channeling Ashtar, and I told them, probably neither one. To be honest with you, you know. I couldn't tell them and I wouldn't tell them.

AUDIENCE: Why are these current times so difficult and what can we do to get through them better?

OMNEC: Do more meditation. When you focus your attention on healing the Earth, you correct the situation that you see that needs it. We use our visualization process to visualize the Earth as we would like it to be, and that's what we can do to help. I did this for years. I was teaching people to form meditation groups – to work together and to work singly, alone. People can do something. You don't have to feel under stress because of the situation on Earth. It is in the process. The money situation is supposed to collapse. That's part of the process. Everything is part of the process. It will get better, but it has to go through hard times first. It will be better, depending on more people who participate.

AUDIENCE: It feels like being tied to rubber bands. Nothing really works out, everything is so stiff, so exhausting. It's as if one is held back from all sides.

OMNEC: I can understand that. I hope it gets better. Maybe some of my information can help. That's what I intended to do on Earth – to give information so that people CAN live in happiness and harmony, so that you can be a regular human being. A happy one, I hope.

+++

Linz (Austria), October 3, 2011

This evening begins with the presentation of Omnec Onec's PR-Trailer which is projected on the wall with a beamer. YouTube Link: **https://youtu.be/uJ4miptxqXs** (or search for "omnec pr trailer")

+++

OMNEC: First of all I want to thank all of you for coming and for being here. These are my first appearances since I had my stroke. A lot of people thought I wouldn't come, but I said, yes, I'm going. [applause]

Yes, because, the reason I am doing so well with my speech therapy behind me and I am learning to walk again, is because of YOU. [applause]

And I appreciate it – thank you! [applause]

A lot of people wonder about the song NURI BANI. It's in the beginning of my Soul Journey CD. I used to sing this mantra in my workshops. It means light and sound in Sanskrit. I created a song, because I thought the mantra was too boring.

I hope that you like the new book that has got all my information from all three books I wrote before – the most important information.

And for those of you who don't know me: I came to Earth at age seven. Before, I lived on the astral dimension on Venus. I manifested a physical body on Venus and came to Earth in a spaceship to fulfill my mission and also for karmic reasons.

I am going to have Anja read to you about the astral dimension.

+++

Reading: Excerpt from *The Venus Plane* – Text see Cologne, September 3, 2011

+++

OMNEC: I am going to answer questions now. If people have questions, I'll try to answer.

AUDIENCE: Are you able to do astral travel here on Earth like you did on Venus? Is there a difference?

OMNEC: We prefer Soul Travel, because you are not limited to the astral. When you astral travel, you are limited to the astral dimension. And of course, when I am sleeping, I am always out of my body going somewhere else. I even work on the other dimensions, especially with children, and the children recognize and know me. I have met them many times. They knew me but they did not know where. I explained it to them and then they were OK and satisfied.

I believe that love is the most important thing that exists in this universe. It's the most powerful force there is. The more you give, the more you receive. It's endless. It's very, very vital to our being. I believe we were all created because of love. God loved Itself and It created everything from Itself in non-ending cycles so it would never cease to exist. God exists through Its creations, which is us. Every Soul is a little part of God. We have the same abilities. We have the free will and we can create as well. That's what I say to people: Think about how you want the world to be and create it that way. What do you want to happen in the future? It's up to you, because you have the choice and nothing can happen unless you want it to.

AUDIENCE: In 1956/1957 there was a group in Washington who claimed to come from Venus – their leader's name was Valiant Thor. Do you know anything about this? And another question: There is much channeling from the Hathors, can you comment on that as well?

OMNEC: I can't say anything about the Hathors, but I heard of Valiant Thor. I know Dr. Stranges[16] – I was on TV with him. I am

---

16 Dr. Frank E. Stranges (1927 – 2008) is the author of *Stranger at the Pentagon*, a book about his encounter with the Venusian Valiant Thor in the late 1950's.

aware of these people that come also from the physical Venus and say they have no finger prints and they have a whole different story. I am aware of that, but I come from the astral and I did manifest a physical body. I accompanied a child during her birth process and I reccived the genetic imprint for my future life when she died. After her death, I took her place. It's a little different situation.

AUDIENCE: What's going to happen in 2012?

OMNEC [laughs]: What do you want? Something is going to happen because too many people are expecting it. I suppose it will be a surprise. Let's hope it's a pleasant one. That's what I wish. Maybe a big spaceship or something will come? I have no idea. I have been asked a lot. So I expect something.

AUDIENCE: In your book you mention a teleportation device that your Uncle Odin is working on. It is some decades ago since you wrote this – does this device exist meanwhile? Why does one not hear anything about it?

OMNEC: Uncle Odin is still working on it. He tried to present it to Earth, but they were only interested in using it for espionage, and of course he refused. That's not what it's for. He is still in a spaceship in a scientific laboratory outside the Earth, along with other ships which are sending energy to the Earth for the Transformation.

AUDIENCE: Do you know if the crop circles are made by Venusians as well?

OMNEC: Of course. Crop circles are always symbols and puzzles for mankind to work on. They are always positive messages and beautiful.

AUDIENCE: Where else do crop circles come from?

OMNEC: From many beings. Some of them are not even in this system, but they are friendly. Most of them are art, for beauty. Of course it's mathematical. I think people love them, as far as I know. I visited several in Germany. I have taken many pictures. I have been in the middle of them with groups from workshops. I love crop circles.

AUDIENCE: What will the future bring us?

OMNEC: In the future, a lot of your ancestors from other planets will come and bring free energy and new technology for mankind. They are waiting for the Transformation to be complete. That depends on the people and how many participate. It's going very fast and it's working very well. I think the more people that participate, the faster it will be. I have faith in people. I believe that you can do it and I believe you will. How hard do you want it? How do you want the Earth to be and how soon do you want it?

AUDIENCE: Are you able to increase your vibration here with your physical body just like you were used to do it on the astral level of Venus?

OMNEC: No. I am limited. Now I am totally in the physical body and I have no help from my uncle anymore, because it's against the spiritual laws to have assistance. So I have to deal with whatever happens to my physical body. So now I have to recuperate from the stroke. Of course, I am getting better and I appreciate all of your help.

AUDIENCE: When you arrived on Earth from Venus with a space-ship, did other people notice your arrival? Or did it happen in the astral dimension?

OMNEC: I'm not positive about that. We landed in a desert area on purpose. Quietly, so that we would not disturb. We snuck in [laughs].

AUDIENCE: I would like to learn more about the Laws of the Supreme Deity.

OMNEC: Yes, they are in my book.

AUDIENCE: Why have you become ill?

OMNEC: Because I chose to be for an experience, to understand.

AUDIENCE: In your book you write about a special spiritual path that all people on Venus go and that there was nothing similar on Earth. You say that there were many religions on Earth, but not THIS direct path. Has this changed meanwhile in the last decades since you wrote your book?

OMNEC: Through Eckankar, I would say.

ANJA: Eckankar are the ancient teachings that Omnec knows from Venus. These teachings were brought to public again in the Sixties by Paul Twitchell – he was mentioned in the videotrailer we showed in the beginning. Paul Twitchell published these teachings for the first time since they had been kept hidden for a very long time. Eckankar teaches this direct path to God.

OMNEC: It's a very ancient way and it was protected in the tem-

194

ples on Tibet and on other planets as well. Now it's available for mankind. It's taught from a living master or teacher to the Chelas or students.

AUDIENCE: *I know one of these teachers, his name was Darwin Gross and he was very controversial. The whole organization was negatively affected by his presence. Do you know the name of the current master?*

ANJA: Sure. Harold Klemp is the living Eck-Master.

OMNEC: I wasn't part of it. I am not part of it. The masters support me and I am supported by the Eck members on Earth but I am not a member in the Eckankar organization. I just teach the same spiritual teachings.

AUDIENCE: *Do you come from the astral or from the etheric level?*

ANJA: From the astral.

AUDIENCE: *What is the difference between the astral and the etheric?*

OMNEC: The etheric is a higher level. The astral level is the level where I originated in this lifetime, and after this I will go to a higher level than the astral. I have a lot of work.

AUDIENCE: *We are all coming from somewhere. We are all searchers – what is the difference between us and you?*

OMNEC: I retained my memory. I was on Venus for 130 years before I came to Earth. I am very old and I had a mission. I am supported by the spiritual hierarchy and sent here to share this information with mankind. Every Soul that's sitting here knows everything I am saying, because you know it as Soul, but your brain in this body in this incarnation doesn't remember everything. Your brain does not have a direct channel to the Soul. So I am trying to reawaken people to what they already know. Otherwise I wouldn't be here. We are all knowledgeable. We all have the information, but you cannot remember what you forgot – but you must not forget what you know. What you know is on the Soul level. It's from experience through many incarnations. Hopefully I am trying to raise the consciousness, because each individual can have this ability. I believe that you CAN – that's my goal. My goal is to have everyone remember everything.

AUDIENCE: *How does one remember what one forgot?*

OMNEC: That's the trick. You can't remember what you forgot, but you must not ever forget what you know. That's a spiritual puzzle.

ANJA: One needs a couple of paradoxes, so that the brain gets a shortcut. Then the wires are differently assembled and everything functions.

AUDIENCE: What are we doing wrong? Why don't we remember and what can we do to remember?

OMNEC: You must ask your Soul every night that you wish to remember what you experienced before.

AUDIENCE: Do you really believe that we can change our world and that the negative forces are not stronger?

OMNEC: I know they are not. Otherwise I wouldn't be here. They have attacked me all through my life. I KNOW we will win. [applause]. Love will win. Always.

AUDIENCE: Is there a connection between the increasingly common disease dementia and the fact that we cannot remember our True Self?

OMNEC: I don't really know, but it's an interesting thought, maybe you should write about it and share your thoughts with others. I thought many times that dementia patients were lost in their memories. It could be. They are in the past, they are not in the present.

AUDIENCE: If most of the people can't remember that they are Souls, what happens to the Earth if we are the minority?

OMNEC: I think we were the minority, but we are the majority now. That's how I see it, that there are more people with a higher consciousness. I think it's much better than before, because I am accepted more and what I am teaching is accepted. I think the people are more willing and open.

AUDIENCE: If I say "I am Soul" and "You are Soul", we are all brothers and sisters – is that correct?

OMNEC: Exactly. We are all connected.

AUDIENCE: Is it correct that we increase our consciousness by aligning our attention – for example by being here this evening?

OMNEC: Of course. Your Soul brought you here.

AUDIENCE: Is it the task of the Soul or our task in this physical world to transform the passions of the mind into virtues of the Soul?

OMNEC: That's one of our goals. Yes.

196

AUDIENCE: That means for example, that if I get a disease, I thereby learn to understand others with their diseases and to tolerate and love them?

OMNEC: Of course! I cannot reject anyone, because I love everyone. Of course, when I go through experiences, then I have more love for the people that are having difficulties. I always thought that these disabled or retarded people were special gifts to Earth as an example for others to be grateful for what you have. You are able and clear and can think and you do everything and you don't have to concentrate.

I have so many "special friends," because I cannot reject anyone. I love everyone and I accept everyone. I always will. I used to love even objects, things, you know, like paper blowing out in the wind or something that nobody cared for. I was ridiculous sometimes, now I don't even think about it, but at that time I was very serious. I have cried over the funniest things, because I am easily touched. I have such deep feelings for everyone. When I see pain, I feel it. It was not an easy life, but I chose it and I am still happy and I still love people and I am still here. I am so happy to see so many people here. Even if only one came, I would be happy.

AUDIENCE: I have an autistic son. Many people say autists have special talents, however, so far I don't know what it is.

OMNEC: I believe they are very special. If you can reach him and if you can communicate with him, that's wonderful. It has a lot to do with trust. You are very lucky.

AUDIENCE: What happens with those people who don't believe in the Transformation Process and who don't consciously participate?

OMNEC: They still go through it. They have no choice. They are going through the Transformation and if they don't wish to participate, then, you know, many people will perish during this time. They have to die and come back in a new body that is able to live with the new information.

+++

[End and autographing session]

Frankfurt Bookfair, October 15, 2011

OMNEC: Hello, my name is Omnec Onec. I came to your planet in 1955. My autobiography was written in the Sixties and published first in America in 1991. Then I came to Germany and since then have written two more books. All these books were recently published by Kouki Wohlwend of the DAS GUTE BUCH Publisher. The whole three books in one are now available.

I am happy that all of you came and took the time to share a little while with me. I hope that you read the book and enjoy it, because most people find that it answers and fulfills things that they believed always within themselves.

Two years ago here in Germany I had a stroke. I am now in the process of recuperating thanks to a lot of love and healing energy that was sent to me from people like you.

Many people said, I should not come. But I said, "I must" because if I am going to continue to inspire people I have to have the courage to appear and go on. Of course, it's a challenge, but on the other hand, I am progressing. I am walking on my own, but not as much as I would like. My speech has improved and I can move a lot more, so I feel I am actually doing a good job.

I want Anja to read to you from the chapter over the astral dimension, so you can have a better understanding of what the dimension where I began was like.

+++

Reading: Excerpt from *The Venus Plane* – Text see Cologne, September 3, 2011

+++

OMNEC: Of course there are many questions and that's why I wrote the book. I try to answer all the questions that people have. I think the most complicated idea is that I manifested a physical body to live on Earth. That means this body came from the astral dimension, but the material is now of the physical world. People always think I'm a walk-in or that my Soul entered another body – no. I have the same form and the same memories and the same Soul that I had in the astral. I lived there 130 of your Earth years. Our time is much different than on Earth. We live to be 500 of your Earth years in one life cycle on Venus. So I am very old. Believe it or not – I am like 350 of your Earth years. I have been here 60 something Earth years.

Now I would like to open up my time for you to ask questions and I will do my best to answer.

AUDIENCE: You already said that you are approximately 350 years old in Venus time. How is dying – on Venus and now here for you on Earth?

OMNEC: Naturally, since I manifested a physical body to live and to work on Earth, I have to continue in this body until it dies or translates on Earth. On Venus, we know when our time is finished that we translate to a higher dimension. We don't die. Our Soul just goes to a higher dimension. We have a ceremony.

The reason I wrote the book is because of the questions of human beings. The Venusians are part of the human races' ancestors from Earth, and I come to bring this knowledge and information and make it available for every human being. My book tells you the origin of all the races, how they migrated to your system, how they colonized different planets and eventually the Earth. Our whole reason for contacting the Earth people is to make you realize that your heritage is much richer than what you have been told. Basically you are all Soul which is immortal, and the physical body is just temporary.

I try to help mankind understand the best and the most generous of all the energy that we possess is Love. It is the whole basis for our creation.

We know of God as a source of energy. We from the other planets call it "It" – "The Creator," but it's really like a big source of energy where everything that's created first existed and everything is a little part of this energy. We call it Soul. It was created because the Creator loved Itself so much that It created everything in non-ending cycles, and therefore It exists always through Its creations which is of course US.

We can create what we want of this world. Everything that exists was once someone's imagination before it was reality, so the imagination is the key to creation. We have the ability to create with our concentration and power. Therefore, if you want to know what lies in the future, it depends on what you really want.

We have the power. We ourselves. We created this world, and we can keep it safe from harm by concentrating positive energy on the sources and the places that are troubled, that are having wars. All you have to do is concentrate and send your peaceful and healing energy. You can solve all the problems.

We say: Wherever your attention goes, the energy flows. When you put your attention on something, energy automatically flows. Whether it is positive or negative is up to the individual.

AUDIENCE: You say that we create our own world. I would like to understand your point of view on your own physical problems and diseases. Did you create them yourself?

OMNEC: I chose it myself. As Soul I chose what I am experiencing in this lifetime. I am responsible myself. I wished to have the experience or I wouldn't be having it. I think that's the same with every experience that humans have. We don't realize that we chose it before –before we began this life term. We choose our experiences, because every experience, no matter how bad it seems, is a highly important evolvement for the Soul.

We have been taught that something is good and bad, but that's part of the thinking process. In reality, it's not. It's just a very valuable experience.

God is not cruel, because we have the free will to choose what we wish to experience. God is not responsible. God only created

200

us with the free will to choose experience whatever we wish and it is a wonderful thing that we have this free will.

I think we search for someone to blame for some situation. That comes with a lower consciousness and understanding. We all go through that, but when you reach a certain consciousness level you become aware that we have to take responsibility for anything that happens to us.

That's why I gave workshops for years. I am trying to teach people how to change this perception of themselves and the world and how to have a greater concept and understanding of themselves starting with the Soul. And, of course, understanding what happens to you after this life and beyond the world here.

What happens to you after this life is over is also up to you. You create what happens to you in the next life and your next experience beyond the physical.

I know that I still have lots to learn and that this brain cannot comprehend all I have to know. So I have to go to a higher dimension with greater capabilities. And I can learn from the Soul level.

I enjoy the things while I am here that I can't experience anywhere else. The greatest thing is the human being, the various beautiful human beings with their individual personalities and beautiful Souls – it's always inspiring for me. The kind of love I have is: I love you just because you ARE, and for no other reason. We call it 'Unconditional Love'. I am trying to share this with the people so that they can also love the same way.

I am very thankful for your attention and for you sharing your time with me. I hope that when you read my books or see a video of mine that you will get some kind of energy and knowledge that serves you.

AUDIENCE: Does free will only exist on the Soul level or also while we are already here in this physical body? Can we change our mind and say "No" to something that we experience?

OMNEC: You have the free will when you were created as Soul and as a human being. You make choices. Nothing is forced on you. If it is, it's against the spiritual law. Nobody has the right to force another individual to do anything. It's totally against the spiritual laws and the social laws that I know of.

I believe that you should obey the social laws of wherever we are and the spiritual laws. If we go by the spiritual laws of God and obey the laws that God has presented and given us, our lives will be very simple. It's simple. You simply love others as you wish to be loved. We must learn to love everyone exactly equally.

I never reject one person. I accept everyone equally. I feel that they are the same as me. I am not better or more knowledgeable than any other Soul. But you may not remember everything that you have experienced as Soul with this limited mind and limited body. On the other hand, as Soul, you know everything.

I always make a joke out of this and say: "You cannot remember what you forgot. But don't ever forget what you know!"

Because when you KNOW something, you never forget. Learning is an experience and when you learn through an experience, it's not like someone is telling you something. It's something that you go through and you'll never forget that.

Knowing is not the same as thinking and remembering. When you know something, it's something that you have gone through and experienced.

It's not really complicated – it just sounds complicated. I'm a very simple person.

My books are very easy to read, because I don't have a scientific mind. The physical world is complicated. Whatever can go wrong, will. Eventually in the physical I found this out. But you know, I am very lucky. I have a lot of people who love me and a beautiful family and the greatest thing of all is my Soul family, which is you.

AUDIENCE: *How do we see things from God's perspective?*

OMNEC: You try to have a greater perspective, a perspective that the person who says or does something says or does something out of an experience, but that's not what they are. You see the perspective that this is an experience a Soul is having – it's that they are not basically cruel.

We can't be judgmental of each other. We have to realize that we are not what we do or say. We are Soul and what we do and say is an experience of this moment or this time that we are in.

We have to remember that. Most people will automatically – like Kouki told me yesterday – for a second she thought, "This person

202

was not paying attention," and then in the next thirty seconds she herself did not pay attention and fell.

We have to be careful, you know, when we look at another person and be aware if we are judging or criticizing this person, because that could be us in the next moment.

That's called "instant karma."

I think that's funny. I love instant karma. I love it when it happens to people, because they are aware that they caused this with their thoughts. It's like calling somebody a bad name and turning around and walking into a brick of wall. I think these things are kind of funny. I have a weird sense of humor.

But actually I am very much like Earth people I grew up here and my habits and the way that I live and behave it's very much like you.

AUDIENCE: You as Soul chose your life and all that you want to go through in your life before your incarnation. Now, when you are in this incarnation, when you are in your body and you go through a certain experience that you feel you don't want to have anymore or you want to change it, do you still have to go through it?

OMNEC: It's too late. Once you made the decision and were born, you have no chance. You have to experience what you decided.

AUDIENCE: So the free will only exists on the Soul level? Or how would you explain a little more detailed the free will? So we don't have a free will?

OMNEC: We do have a free will. Your free will is the fact that you can choose to go left, to go right, to go into the darkness, to be cruel, to be kind – that's your free will. To accept your situation or not to accept. Many people commit suicide because they do not accept what they chose.

It's hard to accept sometimes that you accepted a very heavy body or a very handicapped body, but sicknesses and retardations are something very special for a Soul to experience and for the others around them to observe.

When you have a difficult life, you are a very courageous Soul and other people realize that and admire you for it most of the time. Unless you are a very low consciousness – then you may harm and injure the person that's already having a hard time. That's why God declares that if you behave this way toward others you'll eventually end up in the same situation so that you experience it – and that's your lesson. Perhaps that's why I am in the position I am in. Because at one time or another I am sure that I wasn't perfect and I made mistakes, so now I pay for it.

AUDIENCE: When you chose your life from a Soul level and you chose to experience a certain kind of disease, is it also decided beforehand that you heal from it or that it is permanent and you die from it?

OMNEC: Everything that happens in a life cycle is chosen beforehand, so whether you die or get better, that was your decision.

AUDIENCE: Did we also choose our job and our partnerships? What kind of freedom in our choices do we still have while we are in the physical?

OMNEC: You still have your free will. You choose your parents. You choose where you are going to live and what you wish to experience. The small lessons in your life are your choices at the time while you are living. Only the great points of your life are prechosen. Of course you choose your career and everything based on your parents, where you grow up and how you go to school, what religion you are. All of this is your choice. You make these decisions as you live your life. You have your will and then eventually if you don't go along with your parents' religion, because you have decided it doesn't give you the information you need, that's your choice.

+++

[End and autographing session]

Frankfurt Bookfair, October 16, 2011

OMNEC: My name is Omnec Onec and I came to the planet Earth in 1955 at the age of 7. I manifested a physical body on the astral level of Venus in order to come and work and live in your system. My whole story is written and put in book form since I was advised by a spiritual master in the 1960s named Paul Twitchell. He established the organization of Eckankar and I participated in the organizing of this. Since then I have published the book due to his request. Paul had taken a spiritual journey with Rebazar Tarzs, an older master, to the planet Venus and had met me before I came to Earth. Rebazar told him: "That little girl there will soon be on Earth and will help you with Eckankar." For people who have trouble to understand it, I have written it in a very simple way in my book. There was a physical connection to a family on Earth that I lived with and there is a spiritual background for me to come. I was to accompany her Soul with my Soul during her birth process. I wrote a chapter in my book about the astral dimension, where I lived and what it was like. Anja is going to read that to you so you got a better understanding. I am just recuperating from a stroke that I had two years ago. This is my first appearance here in Germany since I had the stroke. Thank you for being patient.

+++

Reading: Excerpt from *The Venus Plane* – Text see Cologne, September 3, 2011

+++

OMNEC: I want to tell you that we live in a higher frequency, but our time process is much slower than the Earth's. Even though I was in the form of a seven year old child, I had already lived 130 Earth years on the astral before I came to Earth. So I have been living consciously and aware of your time like I am over 300 years old. We live to be 500 years old of your time in one life cycle. I didn't figure this out – my uncle, who is a scientist, told me. He helped me a lot with the technological difficulties of explaining to the people. I want you to feel that you have time to ask questions individually and I will try to answer them.

AUDIENCE: Can you remember the time before you lived on Venus?
OMNEC: Of course I have total recall through my Soul existences in many lifetimes.

When I see people, I see the Soul and I recognize a lot of beings that I shared times in other life existences. Sometimes the people feel this.

All of the memories of your existences are not in this brain. They are stored in the Soul body and your Soul is trying to awaken your physical mind. I feel that you already have all this information. I am just reminding you. I happen to remember. That's my job: to share this information with every human being, and to remind you of what you already know.

AUDIENCE: What was your reason for coming to Earth? Did they give you a special task?
OMNEC: I was in training with the masters for a spiritual mission which I have to fulfill on Earth as well as a karmic debt to the family I lived with.

If you look at my information ... I covered the unknown history of the human beings on Earth as well as the spiritual Transformation of the planet Earth.

ANJA: This information is available on DVD. Omnec shared this about 15 years in lectures and workshops. Due to her health situation, Omnec will probably not give these workshops anymore.

OMNEC: I have been guided through my whole life by many Ascended Masters such as Fubbi Quantz, Lao-Tsi, Rebazar Tarzs. Little by little, as they revealed to me my mission, I set out to give this information to people. That's the reason that I am here. I also work on a spiritual level, a non-physical level, with children and people who are having difficulties. That's my job while I am sleeping. My physical body rests, but I am busy.

I try to explain to people that we are responsible for every decision we make, because any kind of experience that you go through, you have prechosen before you were born. The Soul is immortal and it's forever and every lifetime is just a small grain of sand to the Soul. Any kind of experience that a Soul has is very valuable. The way that you see things as good or bad is a thinking process; in reality, there is no good or bad. Everything is an important process of learning. Of course, when you do things against social laws, you have to go through punishments and trials, but God doesn't punish us. We have the decision and the free will to choose what we experience.

When we look at God on the other planets in our consciousness we think of God as the source of energy through which all creation began.

This source of energy loved itself so much that it created everything that exists out of this love in non-ending cycles. Therefore, it never ceases to exist. It exists always through its creations. I explain to every individual that as a Soul you go through evolution through the mineral, plant, animal and then the human state. Every lifetime you have to serve a certain purpose and then you can evolve. But your Soul has been here for billions and billions of years and God knows how many life cycles. It all began because of love. Love is the most powerful energy. Real love is unconditional. That means you love each other just because you are. That's the kind of love that I try to teach, and that's how I live. I can never reject anyone. I hope that you learn or get something from me sharing my life with you.

AUDIENCE: Do you already know where you will go when this life is finished?

OMNEC: I don't know exactly where I go, but I know I am not coming back to the physical. I am going to be learning and working on a higher dimension.

AUDIENCE: There are so many reports about UFO sightings worldwide, but we don't get this information via the mass media. Do you have an explanation for this?

OMNEC: It's mostly their fear, because we have a technology greater than the people on Earth. We are waiting for the consciousness of mankind to change and then we will come and share our technology with Earth. The governments know that the Earth is changing. The culture will be other than it is now, and the negative powers will not be in control anymore. Money won't be the essence of mankind anymore, but spirituality and sharing and living as human beings really wish to, because that's really up to you. You have the power to visualize and to create the kind of societies you want – and you will. I am here to help and others are coming – not only physical, but the spiritual ones are coming.

AUDIENCE: Can you say when approximately we will experience a higher spiritual level on Earth?

OMNEC: Well, the process is going much faster. Thousands and thousands of beings are participating in the raising of the consciousness and the Transformation of this planet. So many people are waiting to see what happens in 2012 ... I don't know, but something will happen because everyone is expecting it. It's a big surprise – we will see!

AUDIENCE: If all Souls are reincarnating over and over again, does that mean that there is a determined number of Souls or are there new Souls created?

OMNEC: It's constant. Old Souls are moving upward in the spiritual realm in the non-physical, and new Souls are being created in the mineral and the plant form. It's a never ending cycle of change. That's the way it is.

AUDIENCE: Can a Soul that is incarnated on Earth visit Venus?

OMNEC: Of course. Many of them do. Many lived on Venus before they were on Earth. When they read my book, they are aware of it, because they remember.

I want to thank you for being here. For those of you who know me, I realize that you send me lots of love and healing. That has helped me to come this far after my stroke. I love to be here because Germany is my second home. A large part of my Soul family is here. Every time I appear I meet more and more of those.

I would like to give you a Venusian Blessing, a greeting, which is AMUAL ABAKTU BARAKA BASHAD, that means: "May the Universal Love and Blessings be". Thank you.

+++

[End and autographing session]

Dresden, October 30, 2011

OMNEC: For those of you who don't know me, my name is Omnec and I came from the planet that you know as Venus when I was 7 years old in 1955, but from the astral, not the physical. I have been traveling all over Europe and America doing workshops and lecturing and writing books. My first book was written in the 1960's and was published in 1991 in America. Here in Europe I wrote two more books, but I haven't traveled or been in the public since I had a stroke two years ago.

I am happy to be here. I wouldn't be here if it weren't for people like you sending me love and blessings. I am finally walking on my own, but very slowly. At least I go. I told the people in America – they didn't think I should come – but I said: I am going! I really have to go in order to get better.

[A baby in the audience is talking.]

I love babies, no matter what they do. I love them. That's how much God loves us. No matter what we do – we are special. They are just a blessing – and you are a blessing.

Today we are going to have the Soul Journey to a music CD that I composed of many different musicians from different parts of the world. It's a journey through the different dimensions with the mantras and the colors and the sounds. I hope that you enjoy the journey. It's a long one, but when you come back, if you have any experiences, I would love to hear them, of course.

Anja is going to express through the book some passages that tell you a little bit about the dimensions and the mantras.

+++

Reading: *Mantras and their benefit* (excerpt from *My Message*, part 3 of *The Venusian Trilogy*)

This is an introduction to the Venusian understanding of the different dimensions, their corresponding colors, sounds and the mantras that represent the vibrations of these dimensions, also to the benefits that they have on us living here in the physical. It is essential for practicing the Soul Journey[17] as I have described in the last chapter.

On the following pages are individual listings, features, directions and benefits for each dimension to help you in your daily life here. I have found them very helpful to me. I hope you enjoy and practice these!

The Meaning of Mantras and Chakras

Mantras are very special ancient words or sounds which have been chosen by spiritually Ascended Masters of the physical or non-physical planes. They are powerful words or sounds. Repeated by using a special breathing technique and concentrating on the spiritual self, these mantras have the power to generate energies relating to particular dimensions.

Mantras can shift Soul into non-physical dimensions to gain inner experiences. They also have a beneficial effect on the physical, emotional, and mental self as they help to transcendent the physical existence and can transform confusion into calmness, peace, and understanding. So if you sing or chant a mantra you are feeling better because these spiritual realms are the true home and the birth place of Soul. By bringing these experiences back into the physical plane, you will have a clearer and a more balanced perception of yourself and your experiences. Usually, mantras are part of meditations and are chanted with concentration.

Chakras are spots of energy in different parts of the physical body. They correlate to the energies of other dimensions directing them to those parts of the body which are attuned to these energies. Chakra points are also the location of the endocrine glands. Energy

17 also Journey of Soul

is not only flowing into the body through the chakras, but they also serve as valves to get rid of depleted energy. Thus the non-physical bodies can respond to the experiences made during meditation or other stimulating situations. The chakras enable us to consciously or subconsciously keep in touch with the other dimensions. Meditation helps us to become aware of the energy flowing through these areas and to consciously direct it.

Mantra for the physical dimension

ALAYA is the mantra representing the physical dimension and is spiritually in harmony with the specific vibrations of the physical level. Pronounced "Ah-lah-ya" it should be repeated at least three times very slowly while visualizing the color green that symbolizes the physical. The predominating sound is thunder and drums. These represent the basic vibration of the physical.

When involved in physically strenuous activities this mantra is beneficial in creating the balance of energy and strength needed to reinforce the physical self.

Mantra for the astral dimension

KALA is the mantra representing the astral dimension. Chanted loudly it helps to make experiences on the astral dimension. Pronounced "Kah-lah" it should be repeated at least four times very slowly while visualizing the color pink which is the color of the astral.

The sounds that predominate the astral are the sounds of the ocean. This mantra is beneficial for balancing and harmonizing the emotional body. When you are in very stressful emotional states or have difficulty controlling the emotions it affects everyone differently depending on one's feelings. It can make you cry or feel happy – both are beneficial in balancing your feelings.

Mantra for the causal dimension

AUM is the mantra for the causal plane on which the experiences of Soul are recorded. It is therefore beneficial to bring past life remembrances in one's subconscious mind to the surface. It is pronounced "A-oh-m" and should be repeated slowly at least five times. The color of the causal is violet or purple and the sound is tingling bells.

Mantra for the mental dimension

MANA is the mantra for the mental plane. It is pronounced "Mahnah". It should be repeated at least six times slowly while visualizing its representing color of blue. The sound is of flowing or trickling water. This mantra is beneficial for stimulating the thinking process for those who use computers, do typing or are teaching science. It balances and harmonizes the thinking process. It can eliminate confusion and stress related to the mental process.

Mantra for the etheric dimension

BAJU is the mantra for the etheric plane. This is the first shell or body that Soul takes on when after it is created it starts its downward spiraling journey to the lower dimensions and their divisions – the negative and positive planes or dimensions. This is beneficial for inspiring or creative work. It is the closest to Soul. It is pronounced "Bah-ju". It should be repeated slowly seven times. The color gold should be visualized as it represents the etheric. The sound of this dimension is a humming sound or the sound of bees. It can be a deep humming. It stimulates the creative energy within oneself.

Mantra for the Soul Dimension

SHANTI is the mantra for this dimension. It is pronounced "Shantee". It should be repeated slowly at least eight times. The color of the Soul dimension is pale yellow. The sound is stark wind. This mantra is beneficial in harmonizing all the before mentioned bodies and creating a very peaceful feeling of contentment. Also it is beneficial in healing physical injuries, emotional crises, mental illness or depression or difficulty in any area of one's functions.

Mantra for the Anami-Lok – (God) Dimension

HU is the mantra for the dimension called the void of creation where all energy that created all there is and all Souls flows from. It is the center of creation. It is pronounced "Hyoo". It should be repeated at least nine times. The corresponding color is white, the sound is music of the universe, which cannot be described in words. It is beneficial for spiritual enlightenment, helps to raise the consciousness and changes the perspective view of an individual. It is where we began and shall seek to return to for all knowledge.

Each of these mantras raises the vibration of Soul to the level of the dimension it represents and allows a learning process to be experienced there.

Here you find a summary table of the single dimensions and their corresponding mantras, sounds, and colors:

Dimension	Mantra	Sound	Color
Anami Lok (God Plane)	HU	Music of the universe *(cannot be described in words)*	White
Soul	SHANTI	Stark wind	Yellow
Etheric	BAJU	Humming of bees	Gold
Mental	MANA	Flowing of water	Blue
Causal	AUM (OM)	Ringing of little bells	Purple or violet
Astral	KALA	Ocean breeze	Rose/Pink
Physical	ALAYA	Thunderstorm	Green

The different dimensions differ from each other in the density of their vibrations of light and sound.

In the spiritual worlds the separation of time and space, as we experience it in the physical realm, does not exist. In so far, all these levels exist within you or rather within your Soul consciousness simultaneously. When singing a mantra to connect with one of the dimensions consciously, you address to all other levels of consciousness at the same time. This counts especially for the mantra HU (sung as "Hyoo"), as it encompasses all dimensions.

No matter if you sing the mantras inward or outward, by practicing, your range of experience widens and your spiritual consciousness altogether grows.

+++

We are doing the "Soul Journey" Meditation from CD together.

+++

OMNEC: I want to really thank you with all my heart for sharing this time with me. I am very proud to have this young gentleman in the front meditating and listening. The spiritual interest is very unusual for a young person. They are the future of this world. It's wonderful to see someone with spiritual interest – and unusual.

There is another one over there, he is too young to meditate, but he is here. [Omnec refers to the baby.] He was doing his baby mantras for the baby dimension. I am glad to have everybody from all ages here.

AUDIENCE: How important is it to have the thumbs and the feet touching? When I lay on the back, I felt it was a little difficult to touch the thumbs.

OMNEC: Really? Just clasp your hands. I cross my feet. It's very important, because the body becomes a channel for the energy. The energy flows through your crown chakra and circulates through the body and of course you receive energy from the Earth. Then actually the energy circulates through your body. It does the same thing through all the planets. The energy flows around and through the planets.

AUDIENCE: What does it mean to be enlightened? For people who meditate it is something they are striving for, but in reality I don't know what it means to be awakened or enlightened.

OMNEC: I don't know ... My masters said to me: If you think you are enlightened, you have lost your mind – and to be enlightened you got to leave the mind behind.

I don't know ... Enlightened is when you are really aware and you have an overview like God has so that you can look at the worst human being and say THANK YOU for everything and I LOVE YOU ANYWAY. It's being able to actually have the same consciousness and awareness as God. It's just learning to be aware on all levels at all times and to love and be thankful for everything and everyone. And ONLY to be positive and only send love and blessings all the time.

AUDIENCE: Does this mean that the journey is finished and that one is with God?

OMNEC: No. When your journey is over, you won't be here anymore. You will be somewhere else besides the physical. There are very few beings who are enlightened. It's very hard to attain such a goal.

AUDIENCE: Buddha supposedly was enlightened – and he was here!

OMNEC: That's what I said – there are very few! I haven't seen that many.

AUDIENCE: But nowadays many people claim to be enlightened.

OMNEC: Maybe. I am not sure. I really think that we all thrive to be best we can.

AUDIENCE: When you encounter Soul relatives from Venus, how do you recognize each other?

OMNEC: They usually have a very peaceful appearance and they are just outstanding. They are beautiful as well... if they haven't lived on Earth for long time. [laughter]. This is a difficult place. That's why we are here – it's our school. We are still in school. I came back just purposely to be in school and of course to be with my friends. That's more important than learning [laughs].

Anyone else? Does anybody have a nice experience?

AUDIENCE [the father of the baby]: I noticed that during the Soul Journey Meditation it was very easy to observe the body and the mind and that it was going deeper than normally in meditations, and I realized how great the music is – really good! And my son liked the meditation, too.

OMNEC: That's really amazing. My friends tell me their children and their pets really love this meditation.

I worked three years on it and had musicians from all over voluntarily: an overtone singer, a shamanic Indian, different music instruments. Creating this CD has really been a wonderful experience. The birds actually came to the window when the flute was playing. People asked me, "Why do you have birds on the CD?" and I said: "God sent them, that was not me – they just approached the window." It was a beautiful experience, and it was all out of love.

I had to be the one to express to everyone what it should sound like and what music should go with which mantra. It had to be from my own experiences. The music producer had to trust me and I had to trust him that he would do it. It was a wonderful experience for both of us. I love all the music. I was chasing through the garden with a microphone after the sound of a bee. I just found one, so we multiplied his sound in the studio. It was a lot of fun. We had thunder and everything is from nature, out the window with the microphone. I love to share this CD with the people, because it was such a wonderful experience.

AUDIENCE: How shall we deal with all those crises on Earth? And what is your opinion on 2012?

OMNEC: Everywhere I go, people say, "What's going to happen in 2012?" I say: "What do you WANT to happen?" We really have the power to have anything we wish. I spoke the other night about it. The negative powers always create new prophecies and put question marks in front of peoples' heads. Instead that the people are concentrating on their evolution and enlightenment, they are nervous about the future. Especially now, since the negative forces are crashing, because we have been very successful in our spirituality. The Transformation is going much more rapidly than it was expected. We are very successful and the negative forces are very nervous. And of course they are going to try to distract people. We will see what happens in 2012 – it's going to be a surprise, because something has to happen, but I have no idea.

AUDIENCE: During the Soul Journey, I sensed a touch of my Third Eye, and I even had pain in my head – what could that mean?

OMNEC: You'll have a lot of this during the Transformation. Because you have new chakras that are growing in the body and energy flowing through parts of your body that you never had before. The frequency of this planet is changing. You have high pitch sounds in your ears, hunger that goes and comes, sharp pains for no reasons in different parts of the body – there are many things that you can expect to happen. You'll find that you are more telepathic. You are thinking of someone and they get in touch with you. You'll have sleepless nights where you are not able to dream or you'll have very many dreams. There are many things that will happen to the body. But it's just the Transformation, you don't have to go to the doctor.

AUDIENCE: Are there more schools like Earth or is Earth the only one?

OMNEC: Earth is the only one right now. I think later there will be a new planet that will serve the same purpose, because when the Earth completes its Transformation, it will be a beautiful place. You have got lots of help from the space brothers, they are sending energy with their spaceships around the Earth. The spiritual Ascended Masters are doing the same. I started that program called Operation Peace years ago as a part of the Transformation Process. It's a meditation every Wednesday. The day was chosen by a group of people from everywhere, because it doesn't interfere with other religions. You take 10 minutes or half an hour, as long as you want, and meditate. Everybody does it at their own time all over the world, because it's a 24 hours meditation. The masters send energy and blessings from their levels, and you can focus on a place on Earth that is suffering from a natural disaster or a war or whatever. It's for healing and blessing the Earth. I made posters and sold them. I painted them. It was a pink heart around the Earth from the energy. And we had bumper stickers that said, "Ask me about Operation Peace." Some people meet at their homes and have little get-togethers and group meditations with my CD and everything. That was part of the Transformation Process. Operation Peace is just a meditation, but it is something that you can do individually or together, because it's very good for the Earth. You can visualize the whole Earth or you can picture your favorite animals or your favorite place. That way you can do something, even if it's just sitting and sending blessings, because you are doing something. Your energy together is very powerful.

AUDIENCE: Will there always be such a school planet like Earth with Souls living there on their evolutionary path?

OMNEC: There always has to be a place like this in the physical for the younger Souls to have their experiences in their primitive states. That's just necessary in the physical.

AUDIENCE: Which conditions do we have to meet so that benevolent extraterrestrials contact us?

OMNEC: In the future, when the Transformation is complete, there will be complete contact with other aliens and they will bring you new technology. I think there would be more now if it wasn't for the fear of the governments. They know that we have the technology that outstands from theirs. No matter how much peace we bring, they are afraid of people who have the technology to travel from place to place and through time. Also they want it – even by force. They have to take the technology. We can't allow that because it's our responsibility. Our technology is just like we have had during the Atlantean times, it's only for the benefit of humanity, and not for the destruction or the capture of war. When people reach a state of consciousness where they can be responsible for such technology, then it will be theirs. That's our goal. That's exactly part of my mission to inform people.

AUDIENCE: Nuclear tests have such a negative effect on the atmosphere and the spiritual world is really busy neutralizing it. Why doesn't the spiritual world simply abolish that because it is so dangerous for our blue planet?

OMNEC: Because they don't believe in interfering. It's against our spiritual beliefs. We will come if a disaster happens on Earth and help to shut down the nuclear places. We are well protected. Our whole purpose and reason is to protect the Earth, because it belongs to us in a way and the people are part of our own people. We love the Earth and we are the ones that brought some of the stuff here. So, of course, we want to take care of the Earth.

AUDIENCE: Which meaning do crop circles have? Are the patterns supposed to increase the frequency of the Earth? The patterns are always so different.

OMNEC: They are messages of love and peace and they are kind of like mysteries and puzzles for mankind to solve. It's all about balance. Balance is very important. Extremism is very dangerous.

AUDIENCE: Will life on Earth after the Transformation be in a similar dimension like on Venus, for example?

OMNEC: Oh, the Earth will be a lot different. People won't have to be born, but they can manifest. The karma is already dissolved except what you create if you deliberately do something. You have got to be careful.

AUDIENCE: Are there other extraterrestrials on the physical level in our solar system?

OMNEC: No. The atmosphere of the other planets cannot support life. At one time, yes, they could. And that's what we are trying to prevent the Earth from, because during your technical growth sometimes you make mistakes and destroy your planet's atmosphere. I am not the only one, but I have been working a long time. All my messages, all my workshops, everything is actually about this. It's important that humanity changes its consciousness and awareness, because that's exactly where the problem lies, because you have got a lot of misinformation. I can't help you each individually, but I can make it possible that you can get the information.

I work at night when I am sleeping; I am actually on the other dimensions working with children and a lot of people. I had such a person come to me at the Frankfurt Bookfair. He only saw me once on the television years ago and he was heavy into drugs and alcohol. He walked and passed the bookstand and saw me and stopped and started crying. He said: "Are you Omnec?" And I said: "Yes." And he told me that I saved his life. He was going to commit suicide when I appeared to him and begged him not to. He said: "I can't believe that I am actually meeting you." And he had all the people in the stand crying, my publisher, too. He was so overwhelmed. That really touches my Soul, because that is some work that's very special to me, especially when the people are saved because of it. I gave him the CD with the Transformation of the Earth and the Unknown History as a gift – and of course I gave him a hug. We took a photo of us together. I wanted him to remember that I love him and I am happy that he is here.

That kind of work that I do is special to me and I have met many people over the years. Children who cried, "I know her!" They are convinced they know me and they are saying to their Daddy or somebody: "Please, can I talk to her?" I tell them "Yeah, I know you!" and they are happy then. Of course the fathers and others are saying, "Hah? I just brought you because I couldn't get any one to watch you. I don't think you know her." I used to have private sessions all the time. Many children have come to me. Their parents had to bring them because they would not be happy until they did. They know me. They know me, but not in this world. I know many Souls.

AUDIENCE: Are you in touch with Mother Meera, or Sai Baba, or the White Brotherhood?

OMNEC: With Ascended Masters, yes. Like Rami Nuri, Rebazar Tarzs, Lao Tse, Gopal Das. Rami Nuri is the Venusian Eck Master. I lived and worked with Jesus during his time. I was a disciple. I wrote about it in my book...

ANJA: ...this part has been taken out of the new book from the publisher.

OMNEC: The publishers are afraid of the religious reactions. Isn't that terrible if you have to be afraid of the spiritual religions? But at one time, people were killed if they didn't believe a certain way, so the fear is deep in the genetics of the people. Unfortunately.

+++

[End and autographing session]

Luzern (Switzerland), November 4, 2011

OMNEC: Good evening and thank you for coming and spending time with me. My name is Omnec, for those of you who don't know me. I came to Earth when I was seven years old from the planet that you know as Venus. Some of the faces I recognize, because I was in Switzerland many times and some I recognize as Souls that I knew before. All of you are beautiful Souls.

I am very happy to be here. I hadn't done any kind of touring or traveling since I had my stroke. So this is my first time. I had to get up my courage, of course. And I am not really sure that I am not still insecure... [applause and laughter].

At least I can walk and I can talk again. I can't use my left hand as well as I would like to, but I can move it. The only reason I am better is because people like you send me lots of love and blessings. I can only do my best. I remember years ago I had lots of energy and I could talk for hours and jump around, too. I love being active and I miss dancing, but I am happy to be alive. That's right. I am glad to be here.

I don't know if all of you know that my books are now republished and that all three books are now in one book. That's why I am doing the tour – to promote the new book.

For those of you who don't know, of course, I came from the astral dimension to the physical and manifested a physical body. I can't return. For about eight years now, they have discontinued my treatments, my uncle and the others, because it's against the spiritual laws.

Of course, I chose this stroke before this life. I always admired mentally and physically handicapped people. I love them very much, because they are brave Souls, and they have an example for the rest of us. So apparently I chose to experience this – but I am still me and I appreciate you being here.

A lot of people get confused about when I came to Earth that I did not step into another person's body. No, the little girl died and I had a karmic bond with her. I stayed with her parents as her. I had her genetic imprint, because I had accompanied her Soul during the birth process. That was part of my spiritual mission on Earth. The rest of it is in my books and my CDs. I am going to have Anja to read the chapter from my book about the astral.

+++

Reading: Excerpt from *The Venus Plane* – Text see Cologne, September 3, 2011

+++

OMNEC: When I die, I do not want anyone to do any channeling. I said everything I could say when I was here. Any questions?
AUDIENCE: When you are sleeping, are you going back to Venus?
OMNEC: Not really, but I work. I work with children and a lot of people who are close to me – on the astral.
AUDIENCE: You have said that you cannot return to Venus, why not?
OMNEC: Because I have a physical body.
ANJA: In her book, Omnec explains that the manifestation process is irreversible. Omnec has to stay in her physical body until she dies.
AUDIENCE: And after your death – will you go back then?
OMNEC: No, I am finished with the first and second grade.
ANJA: She is finished with the physical and the astral dimension and will go to a higher dimension.
AUDIENCE: When you say that you work with children on the astral, how can I imagine what you are doing there?
OMNEC: Some children I am preparing for when they are born so they find the right teachings. Some children have been abused in their last life and I also am with them, healing them. I meet

with many children and just teach them. I have met many of them throughout the years. They recognize me and then they want to have a private session or see me somewhere. I have the same thing with grown-ups, especially when people have deep troubles. Apparently I work with the ones who need to be rescued; it's obviously people in need of great help. When they see me somehow, they make a connection. I had such an incident in Frankfurt at the book fair. A man walked by and he stopped and looked and said: "Omnec?" He was just crying. I said, "Yes! Hello, come on in." He was a little shy, he came in and sat down and said, "I can't believe you're here. I didn't know you were here." He told me the whole story. He saw me years ago on TV and told me, "You appeared in my room and convinced me not to commit suicide." He said, "I am still here!" And he had the person who published my books and everybody in tears. I was giving him a hug, of course. I wanted him to be happy. I was very happy, too, because I know I am working. Then I see the real importance in my work, so it's wonderful for me. He didn't care if I had a stroke, he was just happy I was really there. I am happy that I was there for him. Both – in the non-physical and in the physical, because, you know, he saw me on TV, but he never saw me physically. I have his address, of course. He has no computer. I said I'll take your address, because I want to also send him a little hello every once in a while. I do that for a lot of people, I write a lot of hellos. I don't talk on the computer, or SMS, no, I am a letter writer. That's the way I am – old fashioned. It shows my age.

AUDIENCE: *How many people from Venus are incarnated on Earth? Do they recognize each other?*

OMNEC: There is a way that we recognize each other. It's the charisma, an outstanding charisma, and a peaceful look about them. And telepathically – we don't usually say anything, because most of them are quietly living their lives.

AUDIENCE: *How did your family react after they noticed that you are not Sheila?*

OMNEC: It didn't matter. They loved me anyway. I told them, of course. I explained the whole thing to them, later, but before they died, of course.

AUDIENCE: *How did you get here?*

OMNEC: Of course in a spaceship.

AUDIENCE: Was it your own decision to come here? Was it voluntarily?

OMNEC: Yes, of course.

AUDIENCE: And why?

OMNEC: I knew I was preparing for a spiritual mission and because I owed a karmic debt to this little girl. It's in my book.

AUDIENCE: Where are the UFOs – or are they there at all?

OMNEC: There are many of them around the Earth. They are sending energy to the Earth for the Transformation. There are people seeing them every day, and there are reports all over the world.

AUDIENCE: And that is positive energy?

OMNEC: Of course. They are trying to help with the Transformation. A lot of their energy is benefitting the human body in the process. When the Transformation is complete, they will come and bring new energy sources.

AUDIENCE: When will the Transformation Process be complete?

OMNEC: It's going faster, but it depends on how many people participate. Everything that has to do with the future of the Earth is up to humankind. It depends on what you want. People have fear, you know, about 2012 and many things. I always tell them, the negative forces' job is to distract you from your concentration and helping with the benefit of the Earth. They start these theories and prophecies and it never happens. There are too many people that love the Earth. Therefore we are sending energy and concentration to benefit the Earth. The whole Transformation was years and years of work and thousands of beings operating, projecting on the Earth. Many people that are not physical – Ascended Masters and angels and people from other planets – are working toward this. There are a lot of people working to keep this Earth intact. That doesn't mean that it can't get bad, because the negative forces are fighting with all their might. They are about to be kicked off the Earth. The money is breaking down, the whole system. Exactly what I told people years ago. I said this is what's going to happen and it's happening. It's just part of the Transformation. It has to get worse before it gets better. It's like a sore, you know, all the poison has to come out before it heals.

AUDIENCE: I would like to know if Venus has a connection to Sirius.

OMNEC: Of course, they are helping in the Transformation. They all have a lot to do with it. We cannot give the credit for the Transformation to anybody in particular. It's lots and lots of years of work. Finally it happened in 1999, we knew it was completely working, and then karma was dissolved.

AUDIENCE: The karma of all human beings?

OMNEC: All, yes. It means that you have a clean slate as long as you don't deliberately do something to hurt somebody. There are some people who deliberately do things. I have no idea why. I guess it's their experience at their time of evolution. We can't judge; we have to say, "Well, that's part of their learning process." It's part of unconditional love that we can be thankful for them. They are doing a good job. But we don't want to do that. We have done that already, I think all of us have that behind us, as far as I can see. I see nice beautiful Souls out there!

AUDIENCE: What can we do to contribute to the Transformation?

OMNEC: I started a program called Operation Peace.

ANJA: Operation Peace is a meditation program that Omnec was asked to establish many years ago. On Wednesday, you chose a certain time and take 10 minutes to send love and blessings to the Earth or to a project of your choice.

OMNEC: The spiritual hierarchy and the brotherhood of the planets are sending energy from their level. Every Wednesday, people get together and have little parties and eat and then they listen to a meditation CD together. Of course, you can do it by yourself, at your own time, when you are not going to be interrupted. It's something you can do. It's creating a spiritual united force. It's worldwide – and of course, it's universal. Everybody is focusing on the same project at the same time. It's a 24 hours program. It's been happening for many years. We used to have posters and bumper stickers, you know, with the Earth and a pink energy heart around it saying "Ask me about Operation Peace". We did that for years. I did the paintings.

[Omnec and Anja are looking around in the shop and notice all the elves and angel figures.]

That's nice company! Elves and angels. I like Heinzelmännchen *[gnomes – Omnec loves the German word "Heinzelmännchen"]*. I met one and I wrote about it in my book.

ANJA: It's not in the book, Omnec.

OMNEC: Oh.

ANJA: Omnec wrote about her meeting with a Gnome, but this has not been published in one of her books yet.[18]

OMNEC: Anja has got a bunch of stuff that the publishers wouldn't publish.

ANJA: Yes, I have a collection of unpublished texts which publishers did not want to include in Omnec's books.

OMNEC: Like the *True Story of Christ* – they were afraid of the religions. So Anja is going to make everything available – I think it's going to be a whole booklet of unpublished stuff from Omnec.

I am not afraid, because the only thing that can happen is I can die. That's only a transition from one kind of life existence to another. There are many people who are afraid of so many things, but I am willing to stand up and fight for what I believe. You have to really – when you believe something or you know something – you have to be willing to die for it. You can't be afraid. The worse thing that can happen is you can suffer – that's worse. I believe that suffering is worse, I wouldn't want that for anybody.

Anyone else?

AUDIENCE: Can you say something about the date November 11, 2011?

OMNEC: It's my granddaughters' birthday. She will be three. It's the only one she will have on 11 11 11. That's it.

She is my oldest son's first baby. His name is Jo, her name is Josey. And she always says, "I love you" to whoever calls. She has been saying it since she was one. That was one of the first things we've taught her. Say, "I love you." It's very important – those three words.

The love is the most important and the most powerful energy there is. It's stronger than anything. It's the very source of our existence. Because God loved Itself and It created everything from Itself in never-ending cycles, so that It would always exist through

18 see in PART TWO of this book *Meeting a Gnome*

its creations. All from love. That's why it is important. Especially the right kind of love: I love you because you ARE. That is the only reason we should love each other. That way it's for no reason at all.

Don't you agree? [laughter] So far I haven't met anyone who argues on that point, because it wouldn't do any good.

AUDIENCE: If karma is finished, does it mean that children who are born now have no karma?

OMNEC: Exactly. That's exactly why we got so many Indigo children and crystal children coming into this world. I was just in Dresden at a beautiful place. There was a young boy, same age as my oldest grandson, 11 years old, and he was listening to everything and meditating. He was really spiritually interested, which is unusual. He knew he was the same age as my grandson, because he read my book. He sends me emails. His name is Johann. A beautiful boy. I am happy when I see these children, because most of them are all caught up in what's really on the market today and don't have much time for spirituality. Although my grandson has always said he can see Souls and he is very interested. When he was only two, he was saying that we are connected, because our birthday is only a couple of days apart. He cried when I had to come to Germany. He was crying when they took me to the airport and he said: "Grandma, why do you have to go to Germanady again and again and again? I hope they close Germany and you can't go anymore ..." Yes, he was always that way, and of course, when he was crying, I was crying, too.

When he was five, he saw me one time when I was in Germany. He made his Mom unlock the door and said I was standing there in the room. His little brother saw me, too, but my daughter didn't see me. When she came, I was gone already. So I must have been there for a minute.

AUDIENCE: Does that mean that you are not always completely aware of what happens? Or do you see everything with full consciousness?

OMNEC: I am not always aware, no. I may be sitting here and maybe somewhere else working, I don't know. I would probably be dancing, if I can.

+++

Nürtingen, November 11, 2011

OMNEC: Hello! I am really happy to see so many people willing to share a little bit of time with me. Thank you for being here.

This is my first tour since I had a stroke two years ago. I had to get the courage to come, so I am here. It's only because so many people send me love and blessings that I am able to walk and talk at all. Thank you for all your love and blessings. I really appreciate it. Somebody has already asked me and Anja also asked that we do a short meditation, because it's 11/11/11 – and I know that, because it's my granddaughter's birthday. She is three today and her name is Josie.

I thought we do KALA, because it balances and harmonizes the emotions. Of course, you carry energy with you, so it will help us balance all that.

Get into your meditation positions. Take three deep breaths. It's going to be a short meditation, because we have a program, but it should be very powerful, because we are a great bunch. So let's take three deep breaths and then we'll repeat the mantra KALA five times. And then we'll sit quietly and I'll say BARAKA BASHAD. Let's begin.

+++

Meditation KALA Mantra – Silence

+++

OMNEC: For those of you who don't know who I am: I'm Omnec Onec. I came to your planet Earth from the planet Venus, but from the astral dimension, when I was seven, in 1955. I had to manifest a physical body. We can do that in a special temple in the city of

Retz on Venus. Very few people do it, because once you manifest a physical body and enter into the physical, you cannot go back and live in the astral. I only did it because I had a karmic relationship to a small girl on Earth from a former life and I had a spiritual mission. I had accompanied her Soul at her birth process on Earth, so I could receive the genetic imprint from her body to prepare me to my physical life here. It was like a non-physical twin. Then, when I manifested a physical body, I had the same genetics as her family. We have the consciousness and abilities and technology far beyond what you understand. A lot of this information I am sharing with people, because a lot of it should be the information of human beings.

Our people are your ancestors. They were living on physical planets in this solar system before Earth was colonized, but they are your forefathers. These same people are the ancestors of YOU. In my books I talk about this and in the "Unknown History." It's a lot of the history of mankind on Earth, but before the Earth even existed. It tells about how the Earth was first prepared for life and created like a paradise before there were people. It was brought here by the four original races. When I came to Earth, I intended to teach people my spiritual understanding. I ran into a man who was teaching people about Eckankar – the science of Soul Travel, which is the same teachings as I have. The Venusians protected these teachings and they were hidden on Earth in temples in Tibet and taught only from master to student until Paul Twitchell organized Eckankar. I helped to organize the organization of Eckankar in its very beginning. I never belonged to the organization, but I had all the initiations, because I was a teacher of the same teachings. Originally, these were the teachings I understand.

We understand God as the source of all energy that everything is created from including our individual Souls. We are all a part of this energy source. Each individual Soul has the ability to create as well. All you have to do is visualize and imagine and it becomes reality eventually. That's how everything came to be in this world. The imagination is the key to creation.

If we use this energy to heal this Earth and balance this Earth, it will work. I have been teaching people that for a long time – you don't realize how powerful you are. You don't know all that your Soul knows. Your Soul knows everything, because you have experienced it and you have learned through experience. You have lived millions and millions of incarnations. You just don't know how beautiful and how perfect you are as a Soul. I see it all the time. That's how I look at people. How beautiful you are! And how much love you have, because, you know, we are all created because of love. Love is the most powerful and the strongest energy that exists. It's the most important. It can overcome ANYTHING. It never ends, it only gets stronger. It's abundant and never ending. God loved everything, including Itself, so much that It created everything out of Itself in never-ending cycles. Everything recreates from Itself, therefore God always exists through everything It created. You, too, because you are a part of this. All of you have been minerals and plants and animals before you were persons.

Now you need all these life forms to exist. Of course you should understand and love these life forms, because you were them. That's our understanding on Venus, from the time we are born, we are taught this. Of course, I want to share this perception and understanding with all. That's why I have the books and the CDs and all the information, so that people can have it – it's available. Information that I have written that no publisher dares to print because they have fear, Anja has available. I want the people to know; even if some people are afraid, I have no fear, because the only thing that can happen is I can die. And that's only a transition from one existence to another. So there is really nothing to fear. The only thing that's terrible is to suffer. I don't want anyone to suffer. I always admired these special Souls who were born handicapped mentally or physically. I think that's why I chose to have a stroke, because now I understand what it's like. I was very independent, now I have to have help.

But it's OK. It's good for people to help me and it's good for me to let them. I hope you enjoy my books and information, and I am hoping that I will become well enough again to have workshops or lectures.

Anja is going to read to you about the astral dimension where I lived before I came to Earth.

+++

Reading: Excerpt from *The Venus Plane* – Text see Cologne, September 3, 2011

+++

AUDIENCE: Is there a day and night rhythm on Venus?
OMNEC: We create it only out of comfort from when we were physical. It's not necessary, but some people like it. So it's individual.

AUDIENCE: If every individual creates his own projection, his own visualization on Venus, how does he deal with the projections of others? And is there time on Venus?
OMNEC: There is no time, no. Time is a concept of human beings, for keeping time of their birth, in the process of their life.

There is no interference of people, what they create. It's all individual.

AUDIENCE: Can others see your own creations?
OMNEC: If they want you to – if you are sharing something with them.

AUDIENCE: So I am kind of a Soul being on the astral level with my own frequency and I only meet other beings who have the same frequency like I have?
OMNEC: If we all happen to live in this society, yes. There are many levels of astral, and Venus is only one small part. We Soul travel way beyond the astral. We are aware of it, and we are aware of the lower astral, but we don't go there. That's a terrible place, where all your nightmares come from – usually they come from the lower astral. It's not a nice place, it's not somewhere you really want to go on purpose.

AUDIENCE: In the night during sleep Soul leaves the body. If I am dreaming that I fly in a UFO, is that reality in another level? Is it possible to physically fly in a UFO, for example, in one from

Venus? There are lots of UFO sightings at the moment and many people have seen them – I saw them, too.

OMNEC: It could have been an astral experience. Of course it's possible to fly in a UFO.

AUDIENCE: You say that one can manifest with thoughts if one wants to. Can I manifest to fly in a UFO?

OMNEC: On Venus, yes. Not on Earth, but it doesn't hurt to keep visualizing, because it CAN happen. Everything is possible. I believe that everything is possible. You can fly in a UFO. In the future, lot of people will. There will be once again a relationship with the people from other planets and Earth people. That's why we are having the Transformation Process, so that people of Earth can reach the consciousness. They have to reach a certain level of consciousness before they can have the new technology. It's the responsibility of using it. It's a lot of responsibility.

AUDIENCE: Is it true that a part of one's Soul can be somewhere else?

OMNEC: I don't think the Soul is divided. I think it's more of a projection. It's possible that I can appear in more than one place at a time. It depends on if it is really necessary. The Spiritual Hierarchy has decided that. I have helped people many times and I wasn't there really, but I kept them from committing suicide and other things. I am with children a lot and other people that are close to me. When I am sleeping I am really busy on another dimension, I am working. I love that work. Many people know it, many people are with me. It's better they tell you.

AUDIENCE: Venusians don't have physical bodies anymore, what is their next evolutionary step? Where do they evolve to?

OMNEC: It depends on their consciousness and what their goal is. Individual Souls decide what their next experience shall be. Whatever your next experience and your life cycle is, is up to you. You chose everything before you live it. It's an experience. You chose experiences that are valuable for you. And you have to do it in the Soul consciousness, because as a human, you would never choose to have cancer and such things, you know – or to have a drug addict life, but these are all important experiences to Soul. You have got to convince people that no matter what their situation is, it was their free will. That THEY chose it! It's an experience. It's valuable for the Soul. Whether or not our mind can accept it, that's another question.

From Soul's point of view, every life is just a small grain of sand. When you get in it, everything changes the perspective. Then you say, "What in the world have I chosen?" That's the way it is. Sometimes we have to laugh about it – or cry which I did a lot.

AUDIENCE: Does a Soul on Venus experience a birth, an aging process and a death?

OMNEC: We have a special time that we have chosen to live and experience on Venus, and we know that time when we grow up there. We know when our time is up and then we have a ceremony for that.

AUDIENCE: How can one imagine that, if there is no time?

OMNEC: Well, there is no time, but you still have time experiences, you know – experiences of a certain length of living. A cycle.

AUDIENCE: Are there men and women?

OMNEC: Of course.

AUDIENCE: How does the transition work from a mineral to a plant and from a plant to an animal and from an animal to a human being? Does the mineral say, "Now I want to be a plant."?

OMNEC: When you are in the mineral state, and you serve as mineral, like salt or something, and you serve a purpose, then your life as salt is finished. Then you seek the next mineral state until you have fulfilled all the minerals possible. It's that way through every life cycle. In the human state eventually it's more complicated because you form relationships as people. That's why there were karmic relations and you are coming back again and again and again. During the Transformation Process, we have ended the cycle of karma, so that people can continue on their evolution and not get stuck. You have got a clean slate, as long as you don't do anything intentionally. Then you create karma, because you are doing it on purpose.

AUDIENCE: Which tasks does the spiritual hierarchy have?

OMNEC: They sort of help when we are teaching. They give us information and tell us when we are breaking a spiritual law or something – and, of course, you know, make jokes about our limits. They are very useful, they do their work. They did their work, so now they are the best ones to teach the ones who are now in this position. Spiritual work is not for everyone. You can do a good job just by being you and doing what you love and what you do best.

That's why I am teaching people to do the Operation Peace Meditation, because you are building a spiritual united force and you are just a part of it. It doesn't take much energy – lots of love, that's all. It takes maybe 10 minutes of your time or however long you want it. But focusing all of your power and attention and love is important. I was coming a long way in my teaching and they had more and more work for me to do – the spiritual masters. Finally I said; "Wow, I can see the whole big picture now!" And I thought I was proud of myself. The masters were shaking their heads. I said, "Why are you shaking your heads? I finally got something!" And they said, "No, your big picture is just a little bitty piece of the puzzle." Exactly, it was a lot bigger than I know. Everything is a lot bigger than I know. They would tell me all the time things like: *You can't remember what you forgot. But you must never forget what you know.*

I had to think about that for a while, but it really means something. Because your Soul knows everything and you can never forget it, because it's accumulated from experiences. It's not something that you remember in your mind. You can forget what you remember in your mind. They told me: *If you think you are enlightened, you have lost your mind. But in order to be enlightened, you have to leave the mind behind.* They tell me things like that all the time. And I am standing there scratching my head for days, you know, to figure it out, but I finally get it.

AUDIENCE: Is the Soul split up into parts – into twin Souls? Is it that way in higher levels or are there even more fragments that are incarnated at the same time.

OMNEC: No, I don't know that. I never experienced that, no. I just know that all the lifetimes I had are recorded in my Soul. They say, it's on the causal, but really, that energy from the causal is constantly flowing through your body. The energy from that level allows the Soul to remember every incarnation. All the energy from the mental dimension allows you to think and to visualize, from the astral it gives you the ability to feel, to have emotions. The etheric gives you the awareness that the Soul is part of the Creator, also that's where the energy comes from that inspires all the Saints. All of these energies flow through the body, through different chakras of the body, this gives you your life support and the ability to relate to the world. I have told more about that in my *Spiritual Handbook.*[19] It talks about your relationship to the other dimensions and their benefits. A lot of things that I wrote are because of sessions like this, questions and answers. I wrote the book and I have covered everything.

When I am gone from this world, I hope nobody comes and says they are channeling me. You don't need to! I have done everything in writing and I spoke it all. My whole life here, that was the whole purpose. I don't need any one to channel me, don't believe it if you hear it! You say: I doubt it!

AUDIENCE: Which role does Christ play for the Venusians?

OMNEC: We know of Christ, but he was sent here for the Earth people, not for Venus. We admire him and we love him for what he has done. That was something that wasn't published in my book: *The True Story of Christ*, because they are in fear of the religions. You have to get it from Anja on the internet. The Venus black market. I think it's funny that we have to have such information that you have to get in another way. That's what happens in the society that hasn't learned to accept to let people be and think what they wish. They are still judging and they are still arguing over small things instead of living their life.

AUDIENCE: Is your consciousness kind of mixed with human consciousness now?

ANJA: Venusians are human beings, too.

AUDIENCE: Oh, OK, I was not aware of that. I thought they are light beings.

OMNEC: I came with my full consciousness.

AUDIENCE: Many people who are living on Earth come from various stars, from the Pleiadians, for example. Do those who come from Venus come from the same Venus like you – from the astral plane – or is it individually different?

---

19 Now included into *The Venusian Trilogy* as part 3 *My Message*

OMNEC: Venus was a physical society at one time. Some people may have lived there. You could have even lived on the astral. I can't be sure. Only YOU can be sure. But many Venusians live in our society and work here. They have a certain mission and they are accomplishing their mission. Some of it is scientific – or artists. Whatever they do, they are bringing something to mankind.

AUDIENCE: And they came physically as well?

OMNEC: Yes, but they usually come as adults. One man said: [years ago in one of Omnec's first appearances in Germany, a translator misunderstood her and translated very seriously into German that "they came as DOGS" instead of "as ADULTS", because it sounds similar]: "They come as dogs". And the people in the audience were thinking: 'My little dog is black, he must come from Jupiter!' [laughing]. Everybody was laughing, I didn't know why they were laughing, you know, and I asked the man, but he didn't want to tell me, he was embarrassed.

AUDIENCE: There are people who can communicate with plants and animals ... some people can hear the consciousness of trees and communicate with them and with animals as well. Are you able to do that, too?

OMNEC: Yes, of course.

AUDIENCE: I would love to be able to do that as well. How can I learn that?

OMNEC: I think there are many books and many workshops over this.

AUDIENCE: So you think one can learn this?

OMNEC: Yes, of course. It's possible. Because you WERE them, you can communicate with them. When you go shopping, you can always say; "I was this mineral once, I need this mineral." It's a good excuse.

AUDIENCE: You have the Venus consciousness, because you were born on Venus. Those who come from other planets, do they have a Jupiter-, or a Saturn-consciousness, for example? Did I understand you right that you have a limited consciousness from Venus?

OMNEC: Consciously, no. We are all equal that way. We are just from different planets originally.

AUDIENCE: So these states of consciousness exist everywhere, and the ability to create and manifest like on Venus?

OMNEC: Exactly.

AUDIENCE: You are always only talking about these four planets. Do you also know something about Uranus, for example?

OMNEC: No, because I only speak of the four that were the main four planets that colonized the Earth, but there are many other planets with people and with non-human like beings. They are not all friendly.

AUDIENCE: What kinds of beings are flying the UFOs?

OMNEC: Many different kinds from different systems. There are many kinds of beings in our universe. They are all from different places. Human-like and non-human-like.

AUDIENCE: Are there also cat beings or snake beings?

OMNEC: Reptoid, yes. Catlike, yes. There is a UFO book that describes all these beings that they know of.

AUDIENCE: Do these beings influence us?

OMNEC: Not really. Not since the Transformation began. The Earth is protected. We are protected from anyone interfering in our lives. Unless you ask.

AUDIENCE: If one asks for help, for example, for receiving positive energies, one can receive these positive energies?

OMNEC: You should ask from your spiritual higher beings. Asking from a being from another place could invite trouble, because they might want something in return. You have to be very careful.

AUDIENCE: Who protects us?

OMNEC: The Transformation Process is a big process. They connected all the hidden temples around the Earth and this forms a barrier to protect the Earth. This is part of the Transformation. The Transformation is a big process involving a lot of beings. It's a cooperation and a lot of UFOs are outside the Earth sending energy for this process. I write about this and it's on the DVD.

AUDIENCE: Do the Santinians participate in this, too?

OMNEC: Yes, and the Sirians and a lot more.

AUDIENCE: Why is there such a big fuss about the Earth?

OMNEC: Because the Earth involves so many beings in its process of becoming what it is today. They are all involved and protecting the Earth, because it's beautiful and it involves so many beings from all over. We want to protect the Earth.

AUDIENCE: If you had to, would you decide to live on Earth one more time? Do you already know what your next experience after this lifetime will be?

OMNEC: I don't really know where I am going, but I am going somewhere higher. This is my last life on Earth. I love the Earth, but I had enough. This is not my first time, I have been here many times.

AUDIENCE: Can we all go there?

OMNEC: Of course. You can choose to go wherever you want after this life is finished. You decide. You have the choice and you can chose wherever you wish to go. Nobody can stop you.

AUDIENCE: I read that the English royal family members are shapeshifting reptoids. Is that true?

OMNEC: I have heard about that also. I am not really sure. I can't say, you know, if something is true or not, because I really don't know.

I thank you very much for your attention and your time with me. I love you.

Amual Abaktu Baraka Bashad.

+++

[End and autographing session]

PART FOUR

Projects

Operation Peace Program

Author: Omnec Onec

𝒥 was asked to create a meditation by the spiritual hierarchy and my people. All I had to do was choose a day, and I got a group together from all over Europe, and all ages, children up to adults, and older people. We decided that we would choose a day during the week, because that didn't interfere with the holidays of the churches and the organized religions, when most people put their attention on church and prayer and attend services. So we chose a day between Monday and Friday. Everybody wrote their request on a piece of paper. Some people thought Monday, the beginning of the week, was the best, some thought Friday, because it was the end of the week. Everybody had their own ideas. I decided on Wednesday, because it's a neutral day, it's in the middle of the week. Apparently, when we counted the votes, there were more requests for Wednesday. So Wednesday became the chosen day for what we call "Operation Peace".

I chose this name, because everybody takes 10 minutes in their own time, and focuses their attention on peace for this Earth, and healing the Earth. You can choose any kind of project, you can take the rainforest, you can take the whales, you can take different projects that involve the Earth, or you can just picture the whole Earth itself.

You do a 10-minutes-meditation. On this day, everybody chooses their own time; there is not a set time, because everybody has different schedules, and different time sequences all over the world, there are different times. So we didn't set a certain time, we leave it up to the individual to choose 10 minutes when they have the free time and quiet to do this. Some people get together on every Wednesday, and then they choose to listen to maybe my CD or so, and then afterwards they do a group meditation and visualize peace on the Earth. This started, I think it was in 1992, I am not really sure of the date.

I was also advised that if I created a day and requested that everybody meditates that the beings on the higher dimensions would also participate with their energy to the Earth, so that we could create a spiritual group consciousness, a united consciousness, where we are all focusing our energy, our meditation, or prayers whichever way you decide to do it of sending healing energy to this Earth. It has been quite successful; it has been going on for years.

That was just to show the people what 10 minutes of really focusing their attention on one project can do, and it didn't matter where you were in the world or what time of the day. So it creates a 24-hour cycle of meditation on Wednesday, if you have been given the different time sites all over the Earth.

It has been very successful. It doesn't take much energy and much time, and everybody is interested in peace and in healing the Earth. It doesn't interfere with religious beliefs or anything.

I believe that every person has the right to choose a certain religion if they do and if they want. I don't say anything is good or bad, because that's not my decision to make. So we created this one day. I found out later that this was part of the Transformation Process. It was part of teaching the people how they could be involved even if they don't really do much.

It only takes a little effort and a little concentration and discipline that every Wednesday you can remember, this is Operation Peace-Day, so your mind is on it and you are thinking about it. So now it's a special day.

That was one project that I found out later on, was a part of the Transformation of the Earth.

Bookproject *Dancing on Moonbeams*

Author: Omnec Onec

Dancing on Moonbeams

The Ocean

I see the light energy reflecting off the ever-moving ocean
like God's life force flowing through all living entities
providing a place to live
for many life forms
and life for many other sources.
Colors radiate off the moving surface
creating beauty in one of nature's strongest forces.
At sunset, sky and water become one
as colors blend together
in an ever changing array of patterns for human's delight.
Then when darkness falls reflecting city lights
the moon creates a shimmering path
that only our Souls can dance upon
because it is made of light.
As whales or dolphins cries are mingled with the seagulls voices
and sandpipers chase and run from the waves
as this is their nature and not their choices
we close our eyes and in the ever-changing powerful sound of the
waves
we can hear the whisper of God's comforting voice.

Author: Anja Schäfer

Collection of Experiences

𝒰 nder the title *Dancing on Moonbeams*, a book with experience reports shall be published. There are many people who had special personal and spiritual experiences together with Omnec or triggered by her, by reading her book, or by dreams.

Dancing on Moonbeams is a metaphor for Omnec's spiritual work. As indicated in the poem in the beginning of this chapter, only the Soul is able to dance on moonbeams, because both consist of light. Similarly, Omnec considers her work as a spiritual teacher as something impossible in the physical, as something that cannot be seen or proven, because the real work, the transmission of information, the triggering of realizations, memories, and consciousness processes occurs from Soul to Soul.

Omnec's request: "Please send us in your own words all funny, exceptional, or spiritual personal stories, for example about experiences which you had before you met me for the first time, or which you had on workshops, or other personal experiences. Thank you! Omnec"

Omnec's Work with Children on the Astral

For many years, Omnec has been working with children on the astral level. Her masters had given her this job when she herself did not have the time yet to do spiritual work and to travel, because she was still occupied with raising her own children. Omnec speaks about this special task in the second part of her autobiography *Angels Don't Cry* and she also mentions it a lot in her lectures and workshops.

I was with her when children came to lectures or workshops

with the urgent wish to talk to Omnec personally in order to tell her their experiences and memories on the dream levels and simply to exchange love. Sometimes, these children were still very young, and they persuaded their parents to go to the lecture with them.

These encounters were always very touching or overwhelming for all people who were there, especially for Omnec herself.

These children are now teenagers or adults, and of course it would be great if some of them would write about their experiences and shared them with us for *Dancing on Moonbeams*.

If you would like to share your personal story with Omnec, please write it down and send us an email to **contact@omnec-onec.com**.

Omnec's Oasis
– A Place in Harmony with the Universe –

"I often presented the project 'Omnec's Oasis' in my lectures and workshops. This project does not represent a certain religion or teaching, but encompasses all beliefs and cultures. It is a place which carries the spiritual headlines 'You are not judged here' and 'Unconditional Love'. Places like this will be needed due to the Transformation of our societies."

Omnec Onec

Author: Anja Schäfer

A Brief History of Omnec's Oasis

The Oasis, how we call this project colloquially, is a vision that Omnec and I have been sharing since the Nineties. In a way, Omnec is the primal visionary, because due to her life story and her remembrance of the astral level of Venus she carries a deep knowledge about life in a higher vibratory rate and about a far more advanced society compared to what we know on Earth. Additionally, it is part of her life task to support the Transformation of the Earth by, among others, sharing information with people and thereby helping them to raise their consciousness.

After I met Omnec Onec for the first time in the Nineties, I went through intensive life and consciousness transforming experiences, these included writing down my first Oasis vision in 1999. At that time, my spirit had been free and I was able to visualize this place without any limitations. After I had written down my vision, I copied it about a hundred times and sent it off to all people I knew at that time – one of them was Omnec. Omnec was in Chicago when the letter reached her and she called me right away, all exited: "That's MY Oasis!" she said very happily. It was the moment when I realized that we share the same vision. In the course of the following years, Omnec and I tried several times to manifest the Oasis. The following words from Omnec are from 2001. We posted this letter to all people who had been saved in the former address database in order to inform them about the Oasis Project and to invite them to participate:

"I would like to invite all who are interested to contribute to Omnec's Oasis. It is to be a Spiritual Center not based on a particular teaching but to encompass all.

It will not exclude or support any particular religion, race, or culture but give all a chance to express themselves as an individual or group.

The doors shall always be open – on a 24 hour basis with someone always there to share time or give you the feeling of acceptance.

You may receive or give from your particular circumstance.

Of course, you will have to contribute either money or time to attend to certain duties to maintain the Oasis.

There will be a music room with instruments and sound system, or you may bring your own musical instrument.

There will be a meditation room and also a place to eat, or drink and smoke. If you need solitude, this is possible.

There will be many types of healings available as well as scheduled topics and workshops. Or course, you may bring sleeping bags or rent a room for sleeping. No reservation necessary.

There will be provided guidelines or ethics which shall be upheld.

The sign over the entrance shall state YOU ARE NOT JUDGED HERE.

Art and sculptures will be displayed or created here also.

Here you can express yourself or share your talents with others. It will be a place of combined efforts belonging to all who wish to contribute.

It is the place of the future supported by co-operation. A place that will stand long after the Transformation. A place of love and support and respect of all living entities as the Creator intended.

If you wish to support this or raise funds with a special project it shall be appreciated.

I of course will be there at appointed times.

Thank you for your support of my mission on this planet Earth. Love and Blessings – Omnec"

At that time, the contrast between Omnec's description and our real circumstances had obviously been still too big, because the Oasis would not manifest yet. Although a house could be rented and a small community developed around Omnec, it has not been the time for the Oasis the way we visualized it. Consequently, the project withdrew into itself again in order to silently continue to ripen.

It was not until 2006 when the Oasis vision demanded my attention again – and more colorful and concrete than ever. After I had done a long meditation, I felt the strong need to describe the Oasis as detailed as possible and to draw some illustrations showing the houses and the place the way I saw them inside of me. It was my intention to share the texts and the drawings with others to the best of my ability. I decided to learn as much about web design as I needed in order to create a little website and to set the Oasis vision online. This way, I thought, people at least have the chance to find our vision and to contact us if they feel in resonance with it. So in 2008, the first Oasis-website went online.

Occasionally somebody found the site, read the concept description and sent an email. However, none of us had real ideas about what we could concretely do to work on the manifestation of the project. Even when Omnec and I were together, the Oasis was not a dominant subject. It was as if the project needed its own time and space to develop in the background, before the next step in the physical world could be done.

This next step was taken in 2013 on the occasion of Omnec's 65th birthday that she celebrated in Germany. We took the opportunity to publicly present the Oasis Project and to invite to the first official Oasis meeting on September 28, 2013.

This first public meeting formed the foundation for the further development towards the manifestation of this project, because for the first time Omnec and I met a group of interested people, shared thoughts and ideas, and exchanged concrete plans for what kind of real steps should be taken next to help the further development.

Since the beginning of 2014, a new Omnec's Oasis Website is online under the domain **www.omnecsoasis.org**. It took me many years before I was able to accept the name "Omnec's Oasis" for this project, because I wanted to avoid the misunderstanding that this project is to put Omnec on a pedestal or to create some kind of cult around her – this is not what we intend to do. On the other hand, Omnec's Oasis is a name that can clearly be distinguished from all other places that include the word "Oasis" in their names. Furthermore I feel it's correct that Omnec's name is included in this place, as she is the primal visionary and bearer of the spiritual ideas behind it. However, colloquially we are still simply saying "The Oasis".

On the next pages follows the Oasis concept description that forms the meditation or working basis.

Omnec's Oasis – The Vision

The Oasis is a place in complete harmony with nature.

In the Oasis, people may live, work and stay as long as they'd like. The Oasis is open 24 hours a day for visitors and people in need of a place to rest and recover.

In the Oasis, peace and calmness rule as a natural state. There are also a variety of events taking place on a regular basis. Everything here is voluntary, but there are some simple rules and guidelines.

The Oasis is a place of balanced giving and taking. Every visitor, guest and inhabitant contributes in whatever way is possible and comfortable for them. The inner order of the Oasis is maintained through the natural intuition of the people there and through meetings of the people who are living there and wish to take part. In these meetings, all points are discussed which are to be addressed, as well as important decisions made.

In the Oasis, the "Communication of the Heart" is relied upon. That means, every person may speak what is on their mind while the others listen.

A central theme of the Oasis is "You are not judged here". Love and acceptance replace judgment and criticism.

The foundation of the Oasis is the Earth itself. Life in the Oasis pulses in harmony with the Earth and is protected and supported by it. The care and maintenance of the Oasis is also in harmony with nature.

The place as a whole offers room for peace, healing, creativity, and learning.

The gardens are full of beauty and are used for the planting and cultivation of fruits and vegetables, flowers and herbs.

The core of the Oasis are people who are living naturally and in harmony with the ideals upon which the Oasis is based. All subjects concerning the daily life in the Oasis are directed by this core. No matter what question emerges, it is discussed by the core; that means the heart of the Oasis is asked, just as every individual in the Oasis asks their own heart for guidance. For those who don't ask the heart for guidance first, it is possible they may therefore not feel comfortable at the Oasis for any extended time, due to a lack of overall resonance.

The heart of the Oasis is a powerful energy that is in harmony with the Earth and the movement of our solar system. This place is a safe place in the holistic sense, in that it grows and develops in accordance with the nature of the times.

The essence of the Oasis is its harmonious energy in which healing, happiness, and peace can be.

The Oasis is built on an acupuncture point of the Earth's surface. Other places like this already exist, are being built right now, and with more to come in the future. All these places of peace, healing, and harmony are connected along the Earth's meridians. In this way, a powerful net of protection is built which also stabilizes the Earth while helping to raise its vibrations.

Omnec's Oasis – The Grounds

*T*he place where the Oasis is situated is spacious and open, but comfortable.

The Oasis consists of a main house, a living house, apartments/bungalows, a place for animals and a camping area.

All houses are connected by foot paths which are mostly covered by sand.

Between the houses are gardens and open green spaces.

There is a lake near the camping area. A small river flows close by the living house, the animal house and the bungalows.

In front of the main house there is a large circular patch of grass with flowers surrounding a fountain.

There is a parking area in front of the entrance to the Oasis property. The Oasis itself remains auto-free. The only cars and big machines in the Oasis are the ones that are necessary for work or transportation purposes.

The Oasis is only accessible to the world of streets in the front. Nature surrounds the Oasis otherwise, including forest, fields, and open space. One can see mountains rising up in the distance.

All the houses are built in an organic style with an emphasis on curves not corners, and this style is continued inside the buildings. In this way, the buildings create a soft and friendly environment. There are also columns and covered areas outside.

The main building of the Oasis is beautiful. Wide gentle steps lead up to the main entrance here. The outside is constructed with columns and invites one to relax and enjoy the view looking out over the round of green and fountain bubbling in the center as well as to feel the peace emanating from the environment.

The entrance is high and rounded. As far as the weather allows it, the doors are open.

There is a big circular mosaic of colored glass above the main entrance door. Above it are letters that convey the meaning of the heart of the Oasis. Underneath is the word Oasis written in the same style of letters. This script used here arc thought forms which transcend the meaning of written language.

Inside the Oasis is a round area decorated with plants and water. Above, the space is open with many plants growing, some all the way to the roof. The roof is open but can be closed during cold or wet weather as necessary.

The main house is three stories high. On the first floor left is a café/restaurant with an al fresco area. To the right, also opening to the outside, is a business with books and crystals and all kinds of related accessories. Integrated into the business is a large area for reading and relaxing where drinks and fruit are freely available.

To the back from the main entrance area is a larger room with a stage for the presentation of various events and music.

All together the interior of the Oasis is flooded with light, full of wonderful plants, and water bubbles gently all around. There is a sense of peace and lightness. A great staircase sweeps up into the second floor.

There is a open landing full of plants that also allows a view onto the main first floor. It is very open and light. The large plants and trees grow from below on the first floor, right past, and up to the roof.

Here are many "color rooms". The "color rooms" are variously furnished and each in a different lovely color. For example, there is a purple room, which is completely purple and in which there are magnificent amethysts as well as a few pictures and decorations that go with the purple theme.

Furthermore, there is a blue room, a green room, an orange room, as well as a yellow room, a turquoise room, a pink room and finally the rainbow room. Unfortunately, not all colors and shades can be represented in the physical, so the core has to decide which colors are currently on display.

The color rooms are available for creative and healing purposes but also open for simple enjoyment. All the rooms have some sort of outer access, like a balcony, which usually includes a lovely view.

Another set of beautiful stairs leads up to the top floor and meditation room.

The meditation room is a dome made of white color, glass, and light.

Here the meetings of the core of the Oasis take place, as well as regular meditations. At all other times, this special room is open for the enjoyment of all.

There is a terrace on the roof full of plants and offering many seating areas.

Besides the main entrance, the main house of the Oasis has three other doors in each of the cardinal directions.

To the left and behind the main house one finds the big living house.

On the ground floor of the living house is a kitchen, dining room, an office, and a large walk-in pantry.

In the upper three floors there are numerous rooms, where permanent citizens of the Oasis as well as guests are living.

Behind the big living house are bungalows. The bungalows are round and sitting on stilts.

All rooms and bungalows can be decorated and adjusted to meet the needs of the people living in them.

To the left and the front of the main house, is a garden where food is grown as well as a house and place for animals.

There are a variety of animals that call the Oasis home, and how their living area looks can be changed or adjusted according to needs.

The people communicate with the heart of the animals so that their wishes and needs are met as well as those of the people.

To the right of the main house is a camping house and area on the shore of a small lake. There are many trees.

The camping house contains all the necessities for living in the camping area. This area of the Oasis is available for all those who enjoy living in a tent or camper or otherwise enjoy living close to nature.

The entire Oasis is crisscrossed by footpaths which connect all houses with each other and lead in various directions into nature.

This description of the Oasis represents just one possibility. The picture is not fixed but changeable according to the emotions, thoughts, and actions of the people whose vision its realization reflects.

Omnec's Oasis – The Realization

The realization of the Oasis is possible.

According to the motto "Imagination is the key to creation," everything can be realized that one can imagine.

The Oasis is a place of the heart and of peace. It emerges through the power of imagination of many peaceful hearts. The attention of the people who love this place enable it to become reality.

No person alone could ever create the Oasis, even if the financial means were available. The Oasis is a project that results from combined energies and efforts. All the people who dream of this place, who long for this place, who wish for this place, send their energy into the heart of the Oasis. Out of the heart this project grows and gathers to it the necessary material. In this way the Oasis is grounded and realized. It is literally created and takes root naturally.

The spirit of the Oasis exists as a vision of planet Earth itself. The Earth is a beautiful planet that lovingly supports all life forms. The Earth is longing for peace and appreciation through its citizens. The development and being of places like the Oasis is wished.

The spirit of the Oasis exists in the ether and is received by numerous people. From here the Oasis finds entrance through the heart.

These people are filled with a vision like this, dream of it, and imagine a place and life which they fill with their joy and energy.

The next step towards realizing this vision is sharing it with other through words and pictures.

It is for this reason that this website was developed.

Step by step the hearts of the people who share this vision are connected and exchange information contributing to its further growth and development.

The heart of the Oasis collects more and more energy and starts to pulse in resonance with the Earth and therefore continues to grow.

Somewhere, sometime the Oasis is real, lives on the Earth in the physical dimension and is connected with other places of this kind.

This net contributes to the development of Earth towards a light and loving vibration that is harmonious with the universe.

Omnec's Oasis Logo

Some Quotes from Omnec

The most important thing that people on Earth have to learn is to replace criticism and judgment with love and acceptance.

Imagination is the key to creation. Whatever you can imagine, is or will be reality. That's how it works.

Where the attention goes, the energy flows.

I don't judge anybody and I am judged the most.

Sometimes it's more important not to question in detail so much how somebody functions, but to see what he has to share with others.

If you think you are enlightened, you have lost your mind. But never mind. Leave your mind behind – then you are enlightened.

Love never ends – it continues and gets stronger. Love is very special. It's the basis of our existence. We are created, because God loved Itself. And we are a part of God. All of our Souls are like a little piece of God. We have the ability to create as well. We do it through our thoughts – we manifest through our thoughts. Everything that exists in this world, man created from first it was a thought, before it was anything else.
So the key to creation is imagination.
That's very powerful.

Contact

Contact with Omnec's Oasis

If you would like to be kept up to date about the development of Omnec's Oasis, if you want to participate in this project or come to one of the next Oasis-Meetings, please connect with us:

Email: **office@omnecsoasis.org**
Web: **www.omnecsoasis.org**
Facebook: **https://www.facebook.com/omnecsoasis**

Public Appearances and Book Translations

If you are interested in inviting Omnec to your country or in publishing her information in your language, please send an email to **contact@omnec-onec.com**.

In case there are public appearances planned, we will always publish the dates on Omnec's website **www.omnec-onec.com**. If you would like to be kept up to date, please subscribe to our newsletter.

Private Sessions and Private Meetings with Omnec

Whenever I, Anja, am together with Omnec, Private Group Meetings and Private Sessions can be arranged, Private Sessions possibly also per Skype.

Omnec Onec Shop

You can order Omnec's material on **www.shop.omnec-onec.com**.

Connect with us

Omnec does not use computers, therefore and for health reasons we ask you for your understanding that she cannot reply to emails personally.

Email: **contact@omnec-onec.com**
Web: **www.omnec-onec.com**
Facebook: **https://www.facebook.com/omneconec**
Google +: **https://www.google.com/+omneconec**
Twitter: **https://twitter.com/omnecfromvenus**

Recommendations

For ordering the Omnec Onec articles please visit

shop.omnec-onec.com

or send an email to

shop@omnec-onec.com.

The CDs and DVD-Interview are also available as DOWNLOADS.

As EBOOKS, the three parts of Omnec Onec's VENUSIAN TRILOGY are available separately. You can find them in any ebook store.

Ebooks
Onec, Omnec: From Venus I Came (Part 1 of The Venusian Trilogy)
Onec, Omnec: Angels Don't Cry (Part 2 of The Venusian Trilogy)
Onec, Omnec: My Message (Part 3 of The Venusian Trilogy)

More Book Recommendations
Adamski, George: Inside the Spaceships
Lemriel, Robert Scott: The Seres Agenda

OMNEC ONEC - THE VENUSIAN TRILOGY

OMNEC ONEC

The Venusian Trilogy

From Venus I Came
Angels Don't Cry
My Message

"From Venus I Came" - **Autobiography Part 1**

A classic in spiritual literature: In her autobiography, Omnec Onec portrays her *life on the astral level of Venus* and teaches *timeless wisdom*. She speaks about the adventure of how and why she decided to manifest a physical body, and about her journey to Earth in 1955. This book was first published by the US Col. Wendelle C. Stevens in 1991. **Contents:** From Venus I Came • Laws of the Supreme Deity • Tythania Canes of Age • In the Womb • The Venus Plane • Teutonia • The Creative Life • Earthward Bound • Brotherhood of Planets • Agam Des • Sheila • My Earth Family • Compared to Venus

"Angels Don't Cry" - Autobiography Part 2

In the continuation of her autobiography, the author describes her experiences on Earth and conveys further valuable insights. **Contents:** Sheila • My Earth Family • Living with a dictator • A light at the end of the tunnel • Chicago • Longing for love and understanding • Renewed confidence • The Girl from Venus • Reencountering my spiritual teachings • Children – Our Future • My way to the public • Fulfilling my mission

"My Message" - Essence of spiritual teachings. The truth is always simple. Practical and current, Omnec writes about the essence of creation, Soul, and life. This essential third part also contains a new and very precious chapter about the evolution of Souls on planet Earth. **Contents:** Understanding the Physical • Learning to deal with the Emotions • What effect the causal has • The Mental Process • The Function of the Etheric Body • The Soul – the real I • The Laws of the Supreme Deity • About Karma • Spirituality and Religions • Meditation and Contemplation • Journey of Soul Technique • Mantras and their Benefits • Healing and Self healing Procedures • Energy – Ways to feel and use it daily • Love and Relationship • Venusian Understanding of Death • Knowing the Life Plan • A Spiritual Journey • The new Supreme Deity or Sugmad Expansion Ray

Smartcover • 544 pages plus colored pictures • 140 x 215 mm
ISBN: 978-3-9523815-2-6

OMNEC ONEC DVD-Lecture

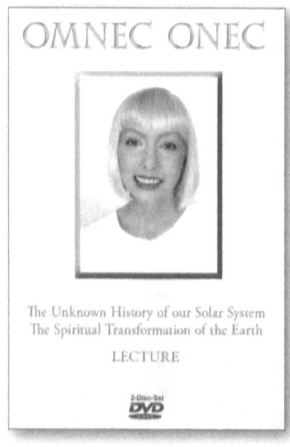

The Unknown History of our Solar System
The Spiritual Transformation of the Earth

LECTURE

3-Disc-Set
DVD

DVD-Lecture "The Unknown History of our Solar System and the Spiritual Transformation of the Earth"

In this lecture, Omnec Onec speaks the story of the inhabitation of our solar system, she talks about the reasons for the spiritual Transformation Process on Earth that is currently taking place and imparts precious information about how every individual can take a conscious part in this process of raising the vibratory rate of planet Earth.

Contents:

DVD 1

The Inhabitation of our Solar System • The Earth Emerges and is Filled with Life Forms • The Battle for the Earth • The First Populations on Earth • A Group of Visitors Wants to Gain Technological Knowledge • The Genetic Manipulation and its Consequences Until Today • The Current Transformation Process and the Return of Lost Knowledge • Our Concept of the Creator • The Design of Creation and the Birth of the Soul • The Complexity of Human Experiences and the Meaning of Unconditional Love • As a Soul on the Journey Through the Levels of Creation • The Creation of a Consciously Desired World

DVD 2

My Journey from the Astral Level of Venus to the Physical Earth •The Preparation of my Spiritual Work • Reasons for Being Here • The Transformation Process of the Earth and Each Individual • Operation Peace Meditation Program • Sharing Information • The End of Manipulation and Control • Many Beings Take Part in the Transformation Process • The Re-Introduction of Technologies • The End of Old Karma • Transformation Phenomena in the Physical Body • An Exercise to Perceive the Life Energy • The Future of the Planet Earth

Languages: English Original and German Synchronization
Double-DVD, length: 162 min.

OMNEC ONEC DVD-Interview

DVD: "The Interview in the Central Courtyard of Kaphof Manor at Hückelhoven, Germany"

Hueckelhoven is a small village located between Aachen and Mönchengladbach in Germany. Just outside the town Kaphof manor is layn where Omnec Onec used to live a few years ago for a few months in every year. Omnec Onec was born on planet Venus. She tells us about her life on Venus. In the interview we talk about life on the astral plane of Venus, hollow worlds, manifesting by thoughts, the cosmic origin of the human races, the relief efforts of the extraterrestrials, the transformation process of earth and about many more items. **Contents:** Living Conditions on Venus • Sleep and Meditation • Manifestation of Pets • Nutrition and Manifestation of Things • About Animals generally • Names of Germanic Mythology • Hollow Worlds • The astral Dimension and Magic • Multiple Levels of Astral • The black Race in Outer Space and on Earth • 'Communication' in the earthly way • Manipulations of Consciousness and Religions • Private Backgrounds • George Adamski • Moon Landing and Alternative A/B/C • Return to Venus?

Part 2 on the DVD: Kurt Abildskov – Contact with Space People

Kurt Abildskov is a former pilot and lieutenant colonel of the Danish Air Force. UFOs and the space people are his special field. Even Kurt had contact to Venusians. We went to Ebeltoft in Denmark and conducted an interview with him. The chapters include: UFO experiences in various Air Forces • Contact with George Adamski and people from Venus • UFO events in Danish airspace • A strange encounter in Paris • A series of weird events happening during slideshows • Open Contact Law and Prime Directive • Alternative Energies and the Status Quo • Possibility of open contacts • UFO crashes • Mayan Calendar and Crystal Skulls • New UFO facts in Brazil • Charles Green and Bashar • Ashtar Sheran and Help for the Earth • Star Children and Indigo Children

Languages: English Original and German Synchronization, length: 56 (Omnec) and 75 min. (Kurt)

OMNEC ONEC CDs

Meditation-CD „Soul Journey": Guided Meditation through the levels of consciousness
A guided meditation with various music compositions corresponding to the levels of consciousness. Mantras and visualizations support the experience of the different dimensions from the physical through the astral, the causal, and the etheric dimension to the God planes.

"Soul Travel is an art and science that allows temporarily the departure of the Soul from the physical existence to visit and explore any or all of the worlds beyond the physical universe, in the Soul body." Omnec Onec
Length: ca. 71 min.

Audio-CD "My Mission on Planet Earth"
Listen to Omnec's fascinating voice, embedded in sound spheres and Venusian inspired music, how she describes in their own words the connection of Venus to the history of the Earth and the purpose and goal of her adventurous transfer from the astral plane to the physical Earth.
Excerpt from the contents: Solar civilizations • Earth's heritage • Planetary Brotherhood • Birth of individual Soul • Evolution and Karma
Length: ca. 53 min.

Audio-CD "From Venus with Love": All about Love
Omnec speaks and sings about "Love" with spherical background music.
Excerpt from the contents: Venus Love • Love of Twin Souls • Friendship and Lovers • Making Love • Freedom and Love • Love is All • From Venus with Love
Length: ca. 65 min.

Audio Samples on shop.omnec-onec.com

Thank you

Omnec Onec and Anja Schäfer, 1998

www.ingramcontent.com/pod-product-compliance
Lightning Source LLC
Chambersburg PA
CBHW020440130626
46549CB00001B/225